Rambles
About Portsmouth

Rambles About Portsmouth

by Ray Brighton

The Portsmouth Marine Society
Publication Nineteen

Published for the Society by

Peter E. Randall
PUBLISHER

Designed and produced by
    Peter E. Randall Publisher
    Box 4726, Portsmouth, NH 03801

A publication of
    The Portsmouth Marine Society
    Box 147, Portsmouth, NH 03801

Library of Congress Cataloging-in Publication Data
Brighton, Ray
        Rambles about Portsmouth / by Ray Brighton
            p. cm. -- (Publication / Portsmouth Marine Society :19)
        Includes index.
        ISBN 0-915819-18-X : $25
        1. Portsmouth (N.H.) --History. 2. Portsmouth Region (N.H.) -
        -History. I Title. II. Series: Publication (Portsmouth Marine
Society) : 19
        F44.P8B834 1993
        974.2'6--dc20
                                                                    93-7851

Other Portsmouth Marine Society Publications:
        1. John Haley Bellamy, Carver of Eagles
        2. The Prescott Story
        3. The Piscataqua Gundalow, Workhorse for a Tidal Basin Empire
        4. The Checkered Career of Tobias Lear
        5. Clippers of the Port of Portsmouth and the Men Who Built Them
        6. Portsmouth-Built, Submarines of the Portsmouth Naval Shipyard
        7. Atlantic Heights, A World War I Shipbuilders' Community
        8. There Are No Victors Here, A Local Perspective on the Treaty of Portsmouth
        9. The Diary of the Portsmouth, Kittery and York Electric Railroad
        10. Port of Portsmouth Ships and the Cotton Trade
        11. Port of Dover, Two Centuries of Shipping on the Cochecho
        12. Wealth and Honour, Portsmouth During the Golden Age of
            Privateering, 1775-1815
        13. The Sarah Mildred Long Bridge, A History of the Maine-New Hampshire
            Interstate Bridge from Portsmouth, New Hampshire, to Kittery, Maine
        14. The Isles of Shoals, A Visual History
        15. Tall Ships of the Piscataqua: 1830-1877
        16. George Washington in New Hampshire
        17. Portsmouth and the Montgomery
        18. Tugboats on the Piscataqua: A Brief History of Towing on One of America's
            Toughest Rivers

Regretfully, he'll never know,
but this book is dedicated to the memory
of a valued friend—the late

JOSEPH P. COPLEY.

Portsmouth and New Castle will never appreciate
how great his contribution was in preserving
their stories, legends and traditions.
"Joe" will always be missed by those
who benefitted from his help.

Contents

Acknowledgments

Probably the hardest part in writing a book like this is to thank properly those who have been of great help during this preparation. In the past few years I have become particularly indebted to people like Richard E. Winslow III, one of the most indefatigable researchers I have ever known; the man is a bulldog when in search of prey. David Goodman, a close student of the municipal phases of Portsmouth life, was ever offering suggestions. The Portsmouth Public Library's reference staff can't be thanked enough for patience in answering foolish questions.

Peter E. Randall, the guiding genius in Portsmouth Marine Society publications, even when seriously ill, was willing to spend endless time in planning and advising on arranging the manuscript. Strawbery Banke helped with photos, as did Carolyn Eastman at the Portsmouth Athenaeum. The names are legion and the listing of all would be impossible.

Over the years, however, one person's help has been invaluable. The then Betty J. Nelson edited all the books I have done since 1973, and nothing has changed because she is now my wife. Between watching for dolphins, while down in Florida she "read copy" on this volume, although she had edited many of the columns before they appeared in the *Herald*, and found a second dose a little much.

Foreword

CHARLES WARREN BREWSTER—"THE RAMBLER"—devoted many columns in his newspaper, the *Portsmouth Journal of Literature and Politics*, to essays about a Portsmouth and its suburban towns that existed largely before he arrived on the earthly scene early in the 19th Century. His *Rambles About Portsmouth*, as he styled them, spanned several decades in the life of the *Journal*, and, being owner, publisher and editor of the weekly newspaper, he could write much as he pleased. Eventually, these "Rambles" were compiled into two volumes, published a few years apart, the second about the time of his death in 1868.

It's well that he did carry this tremendous task to such an extent because every student of Portsmouth history is heavily indebted to his work as a starting place for further research. Without in any way denigrating Brewster, latter-day scholars have been able to widen the scope of his efforts, for the simple reason that each passing year long-hidden sources come to light. For example, the Portsmouth Athenaeum is fast becoming a repository for many collections of family, business, church and organization papers that weren't accessible to Brewster.

Although some of his idolators refuse to accept the fact, Charles Brewster did make mistakes, and, unfortunately, errors, some of them horrendous, will undoubtedly be found in the pages that follow this foreword. Quite frankly, after a lot of thought, the general pattern Brewster used in preparing his two volumes will be followed. Brewster wasn't a stickler for chronological development, simply because he didn't pretend to be writing a definitive history. Further, items of differing genre often were included within the pages of a single Ramble. That concept will be followed in this volume.

Pretentious though it may be, the present author is hopeful that it, too, may be seen, in the years to come as a continuation of the Rambler's fine work. In the main, except where background necessitates it, the period covered by Brewster will get little attention. It has long been my contention that too much city and area history and folklore have been neglected in favor of colonialism. In recent years that shortcoming has been in the process of being remedied. Writers like Richard Candee, Richard E. Winslow III, Woodard Openo, David Goodman, Peter E. Randall, and others, including present company, have been making forays into more contemporary times, although ever genuflecting to the deeper past—if necessary.

The larger part of the material presented here has already appeared in print through the pages of the *Portsmouth Herald*. While on the staff of the *Herald*, I wrote many historical features. After my retirement from active duty in 1979, I continued to write for the newspaper. At the urging of Azio J. Ferrini, the then general manager, I committed to producing two such essays each month. After Ferrini's retirement in 1988, Derek L. Wood, the present general manager, asked me to write a feature for the Sunday edition each week. That pattern has continued ever since, and it can be candidly said that the writer will run out long before the material is exhausted. After all, history is happening in the passage of each 24 hours. So with Derek Wood's express permission to re-use the *Herald* articles, I can only hope, at best, to put more of the Portsmouth story into print as my contribution to the community which I have made home for almost half a century. Nearly sixty years ago, I was kicked out of Antioch College, being told to go forth and "Find a purpose in life." Perhaps, at last, I have found it.

But enough of all that! What must be faced is the problem of finding a starting point. When Joseph G. Sawtelle, one of the founders of the Portsmouth Marine Society, the sponsor of this volume, asked me to "put some of your columns into a book," he offered no suggestions as to how to proceed. As many people realize, the Portsmouth Marine Society has been responsible for the publication of nearly 20 books involving local history. Originally, the PMS was an organization dedicated to helping mariners and/or their families in hard times. It was re-incorporated in 1982 by Sawtelle and the late Joseph P. Copley with the avowed purpose of telling the Portsmouth story. So, at the risk of reiteration, what will be found within these pages is another effort to perpetuate that story. Basically, this book isn't, nor is it intended to be, a chronological political saga. If it's anything of substance at all, it's a series of sketches depicting the life and times in Portsmouth and its neighboring communities in the 19th and early 20th Centuries.

To my mind, there's no better way in which to make a start than to tell a little about the lives of two of Portsmouth's most influential citizens in the middle and latter years of the 19th Century—Daniel Marcy and Ichabod Goodwin. Those knowledgeable of the Portsmouth story will immediately ask: "What about Frank Jones?" And, as the politician always responds, "That's a good question." The answer, from the point of view of the writer, is simple: The story of the almost legendary Frank Jones was rather fully told in *Frank Jones, King of the Ale Makers*, and need not be repeated here. So Daniel Marcy's story will pave the way.

Ray Brighton

Hon. Daniel Marcy

I Daniel Marcy, Sea Captain, Ship Builder, Businessman and Politician

Everyone in the seacoast knows there's a Marcy street in Portsmouth. A few people know that Marcy street, between State street and the South Mill Bridge, was once known as Water street, and was one of the most notorious "combat zones" on the East Coast.

But even a smaller number of people know anything about the man—Daniel Marcy—for whom the street was named. And yet, in his time, Daniel Marcy was one of the old city's most influential citizens. At the end of his long life, Marcy was viewed in sort of reverential awe, but there had been times when he was reviled by his foes and they were legion. In a way, Daniel Marcy is a human symbol of the ambivalence that prevailed during the divisive Civil War era which saw the United States torn in two.

Daniel Marcy's story begins with his birth on Nov. 7, 1809, the third of three sons born to Peter Marcy and his wife, a former Miss Knight of Eliot. Peter Marcy was a native of Bordeaux, France, who had come to America in his youth under the sponsorship of Capt. George Huntress. Eventually he went to sea, and was engaged in the coasting and West Indian trades; he became a shipmaster and prospered financially.

Samuel was first son of Peter Marcy. At the age of 12 he went to sea, serving under Capt. Titus Salter. In early manhood he settled in

New Orleans, and became a successful businessman. The second son was another Peter who was apprenticed at the age of 14 to Isaac Nelson, a ship carpenter, and, after serving out his time, he left Portsmouth with his tool chest and worked his way to New Orleans, a bustling, prosperous city above the mouth of the Mississippi River, which provided a major backdrop in the lives of all three of the Marcy brothers, although Daniel, ultimately, made Portsmouth his permanent home.

Daniel Marcy's mother died when he was two, leaving the father to cope with rearing three active boys. When Daniel was 12, his father died. For a time, he lived with a farm family, but eventually, like his father and brothers before him, he went to sea.

A biographical sketch about him, published in May, 1878, in the *Granite State Monthly*, notes that between voyages he often attended Portsmouth Academy and studied under the famed master, William Harris, However, during his political career his lack of literacy was often harped on by opposition newspapers, so perhaps his schooling wasn't very extensive.

In 1831, young Marcy joined brother Peter in New Orleans, and they both were associated with two enterprising merchants: Judah Touro and Rezin D. Shepherd. Daniel Marcy commanded vessels owned by the syndicate, sailing in the triangular cotton trade between southern ports like New Orleans to Liverpool and Le Havre and then back across the Atlantic to northern cities like Boston and New York. During one of his voyages, he made his way back to his native town and married Henrietta Priest. That was in 1839, and in 1842 the couple returned to Portsmouth to live as part of an agreement with Shepherd, Touro and Peter Marcy.

Marcy had contracted to supervise the construction of at least one three-masted, square-rigged vessel each year and to take each new ship to sea on its maiden passage. One result of the arrangement was that Daniel Marcy took more newly built Piscataqua square-riggers to sea than any other master. For a decade, Marcy was engaged in this pursuit. His last command was the ship *Frank Pierce* named in honor of New Hampshire's Franklin Pierce, the 14th president of the United States.

Henrietta Marcy died on March 19, 1850, at the youthful age of 29. Twelve years younger than her husband, she was the mother of two sons, and a daughter. The sons, Henry L. and Judah Touro Marcy, became outstanding shipmasters. The daughter, Henrietta, married

Marcy's home. Here Captain Marcy, prominent mariner, businessman, shipbuilder, and politician lived out the last years of his life. Author photo.

Capt. Samuel B. Cunningham of Portsmouth. Six years after Henrietta's death, Daniel Marcy named one of his new ships in her honor—the thousand-ton *Henrietta Marcy*. However, on Nov. 23, 1852, Daniel Marcy had married Catherine T. Lord, the youngest daughter of Portsmouth's Ebenezer Lord. The couple had one son, George D. Marcy. Unlike his half-brothers, George Marcy was a landsman all his life, although he once made a trip to England with his father on a steamship. George Marcy served as Portsmouth's mayor in 1903-04, and was one of the founders of Portsmouth Country Club.

Although an ardent, committed Democrat, in a day when party loyalty was valued only secondary to religion, Daniel Marcy had played no leadership role in party affairs. All that changed in 1854, when he learned, while on a trip to New York, that he had been elected to the State Legislature.

That marked the beginning of an extensive political career, one that had some successes and many disappointments. Even in those days, New Hampshire Democrats were ever swimming against a

Republican tide that always seemed to be at flood stage. Marcy was elected state senator in 1857, and re-elected in 1858. (State elections were annual at that time, and didn't become biennial until 1877.) His work in the State Senate prompted a Democratic effort to get him elected to the U.S. House in 1859. Although the Civil War was still more than two years in the future, the pro-secession policies of the Pierce and Buchanan administrations were making a split between North and South inevitable. The Democrats, by and large, were willing to let the individual states determine whether or not they wanted to continue as part of the Union. Slavery, or the continuation of it, was the basic emotional issue, and the *Portsmouth Journal* on Feb. 19, 1859, published a statement taken from the *Dover Enquirer*:

"The Portsmouth Gazette denounces our statement that a vote for Daniel Marcy is a vote to legalize and re-open the foreign slave trade as a foul calumny.

"The re-opening of the African slave trade is now a favorite measure with the Southern democracy. It will have to be met by the next Congress undoubtedly. It is stated on good authority that there are upwards of 50 Southern Democrats in the House now who are not only ready to repeal the laws declaring the slave trade piracy, but are pledged to do it.

"Capt. Marcy, if elected to Congress, will go there as a party man, ready and willing to vote for all the measures required of him by his party.

"If the annexation of Cuba, the establishment of slavery in Kansas, the re-opening of the African slave trade, or any other abomination, is decided in caucus to be 'democracy' he will go it blind.

"There is no doubt of that, not the least. Even if he should hesitate and dodge such foul work at the bidding of the slave drivers, the party to which he belongs advocates these measures . . . "

Marcy lost his election bid. His opponent was Gilman Marston of Exeter and the anti-secession movement was gaining strength. However, Marcy found a little solace in the fact that he carried his home city by 259 votes, 976 to 717. Marston won in only one of the three wards, the second, and that by only 27 votes. The *Journal* published a flamboyant item on March 12, more or less congratulating Captain Marcy on his "escape" from election:

"The Ship of State.—The Democratic candidate for Congress in this District must console himself with the idea that he is regarded by his political opponents as well as his supporters, as a very good citizen, and one who has the means of doing very much good.

"He knows every rope in the ship and track in the ocean—and the ships he sets upon the ocean are always 'A No. 1.' If the 'owners' have of late changed the order of his voyage, he should feel grateful for his narrow escape from a port where the breakers are dangerous, and where he could not represent the true interest of the north without 'disobeying orders,' and infringing on the specifications of the southern 'Charter-Party.'

"The captain we would trust among the pirates in any sea—but when he submits to the pirates who offer themselves as pilots into political havens, he must expect after bleeding freely, to reach the 'Hole in the Wall.'

"Three cheers for the escape of the Captain! Long life, prosperous voyage to him!"

Nevertheless, Daniel Marcy was a bitter man, one who earnestly held to his political philosophy no matter the sentiments of the North. In fact, his feelings were so strong that they led him into an emotional tirade when some friends called on him in his home at what is now 383 Pleasant street. His outburst, as will be seen, was used against him in the election of 1863.

Daniel Marcy was in New Orleans, visiting his brothers, when the news reached him that the New Hampshire Democrats had chosen him as a delegate to the 1859 national convention in Charleston, S.C. Marcy traveled to Charleston in company with many of the delegates from Louisiana who were hell-bent on seceding from the Union. The *Granite State Monthly* said this in its sketch of Marcy's life:

" . . . The spirit of the secession had already begun to manifest itself and many of the party leaders at the South were outspoken in their determination to withdraw from the Convention, if they could not control its actions, even as they proposed that the South should secede from the Union if the result of the election should not be satisfactory.

"With these men, both on the way to Charleston and during the exciting day of the session, he used all his powers of argument to induce them to stand by party and country but to no avail. Other delegates from New England however, including such men as Benjamin F. Butler and Caleb Cushing, then high in the councils of the Democratic party, encouraged them in the course they had determined to pursue. They withdrew from the Convention. The party was broken and defeated as a result. Secession followed, with all its terrible consequences to the South and to the nation. More than one of the Southern delegates whom Capt. Marcy urged to stand by their associates of the North, have since acknowledged to him the grievous error of their course."

History shows that the bolt of the Secessionists assured the election of Abraham Lincoln over Stephen A. Douglas. The South put up John C. Breckinridge, but his electoral votes, combined with those from Douglas, wouldn't have defeated Lincoln. The Republican victory, which provided the last impetus toward creation of the Confederate States of America, put Daniel Marcy into a real dilemma. Despite what his critics said in the heat of campaigning, Marcy was a strong Union man, but one who had strong economic and familial ties to the South, especially New Orleans. War broke out in April, 1861, when South Carolina hotheads fired on Fort Sumter in Charleston harbor. And a quick glimpse at the situation of the Marcy brothers, Peter and Daniel, is found in an item in the *Chronicle* for September, 1861:

"The brothers Marcy, one residing in Portsmouth, and the other in New Orleans, owned jointly four ships. The Southern brother hoisted the secession flag on two, and the old stars and stripes floated over two. The fortunes of war have so turned that the two secession crafts have been seized by the United States authorities, while the Confederates have captured the two belonging to the loyal Northerner."

Actually, Peter Marcy's two ships, captured and taken into Eastport, Maine, were subsequently released through Daniel's intervention.

While the war raged, Daniel Marcy was again preparing to seek election to the U.S. House. For example, in December, 1862, it was reported by the *Chronicle*:

"We learn that a paper to be called the *States and Union*, got up to press the claims of Capt. Marcy, the Democratic candidate for Congress, will be published at the Old Gazette office, in January next, by Mr. J. L. Foster, formerly of the *Dover Sentinel*.

"J. L. Foster" was of course, Joshua L. Foster, progenitor of a Dover newspaper family. His office was in a building at the corner of Penhallow and Daniel streets where the Thomas J. McIntyre Federal Building now stands.

The election in March, 1863, was preceded by the usual journalistic viciousness, of which both sides were guilty. Daniel Marcy was constantly raked by the *Chronicle* and *Journal*, a sample of which was published Feb. 21, 1863, in the latter paper:

"Remember that the election of Ira A. Eastman for governor, and Daniel Marcy, John H. George and William Burns for Congress will cause rejoicing in the Rebeldom, as did the election of Seymour, Fernando Wood and Co., in New York, over which Charleston was illuminated in rejoicing.

"That the sympathizers with treason, all over the Union, are not only turning their eyes to this state, but doing everything in their power to destroy the Republican ascendancy, we have the most conclusive proof. Ten thousand dollars have already been raised in New York to be expended here.

"It is seen that the three Representatives to be elected will in all probability decide the political complexion of the next Congress. As they stand that body will stand, in firm support of the administration, or in sympathy with treason.

"Their votes will elect a Republican speaker, or a Fernando Wood. Need we say another word to arouse every friend of the Union to his duty."

Not all newspapers took the extremist view of the *Journal*. Joshua L. Foster's *States and Union* was ecstatic with the outcome. Above it was mentioned how Foster came to Portsmouth from Dover to found a paper that would support Marcy and his fellow Democrats. On March 13, Foster wrote:

"We have the cheering news for the brave and gallant Democracy of First Congressional District that, that true, tried and unswerving Democratic patriot and whole souled man, Daniel Marcy, is elected to Congress by at least 150 over all opposition. We can hardly find language to express the gratitude and joy we feel at this glorious result. The news sends a thrill of rejoicing and gladness through the souls of all true Union and Constitution loving people from one end of the nation to the other.

"The people of this district have boldly rebuked the rampant Abolition treason and disunion which has for two years past stalked with a high hand all through the eastern borders of the Granite State. Thanks be to God, the people are victorious. Slander and detraction have done their worst. The gallows erected by the modern Haman upon which to hang all the Democrats of the District, now bears Haman himself suspended by the neck, writhing in the agonies and contortions of an ignominious political death."

On Feb. 21, the *Journal* harked back to the evening after the

1859 election and Marcy's bitterness in defeat. Several of Marcy's friends called on him to express sympathy over the outcome.

The *Journal* said:

"The gentleman soon returned from their call, and the mutual feeling they expressed was 'had Daniel Marcy been elected by our vote, we should never have forgiven ourselves.'"

This was sometime in advance of the opening of the rebellion, and of the day when his brother, Peter Marcy, took a prominent part in one of the preliminary meetings in the neighborhood of New Orleans, to fan up the incipient flames of the rebellion, which was now raging with fiendlike fury in the South.

Despite repetition of such material in every issue before the March election, the *Journal* failed in its mission of defeating Marcy's bid for a seat in Congress, and he was the only Democrat elected at the top of the ticket. However, the *Journal*'s view did prevail in the City of Portsmouth. Marcy trailed his opponent, Joel Eastman, by 166 votes, 922 to 756. Ward 3 was the only one to give Marcy a helping hand; there he led by a margin of 84 votes, 222 to 138. Even as late as March 21, there was some doubt as to whether or not Marcy had won. The *Journal* dourly commented:

"On Thursday evening, the Republicans of Dover celebrated the grand results of the Election in New Hampshire, and the probable election of Hon. Joel Eastman to Congress from the 1st District.

"On the same evening, the 'Copperheads' of Portsmouth . . . they so announced their party name on their handbills . . . celebrated the election of Capt. Daniel Marcy to the same office.

"The Hungers [Copperheads] are carrying out the joke to the very point with Capt. Marcy, and will whittle it out to as near nothing as possible. They are bound to make their nominee believe that he is elected until they derive all possible benefit therefrom."

Well, the joke, as such it was, was on the *Journal*; Marcy did win and took a seat in the U.S. House.

It must be said he didn't have to run against the highly popular Gilman Marston. The latter was in the Union army serving as a brigadier general. And it has to be added that Marcy wasn't able to carry his own city, although his margin in the district was about 800.

In the next chapter, the story of Marcy's service in the U.S. Congress and the last 30 years of his life will be told.

II *Daniel Marcy in Congress and the Following Years of His Life*

Daniel Marcy's two years of service in the U.S. House of Representatives were stormy indeed. As might be expected, the Republican newspapers in both his home city and in the state beat a constant tattoo on him, and ferociously condemned nearly all of his stands. For example, in December, 1863, a bill was brought in that called for paying bounties to recruits for service in the Union army. The Democrats offered an amendment which would have barred bounties to black recruits, in effect blocking a substantial source of much needed manpower. The *Journal* remarked:

" . . . if this proposition had succeeded, it would do more to aid the rebellion than any army of 50,000. Capt. Marcy voted for the amendment. If any of our readers yet believe that Capt. Marcy was not elected to Congress for the purpose of embarrassing his own Government and to aid the rebels—let them turn back and read the Resolutions which were adopted by the Convention which nominated him . . . Then let them examine this measure of refusing to employ or pay black soldiers, which Capt. Marcy attempted to carry out . . .

"1. Whether Capt. Marcy is not faithfully reflecting the opinions and supporting the policy of those who elected him?

"2. Whether he and his supporters could not more effectually aid the rebellion if they were in the rebel army then they would if they could carry out their policy in the American Congress?

9

"We again remind our readers that the country is in more danger from Northern than Southern rebels."

The attacks continued all through Marcy's two years in Congress. In January, 1864, the *Dover Enquirer* opined:

"Daniel Marcy, as everybody who opposed his election predicted he would, votes with the most ultra and hide-bound supporters of slavery in favor of every measure which will embarrass our own government and aid the cause of the rebels.

"In giving his vote against employing negro soldiers, he stood with only 41 others of his party. More than half of the Democratic members refused to go with him. Even Fernando Wood refused to be counted in such company, and gave his vote in favor of raising negro soldiers."

Marcy returned to Portsmouth for the March elections, and the *Journal* told a little tale that well demonstrates the bitterness of the Civil War years:

" . . . An incident of Tuesday shows he (Marcy) has no more real sympathy for a white soldier than he has for a slave, and that he lacks the first particle of humane feelings for those who have sacrificed upon the altar of their country, the dearest offering, a beloved son. Among the first to volunteer for his country's cause was Mr. William F. Oxford, who was wounded at the first battle at Bull Run, and died a prisoner in rebel hands soon after, leaving a circle of bereaved friends at home, whose hearts have never healed from the agony of the affliction. Mr. John R. Oxford, the father of William, has in his employ as a teamster a worthy and intelligent contraband (former slave) the ideal of degradation to the eye of Captain Marcy. To this black man, on the eve before election, Captain Marcy took occasion to say: 'Don't none of you niggers go down to vote tomorrow—if you do, you will get your– necks broke.'

"On the morning after the election, Marcy in passing on Market Square, heard Mr. Oxford talking with another man on Copperheads. He turned at once and volunteered the unfeeling remark: 'You have lost one son by war—but you have got one to take his place' referring to the contraband. Mr. Oxford felt the uncalled for and inhuman insult, and in no measured terms denounced the contemptible spirit which prompted it—alike disrespectful to personal feelings, and to the cause for which his son had given his life."

The attacks on Marcy, perhaps deserved at times, continued. In June, 1864, the *Journal* observed:

"The vote in the House, repealing all acts for the return of fugitive slaves, was 82 yeas, to 58 nays. Every Democrat, including our Representative Marcy, voted nay. They appear to love slavery better than ever—or rather they mourn for the return of the seceding States, with the slave influence, which has given them, and can alone, in future, give them influence and office."

The next week, on July 2, the *Journal* whacked the congressman again:

"Who wrote Daniel Marcy's speech?

"A speech by Capt. Marcy, occupying about four columns, is reported, made June 14, 1864, in the House of Representatives, on the proposed amendment to the Constitution.

"The writer of the speech is not announced. In its scholastic and rhetorical flourishes, there is so strong a resemblance to the classic style of Frank Pierce, that there is little question of the source from whence it came.

"Capt. Marcy, not being capable of writing ten lines grammatically, was incapable of composing such a speech."

Occasionally even the *Journal* found something good to say of Daniel Marcy. One instance was a reprint of an item in the *Concord Statesman*, and was published on July 16, 1864.

"Sergeant Henry C. Russell, 12th N.H.R., Sanbornton Bridge, wounded in late battles, bled to death from a wound of the artery in the neck, at Emory Hospitals, last week.

"The father, a poor man, had come to take care of him, and had no money even to get home himself. Mr. Marcy met him accidentally, and finding his destitution, not only paid for embalming and sending the body, but furnished the old father ample means to go home. The old father wept at the unexpected generosity. Two days afterwards I saw him put a fifty-dollar greenback into the hand of another man who had been watching over a wounded brother. This is only a specimen of the manner in which Mr. Marcy has been, from the commencement of this campaign, administering to our soldiers. He goes nearly every day to the hospitals, and always proceeds first to the market, and his purse is always open, and without ostentations or pretension, the unbidden tears going with the charity."

Marcy was renominated by the Democrats in 1864, but time was running out on him. A steady accumulation of votes that New Hampshire Republicans saw as detrimental to the Union became too much of a weight for him to carry. For one thing, he voted against the

Gilman Marston, Marcy opponent.

constitutional amendment that would abolish slavery. Only four House Democrats approved.

Excerpts of a letter to the *Journal* from a soldier in the 18th New Hampshire Volunteer Regt. express typical anti-Marcy sentiments. It was published a couple of days before the March, 1865, election:

"I was surprised to see what claims Captain Marcy has on the people for re-election. That he has done nothing towards putting down the Rebellion is one claim which is presented by the editor of the N.H. Patriot, why do the people of the old First District give him their hearty support? Now, allowing me to be judge, (and I think I know something about it), Captain Marcy has been the cause of more misery and suffering than almost any other man. And why? First because he has failed to give the Administration that warm support he should, and the rebels have taken courage that perhaps in time the North might become divided, and then their chances of independence would be much better. He has, therefore been the means of prolonging this gigantic struggle, and his hands are not without the stain of blood upon them . . . "

There was more, much more, but the above demonstrates the way the tide was running. A Republican flood was in full spate, and, to compound Marcy's troubles, the Republicans nominated a war hero, Brig. Gen. Gilman Marston of Exeter, as his opponent. Marston had defeated Marcy before the war began, served out his term and then joined the army. Marcy fought back. In a letter to the *States and Union* on Jan. 21, 1865, he denied that he had dodged paying income taxes on his salary as a congressman. Then he added:

"As to what the abolition papers say of me, I pass it by as idle wind. I have found but one to account to for my actions; and that is He who knoweth the heart, seeth all, and who will give our reward where the tongues of men cannot lie or slander. You allude to my relations with the suffering soldiers. I have only tried to do my duty to them, as all men should do. If we differ as to the causes and management of the war, that cannot relieve us from the obligations of humanity. I never asked a soldier in regard to his political faith—but only if I could assist him. Although I am for peace and union, under the Constitution of the fathers, I trust I shall never permit my politics to lead me to barbarism, nor be so ill-liberal as to ask what one's faith is, before rendering him that assistance God demands for the needy everywhere . . . "

But it wasn't enough. Gen. Marston recaptured his old seat in Congress, and Marcy returned home, but not to idleness. Even while in Congress, Marcy had, in 1863, built a ship in partnership with his brother Peter. This was the 1,031-ton *Daniel Marcy*, which was constructed in a yard at the foot of Pickering street, where Frederick W. Fernald had built the *Harriet Rockwell* nearly 30 years before. His partner in ship construction at this time was William Pettigrew who had been associated with Fernald for several years. In 1866, Marcy built and launched the 488-ton bark *Aphodel* for a Boston merchant, S.C. Thwing. He followed that in 1869 with the ship *William Ross*, named in honor of one of Marcy's favorite shipmasters.

In 1875, Daniel Badger built for Daniel and Peter Marcy the *William H. Marcy*, one of the largest square-riggers ever launched on the river. She was the last Daniel Marcy built on the Portsmouth side of the river.

The States and Union.

PORTSMOUTH, FRIDAY, MARCH 13.

New England's Abolition Chain Broken!

"COPPERHEAD"

TRIUMPH!

The Charcoals and Paperheads Squelched in the First Congressional District!

HON. DANIEL MARCY

ELECTED

To represent the First N. H District in

CONGRESS.

In his *Tall Ships of the Piscataqua* the present writer expressed great puzzlement as to the source of the name for the ship *William H. Marcy*. Recently, thanks to the research of Richard E. Winslow III in preparation for his forthcoming volume on Portsmouth in the Civil War, it's now known that the ship honored the memory of 19-year-old William H. Marcy, a son of Peter Marcy. Young William was killed in action on April 6, 1864, at Mansfield, La. Why the father and uncle delayed 11 years in honoring William obviously isn't known, but his death well demonstrates the awfulness of civil war. Quite probably, Daniel and Peter Marcy simply needed time to face the reality of their loss. It seems appropriate that the *William H. Marcy* had the honoree's cousin, Judah Touro Marcy, as her first commander.

Marcy & Pettigrew in 1857 had built the *Sarah E. Pettigrew*, and she was followed the next year, even as Marcy was getting ready to run for Congress, by the ship *Orozimbo*. In 1859 came the *Georgiana*.

However, Daniel Marcy wasn't yet ready to turn his back on politics. In January, 1867, he was drafted to run once again for Congress on the Democratic ticket. The nominating committee was headed by Frank Jones, the brewer, and the letter informing Marcy of the nomination read, in part:

" . . . We assure you, Sir, that this convention comprised as true, patriotic and earnest a body of men as ever assembled for such a purpose and this nomination is tendered to you with entire confidence in your integrity, honesty and fidelity to Democratic principles . . . "

In his acceptance, Marcy was almost excessively modest in wishing the convention had chosen someone else, and in conclusion, he said, " . . . Come what will, the Federal Union must be restored and preserved on firm foundations, of the Constitution made by men of '76 and '87. Anything more or less will result in confusion and anarchy to be superseded eventually by absolute despotism . . . "

Marcy once again met defeat, this time at the hands of Jacob H. Ela of Rochester. Not until 1875 were the Democrats able to win in the 1st Congressional District, when Frank Jones was elected to the first of two terms.

The campaign of 1867 followed the unusual pattern of vilification of Marcy by the papers like the *Chronicle* and the *Journal*, and stout defense by the *States and Union*.

The *Manchester Union* published Marcy's "admirable letter of acceptance," and the *Journal* promptly declared it had been written by ex-President Pierce. The *Journal* quoted a letter written by Marcy in 1864 in which he said:

" . . . We had a speech yesterday that will do good from Allen of Illinois. All the speeches are written. If you or Reding or Jenness should get up a good one, perhaps I could read it to the disorganizers and traitors to our country."

The *Journal* added:

"Those who vote for Capt. Marcy may be assured that they vote for a man of straw—an echo of such speeches as his friends may write. That Capt. Marcy sometimes makes speeches of his own composition we are not disposed to deny. That naive speech he once made in the Temple [where the Music Hall now is]. 'I was born in Portsmouth and was always born there' — and that in Jefferson Hall [where Fleet Bank now is] 'that fellow at the *Journal* [Charles W. Brewster] ought to be hung' were his own." Much the same kind of anti-Marcy propaganda was employed by the Republican newspapers such as the *Dover Enquirer* and the *Portsmouth Journal*. On March 2, the *Enquirer* was quoted by the *Journal* as saying:

"Daniel Marcy, for the fourth or fifth time, is thrust before the people of this Congressional District, for the purpose of extorting from them an endorsement of the principles which he professed as well as the course which he pursued when he took sides against his country.

"A vote for him, therefore will be a vote against everything which loyal men have done to preserve and restore the union and in favor of everything the rebels have done to destroy it . . . " In the voting Portsmouth was a lot kinder to Marcy in 1867 than it had been in 1865. In the latter year, Marcy was up against the war hero, Gen. Gilman Marston, and lost the city by 660 votes — 1,211 to 511. Against Ela in 1867 Marcy lost in Portsmouth by 139 votes— 1,059 to 920, and lost the district by only 1,082 votes.

Marcy apparently stepped back from the front line of New Hampshire politics after that defeat. He may well have been devoting his energies toward rebuilding the shattered mercantile interests of his brother Peter and himself. However, in 1868, he was president of a Democratic club which was backing the candidacy of Horatio Seymour for president in opposition to the war hero, Ulysses S. Grant. Serving with him were local luminaries such as Frank Jones, Richard Jenness and attorney Albert R. Hatch. Marcy took advantage of his family's being on vacation to remodel his home on Pleasant street, "and when the work is finished he will have as neat and commodious a home as can be found in the city. The work is going on under the charge of Chas. H. Downs."

The Seymour campaign was an exercise in frustration for the Democrats. Grant won in the Electoral College, 214 to 80. Not until 1884 would the Democrats capture the presidency. By 1876 Marcy was busy both with politics and shipbuilding. The Democrats nominated him for governor to run against Person C. Cheney of Manchester. It was the usual mud slinging vendetta. A classic example of which appeared in the *Chronicle* on Feb. 11.

"We are informed that on Thursday, at about noon, Hon. Daniel Marcy (he then in company with Messers. Osgood and Drew, the temperance reformers, Mr. John S. Treat and others, near the corner of Daniel street and Market square) expressed as his opinion that a dollar a day is sufficient pay for any working man, our informant asserting that he distinctly heard the statement made and that the others present must have heard it also. If Mr. Marcy did not say so he can easily disprove it if he chooses; but he did say so, and meant it, we may presume a dollar a day is what he proposes to pay the working men he may employ in his ship-yard, after the appropriations for work at this navy yard have been cut off 'for good,' as he long ago intimated would be done when the Democrats secured control of the National government."

The *Portsmouth Evening Times*, an afternoon paper with strong Democratic beliefs, couldn't let the matter rest there, heading its rebuttal:

"The *Chronicle* of this morning contains the following article." It then quoted, in full, the *Chronicle's* charge, and added:

"That the statement is absolutely false, — a deliberate lie manufactured 'from whole cloth' for political purposes, is shown by the following communications to this newspaper:

Portsmouth, Feb 11, 1876

"To the Editor of the Daily Evening Times: The article in the Chronicle of this morning purporting to give the substance of a conversation between the undersigned and Hon. Daniel Marcy, in which the latter is alleged to have stated certain views in relation to labor is unqualifiedly false in every particular. The subject was not mentioned directly or indirectly, and Mr. Marcy made no allusion to the labor question whatever.

Alfred W. Haven

John S. Treat"

And, to cap the refutation of the smear by the *Chronicle*, on Feb. 15, John W. Drew of Concord came to Portsmouth, and demanded that the *Chronicle* publish a copy of a letter he had sent to Daniel Marcy:

"Dear Sir: — I have your letter of 11th inst., calling attention to an article in the *Portsmouth Chronicle*, containing the statement that you expressed in the presence of Mr. Osgood and myself the opinion that a dollar a day is sufficient pay for any working man. The informant of the *Chronicle* is certainly mistaken. No such opinion was expressed by you, and our conversation with you had no reference to that subject. I trust you will do Mr. Osgood and myself the justice to believe that neither of us has said anything to warrant such a publication. Mr. Osgood is now in Maine; if he were here he would join with me in that statement."

Marcy's leading role in shipbuilding would seem to give the lie to the charge. At that time he was engaged in the preliminaries for construction of the second *Granite State*, probably the largest three-masted, square-rigged merchant vessel ever built on the river, and it's doubtful he could have hired many craftsmen at the rate of a dollar a day. Even the *Chronicle* was getting a bit ambivalent in the manner in which it reported on Daniel Marcy, especially if he wasn't a candidate for office.

To the end of his days, Daniel Marcy maintained an interest in New Orleans and what was going on there. The *Portsmouth Times* on April 30, 1878, observed that Marcy had been down south for some little time and quoted an item which had appeared in the *New Orleans Democrat* on April 26th:

"Capt. Daniel Marcy, the old war-horse of the New Hampshire Democracy, returned yesterday from a fortnight's visit to the eastern shore of Mobile Bay, where for many years he had lived, as well as in this city, prior to the late unpleasantness. Capt. Marcy paid a visit to Mayor Pilsbury to announce his departure for home on Monday. The interview was a long and pleasant one, during which old times were spoken of, bringing back many reminiscences of the palmy days of New Orleans. Politics were touched upon a little, Capt. Marcy expressing it as his decided opinion that the Hayes Southern policy would be the main issue in the next presidential campaign. As for himself, Capt. Marcy has no political aspirations, but entertains strong hopes that next fall New Hampshire will elect a Democratic Governor. What he says of the prospects of New Orleans is worthy of consideration, coming from a man of his fine business abilities and keen observation. He thinks that at an early day our city will resume its greatness, and shine again as when the Touros, the Peters and the Marcys themselves were among our most promising and enterprising citizens, and he advises young men from all parts of the country to visit New Orleans, in order to learn for themselves something of her present importance and brilliant future.

"Finding our old friend entertaining such excellent ideas about our city, we ventured to ask him why he did not return among us. 'Oh,' he answered, 'I am too old now.' 'Well, what of that, Captain, come and live here and get a new lease on life?' 'Yes,' was the reply, 'as my brother says, *to let me down easily*.' And he gave one of his hearty laughs and took his leave of the Mayor."

As it does for all mortals, death came for Daniel Marcy on Nov. 3, 1893, after a long illness, during which, in order to ease the ordeal, the city kept the section of Pleasant street outside his door covered with deep layer of sawdust to cushion wagon wheels, lessening their clatter on the rocks.

In its farewell, the *Chronicle* said:

"Capt. Marcy was one of the best known of our citizens and no one who was ever brought into contact with him but loved his rugged honesty of purpose and unswerving devotion to what he believed was right."

Ichabod Goodwin

III Ichabod Goodwin: Sea Captain, Merchant, Banker, New Hampshire's First Civil War Governor

THE EARLY AND MIDDLE YEARS of the 19th Century saw an influx of men who for the most of the 1800s dominated Portsmouth's economic and political life. Frank Jones, king of the ale makers, comes immediately to mind. Jones, as everyone knows, left an imprint on the city that continues to this day. But there were others who played leadership roles, although not in the flamboyant manner of Frank Jones. One such was Samuel Lord, banker, insurance man and investor, who came to the city in his youth from South Berwick.

Another was the man who is the subject of this Ramble: Ichabod Goodwin. His mansion is familiar to all who have visited Strawbery Banke, although Goodwin might be a bit surprised to find it in that location. When he knew his house, it was on Islington street, across the way from what is now Goodwin Park, but in his day was Goodwin Field.

To begin at the beginning, which seems a logical procedure, Ichabod Goodwin, who became New Hampshire's first Civil War governor, was born in what is now North Berwick on Oct. 8, 1794, the son of Samuel and Anna Thompson (Gerrish) Goodwin. Goodwin's early years were typical for a boy living in a community that had ties to agricultural, industrial and commercial interests. His formal education was at Berwick Academy. After a few years Ichabod Goodwin left

21

and came to Portsmouth to seek his fortune. Earlier it was mentioned that Samuel Lord, who had moved to Portsmouth, was a native of the Berwicks.

And it was Samuel Lord who became young Goodwin's sponsor and mentor. Whether or not there was a family connection, or merely friendship, that led Lord to do this is a question best left to Goodwin genealogists for the answer. Samuel Lord, who was then making his home on High street, was only six years older than Goodwin. The latter probably came to Portsmouth around the time of the War of 1812, or perhaps a little before. Goodwin quickly fitted into the activities in Lord's business office, or counting room as it was then called, and also made his home with the Lords.

It soon became apparent to Samuel Lord that Goodwin possessed business acumen beyond the lowly post of clerk, and so the younger man was trained for service as a supercargo on a ship in which Lord had an interest — the *Elizabeth Wilson*. While the master of a vessel had absolute authority over sailing it, the supercargo was charged by the owners with business matters, acting as a superior type of clerk. With many idle hours to be filled on long passages, Goodwin utilized his time to good advantage by learning all he could about navigation and the handling of a sailing ship.

About 1820, Goodwin became master of the *Elizabeth Wilson*, and followed the sea for a dozen years. In 1832 he came into port for the last time, and settled into a merchandising career, and for a long time was associated with Samuel E. Coues. The latter was a bit of an eccentric scientist and philosopher; one theory he espoused was that the moon had nothing to do with the ebb and flow of the tides.

One of the ships commanded by Goodwin during his career as a mariner was the *Sarah Parker*, which was named for the woman Goodwin married on Sept. 3, 1827. Sarah Parker Rice was the daughter of one of Portsmouth's leading captains and merchants, William Rice. Five years after his marriage, Goodwin quit the sea, and apparently had never taken himself too seriously as a career ship master because he was once heard to remark that he was only a "cabin window sailor."

The Goodwins were the parents of seven children, but, in 1880, when a son, Frank, wrote an article about his father for the *Granite State Monthly*, only two daughters and Frank Goodwin were living. One son, Samuel Coues Goodwin, died at the age of 12 months in 1838.

Ichabod Goodwin's house once stood on Islington Street where Atherton's stands. Dressed in patriotic finery for the Fourth in 1992, the house is an important part of Strawbery Banke, Inc. Author photo.

Having given up the sea, Goodwin at first contented himself with building up his mercantile interests, and then soon became involved in politics. He devoted many years to the interests of the Whig Party, and was an ardent opponent of Jacksonian Democracy. He was elected to the State House of Representatives in the years 1838, 1843, 1844, 1850, 1854 and 1856. Beyond that, he attended the Whig presidential conventions that saw the nominations of Clay, Taylor and Scott. At the Clay convention in Baltimore in 1844, Goodwin was elected a vice president of the convention, representing New Hampshire. Henry Clay was the unanimous choice for president of the United States. Goodwin was the Whig choice to head a list of candidates for the U.S. House in 1846. The *Journal* said of him on Feb. 15, 1845:

"Mr. Goodwin is at the head of the Whig ticket for Congress. A better selection could not have been made. In his enlarged views and generous purposes he as truly represents the genuine Whig spirit as in the sound measures of Government to which he has always given an unwavering and efficient support. He is eminently a practical man, and is well-suited to such a body as the popular branch of Congress ought to be. Besides, Mr. Goodwin is a successful merchant. The important branch of our national interests with which he is familiar and which he would represent, is but imperfectly understood by the politicians in Congress. It is strange that a country with such great and growing commercial interests and relations has so few merchants in Congress and so few men acquainted with commercial affairs . . . ”

The next few paragraphs might easily have been published in today's *Portsmouth Herald*, and add weight to the belief history simply repeats itself: “There are few men who have reflected upon the subject who do not see the necessity of doing something to elevate the character of the U.S. House of Representatives. When the people see the evil and discredit which these men are inflicting upon the country, they will call into their service such men as will give practical direction to the legislation of Congress, and impart dignity and decency to its deliberations . . . ”

Despite the *Journal*'s strong views on the worthiness of Ichabod Goodwin's candidacy for the U.S. House, the Democrats prevailed in the election. Elections for state and municipal offices were then held annually in March. In 1849, Goodwin was the Whig candidate for the State Senate from the Portsmouth district, but the victory went to Richard Jenness, another prominent local merchant who lived in the former Elks building at Court and Pleasant streets.

However, in the election of 1850 Goodwin was again elected to the Legislature. The death of President Zachary Taylor on July 9, 1850, gave Goodwin the opportunity to speak in the House in support of a resolution relative to the President's passing. His remarks were quoted in the *Portsmouth Journal*:

“Mr Speaker: — Upon coming out of my chamber this morning, in Boston, I was met by the startling intelligence, 'The President is dead!' This event may well fill the nation with mourning. It is a national calamity. There are troubles and dissentions in our country, which the late President, from his character, services and position, was eminently suited to control and adjust.

“His genius as a soldier had drawn him to the attention and admiration of the whole country. As the chief magistrate of the nation, he had obtained a hold on the affections and confidence of the people, which would have enabled him and the country to surmount every difficulty and danger. He had the first requisite for success in public or private station — inflexible integrity.

"He had in all situations, a modesty which never offended, a firmness which never faltered, and a sagacity which never failed. May this sudden and deep affliction soften the bitter sectional feelings which distract our union. — May it produce upon our national councils and the people of our country, that national and fraternal feeling — that love of justice — that purity and patriotism to which the life of our lamented President was devoted."

Ichabod Goodwin's earnest hope that President Taylor's death would bring the nation back together was, as we know from history, already doomed. The "dissentions" he touched on in his short speech were already running out of control. Ironically, it was a New Hampshire man — Franklin Pierce — who, as the 14th president, helped push the United States into a path that led to civil war. And the onerous duty of governing the state in the early months of that civil war fell on the shoulders of Ichabod Goodwin.

However, when that time came, Goodwin was no longer a Whig. Zachary Taylor's successor, Millard Fillmore, was the last Whig to preside over the nation. By and large, the Whigs simply disappeared. In their stead came the Republican Party. The fast development of Ichabod Goodwin's leadership in the Republican Party was clearly demonstrated at the state convention in Concord's Phoenix Hall on Jan. 4, 1859. A snowstorm kept attendance down, but there were 373 delegates present. Although Goodwin wasn't there, he received 368 votes for governor. The campaign ran the usual course of such affairs with even the Democratic *New Hampshire Gazette* finding words of praise for the candidate:

"Of Mr. Goodwin, the nominee, we have at the present time but little to say. His private character is above reproach, and as a neighbor and citizen is deservedly esteemed. Many necessitous people and worthy objects have been the recipients of his unostentatious charity and generosity. As a businessman, he has been successful, and has a reputation for liberal enterprise and honorable dealing which no one will gainsay."

Ichabod Goodwin won the election over Democrat Asa P. Cate, but there was a touch of irony in the victory, he didn't carry Portsmouth, his home city, Cate polled 857 votes to Goodwin's 834.

Adding a bit of insult to the injury was the fact that Daniel Marcy, Democratic candidate for the U.S. House, outpolled his opponent, Gilman Marston of Exeter, by 259 votes, yet lost the election. However, that didn't deter Goodwin's jubilant supporters as the *Chronicle* reported on March 15:

"The Republicans of this city commenced their demonstrations of joy at the result of the late election, by the firing of one hundred guns at sunset on Monday. This was the signal for their assembling on Market Square, which took place at 6 1-2 o'clock, when, with the music of the Portsmouth Cornet Band, they marched to the house of the Governor-elect, Hon. Ichabod Goodwin, cheering as they passed numerous houses which were illuminated.

"In the procession was a company from New Castle, with music, citizens from Newington, Greenland, Rye &c., — and a company of young Republicans from this city. The governor-elect, and other gentlemen were then escorted to the Temple by this very large procession, only a small number of which could get into the building, and hundreds had to leave for want of room. Those who could get in were entertained with speeches agreeable to the programme, congratulatory of the Republican success, and declaratory of Republican principles in the State and National Governments. At about 9 o'clock, the procession again moved, to Jefferson Hall, where a social collation was enjoyed, and the company separated, well pleased with the occasion."

Goodwin began his first one-year term as governor in June, 1859, and it was the calm before the coming storm. Any man with vision could see that secessionists and unionists were on a collision course. In March, 1860, Goodwin was re-elected governor, and in the last two months of that term he met and solved enormous problems.

Despite all the months in which the war clouds were gathering, New Hampshire, like the other northern states, was about as prepared for war when the Confederates fired on Fort Sumter as was the United States when the Japanese staged their "Day of Infamy." Gov. Goodwin showed sensitivity to the impending disaster early in March, issuing a proclamation calling for a day of fasting on April 11, saying in part:

"Never in our national history has there been greater occasion for humility, persistence and prayer; never was our national political horizon so darkened by the clouds of discord and rebellion, never were our dearest social and national interests in such eminent peril . . . "

Ironically, the day after Goodwin's day of fasting, the South Carolinians shelled Ft. Sumter in Charleston Harbor. President Lincoln, with only five weeks in office, called on the loyal states to furnish 75,000 volunteers for three months' service. New Hampshire's quota was a regiment. New Hampshire had always had (on paper) a well organized militia, but, in reality, there were only two effective units: the Amoskeag Veterans and the Governor's Horse Guard; the latter having been formed largely to honor Gov. Goodwin.

One of Goodwin's immediate problems in meeting the President's call for men was that there was no money in the state treasury for raising or equipping troops. The State Legislature wasn't in session, so proper appropriations couldn't be made. Further, from years of personal legislative experience, Goodwin knew that convening a special session would not only be costly but time-consuming. Teaming up with Secretary of State Thomas L. Tullock, a native of Portsmouth, the governor took advantage of his wide contacts with industrialists and other key men to raise funds on his own responsibility.

The response was overwhelming, with $680,000 guaranteed to meet the emergency. More than a thousand men volunteered, and they were sworn in and equipped and ready for shipment in May. A second regiment was raised, but these were all three-year volunteers. When Goodwin left office, he had spent only $100,000 of the funds that had been raised. Nathaniel Berry took over the governorship on June 4, and the State Legislature unanimously ratified all of Goodwin's actions, thus freeing him from any personal responsibility.

The governorship was Goodwin's last elected public post, and he returned to his business interests in Portsmouth and elsewhere in New England. For many years, Goodwin had been in the forefront of promoting railroad interests, not only in the state but also throughout New England. He was the first president of the Eastern Railroad of New Hampshire, a post he held for a quarter century. Tied closely to that was his association with the Portland, Saco & Portsmouth Railroad.

Goodwin was one of the organizers of the Portsmouth Whaling Company, which operated for some years, sending vessels like the ships *Ann Parry, Triton* and *Pocahontas* to sea. The ex-governor became president of the First National Bank in 1878, and for many years was associated with the Portsmouth Bridge Company, which built a span across the Piscataqua about where the Sarah Long Bridge now stands.

For a long period he was president of the Howard Benevolent Society, a charitable institution that's still in existence. Goodwin also served for years on the board of managers of the Portsmouth Marine Society, an organization dedicated to assisting mariners who had fallen on hard times. Another of his many interests was the Rice Public Library in Kittery. The library was established in the memory of

Portsmouth merchant Robert Rice by his daughter, Arabella. In setting up funds, Miss Rice consulted frequently with Ichabod Goodwin.

Goodwin was a member of the library's board of trustees, and, on the death of the Rev. Daniel Austin, became chairman, a post he held until his death. In 1823, when the second block of 50 shares in the Portsmouth Athenaeum was offered, Goodwin became a proprietor, and his share, No. 94, was held in the family until 1935.

Ichabod Goodwin's own death on July 4, 1882, as might be expected, occasioned lengthy newspaper coverage. For example, the *Chronicle*'s lead paragraph read:

"It has been known to our citizens for some time that Hon. Ichabod Goodwin, ex-governor of New Hampshire, was failing in health, and that owing to the weight of the years which he had borne so well until within a brief time, it was improbable he would recover, yet this knowledge did not prevent a feeling of sorrowing surprise when it was announced on the morning of the 5th inst. that the honored and beloved old patriot had passed away on the previous night."

IV Susie Goodwin's Romance with George "Dandy" Dewey and the War Memorial in Goodwin Park

SAILORS HAVE LONG BEEN KNOWN for their pursuit of the tender passion, and George Dewey, of Spanish-American War fame, was no exception.

Lt. George Dewey was assigned to the Portsmouth Navy Yard early in 1867. A news item, published shortly after the end of the Spanish war, said he was so meticulous in his dress that had the word "dude" been in use, it would have applied to George Dewey. As it was, behind his back, he was known as "Dandy" Dewey.

The night after his arrival at the Navy Yard in Kittery, Dewey was invited to attend a ball in the home of one of Portsmouth's leading citizens. As he entered the mansion, his host introduced him to a trio of people. It included the first Civil War governor of New Hampshire, Ichabod Goodwin, his daughter, Susan, and a naval commander, Alexander C. Rhind, who was captain of the warship *Narragansett*, then stationed at the Navy Yard.

Dewey bowed to his senior officer, Rhind, and bowed very low over the hand of Susan Goodwin. When Rhind and the Goodwins moved along, another junior officer told Dewey that Rhind's pursuit of Susan Goodwin was the talk of Portsmouth. In addition to her beauty, Susan Goodwin had the additional virtue of being the daughter of a wealthy man, a matter worthy of consideration by a young naval officer.

29

*Late in life. No longer a dashing, young dandy, this
Library of Congress photo shows Adm. George
Dewey as still a handsome man, and was probably
made after his Spanish-American War triumphs.*

Dewey danced with Susan Goodwin three times that evening, a
circumstance noted by Cmdr. Rhind. Two days later he went for a
drive with her, and the next evening he met her at a dinner and
escorted her to the table. Later, Lt. Dewey was among those invited to
dinner at the Goodwin Mansion, then on Islington Street where
Atherton's is, but now in Strawbery Banke. Gov. Goodwin chose to pay
deep attention to Cmdr. Rhind, while the junior officer gave Susan his
undivided attention.

A bit of luck in the form of naval orders then played into Dewey's
hand: Cmdr. Rhind and his *Narragansett* were ordered to sea, thus
leaving Dewey a clear field. On Sept. 16, 1899, the *Portsmouth
Journal* published a feature article about Dewey's romance with
Susan Goodwin:

"He (Dewey) embraced this opportunity with his usual impetuosity. Soon the good-natured gossips noticed that Susie Goodwin wore a sparkling new brilliant on the third finger of her left hand . . . And it was reported that Gov. Goodwin was quite pleased with his prospective son-in-law, being quoted as saying: 'There's a lot in George. He has the right sort of grit. We'll hear from him in a time that's coming.'"

Not even Goodwin could have foreseen the role that Adm. George Dewey played in the Spanish War. The governor was long dead, as was his daughter Susie. The *Journal* article continued:

"Wedding cards put an end to the speculation of the gossips. 'Commander Rhind or Lieutenant Dewey?' they said tremblingly when they saw the Goodwin crest on the envelope. Dewey it was and their delicious fevers of uncertainty were over. The wedding took place at the Goodwin mansion Oct. 24, 1867.

"Again fortune had favored the young wooer. The impending orders came, but not until after the wedding. Shortly thereafter, 'Dandy' Dewey was ordered to duty in European waters, and for nearly two years he was separated from his young wife. When he returned he was not only a commander, but he was assigned to the *Narragansett* instead of his one-time rival, Cmdr. Rhind.

"The young couple spent their second honeymoon, a prolonged one, at Newport. Here, in the closing hours of 1872, their son was born. The young mother lived long enough to rejoice in the new happiness that had come to her. Five days after the birth of little George Goodwin Dewey, his mother died. Cmdr. Dewey's grief was not demonstrative; he would never talk of his loss, nor permit anyone else to do so, and he took up his naval duties again with a grim determination and absorption that were more pathetic than tears. He ordered two medallion portraits of his wife painted on ivory by an eminent Roman. One of these he carried with him until it was lost at sea."

As American history shows, Adm. George Dewey became one of the nation's great naval heroes with his victory over a Spanish fleet at Manila Bay. While Dewey mourned the loss of his beautiful Susie, he didn't stay celibate. He married again and even visited Portsmouth after the war, and spent some time at the famed Wentworth-By-The-Sea.

Goodwin Park

(Editor's Note: Although Goodwin Park was dedicated as a memorial ground to those who served the Union in the Civil War, it's also a memorial to the man who served New Hampshire as governor in the opening weeks of that bloody conflict.)

It was on Monday, the Fourth of July, 1888, that Portsmouth paid tribute to its Civil War heroes. The occasion was one of the old city's great communal celebrations, events that are always thoroughly enjoyed by the populace. It's an endearing characteristic of the "Old Town by the Sea" that when it takes an interest in something, its enthusiasm knows no bounds. One has only to recall the gala week of the 350th anniversary celebration in 1973 to realize that. For those a bit older, it's possible to remember the 300th, 50 years earlier. We'll rule out the 200th in 1823. And so it was with the erecting and dedicating of the Soldiers' Monument.

In the 1800s, the beautiful little open space known as Goodwin Park was an open field, at one time owned by Ichabod Goodwin, the first Civil War governor.

Portsmouth, as it always does in times of national peril, sent many of its men into combat on the battlefields of the Civil War, the struggle that confirmed once and for all the United States is indeed "one nation indivisible." The Civil War still ranks as the bloodiest conflict in which the United States has engaged, and made all the more horrible because two sections of a great nation were battling each other. For years after the war came to its final bloody conclusion, there was a talk of creating a monument of some sort to honor the men from the city who had fought in the many battles.

Many New Hampshire towns and cities very soon put up memorials to their fighting men. Driving through towns in the New Hampshire hinterland, the motorist speeds by these ancient monuments, usually employing the heroic figure of an infantryman. Portsmouth did nothing. In many ways it was understandable. The citizenry was ambivalent over the war. Many of them opposed it, more on the grounds of disruption of trade than anything else.

The noted antiquarian, the late Garland W. Patch Sr., was the proud owner of an *1864 City Directory* which made entertaining reading for the simple reason that on page after page a former owner had marked the names of those he termed "Copperheads," or southern

This monument in Goodwin Park honors the service peo-
ple of the Civil War. Originally, the monument stood
much higher, but in 1955 it was found that the section at
Miss Liberty's feet was deteriorating. It was removed and
then Miss Liberty was restored to her post of honor.
Author photo.

sympathizers. Oh, the city's young men went to war, although there were many who paid $300 for a substitute to fight for them. However, as such things have a way of doing, the bitterness ebbed with the years, and, in 1886, 21 years after the end of the conflict, then-Mayor Marcellus Eldredge made a proposition to the Storer Post, Grand Army of the Republic, which in substance said:

"If the comrades of your Post will raise by subscriptions among our citizens, or in any other manner, the sum of $2,000, I will contribute a sum in addition sufficient to build a monument 27 feet high, appropriately inscribed and beautifully decorated, the apex to be surmounted with a statue in white bronze of a Union soldier at parade rest."

That was in April 1886, and Storer Post immediately called a meeting to consider the proposition. (The Storer Post, GAR, was to the Civil War veterans what the Frank E. Booma Post, American Legion, is to the veterans of America's 20th century wars. Within a week there was a call for a meeting of the citizenry to consider Mayor Eldredge's proposal. Twenty-three other prominent men joined in sending out invitations to the meeting. There were about 25 present at that first session, and the names read like a who's who of the city's leaders: Mayor Eldredge, J.J. Pickering, Frank Jones, Charles A. Sinclair, Fred E. Potter, William E. Sise, Francis E. Langdon, Ezra H. Winchester, C.M. Gignoux, John S. Treat, John Laighton, W. Freeman, W.H. Rollins, H.F. Eldredge, Henry M. Clark, Calvin Page, C.C. Jackson, J. Albert Walker, T. Salter Tredick, John Conlon, Edward P. Kimball, John Sise, James P. Bartlett, Charles H. Rollins, Daniel Marcy, Wallace Hackett, Samuel J. Gerrish, Benjamin F. Webster, John S. Pray and Joseph W. Peirce. Some of these men were too young to have fought in the war; others had hired substitutes. And, ironically, John S. Treat had fought for the Confederacy.

A committee to arrange financing met the next week, under the chairmanship of C.M. Gignoux, with J. Albert Sanborn, one of the most honored Civil War veterans, as secretary. Gignoux became treasurer and thus was custodian of the first money raised—$81 from the employees of the Eldredge Brewing Company. More names were added to the overall committee: Thomas A. Harris, Joseph Thatcher, Andrew P. Preston, Arthur W. Walker, E.S. Fay, William Ward, George B. French, Josiah H. Morrison, C.W. Tracy, Mark Scott, Michael Crowley, Hiram C. Locke, Thomas Entwistle and Frank L. Pryor.

The Soldiers Monument project dithered along for the next few months as such efforts are inclined to do. Subscription boxes were placed in various stores in order to catch the odd penny or two. Jacob Wendell of New York sent a gift of $200.

By September it was estimated that the fund had between three and four thousand dollars, and so a committee was appointed to select a site for the memorial. Winchester, Dr. John W. Parsons, and Maj. D.J. Vaughan were on it. In February, 1887, the total collected was $2,821.32, and another $385 had been subscribed but not turned in. More importantly, however, Mayor Eldredge reported that the Eldredge family would donate the Goodwin field to the city, provided the monument fund reached $5,000, and that the city would accept the lot and maintain it "forever as a park." The *Portsmouth Journal* reported:

"A committee was appointed to present this gift to the city government, and the meeting adjourned after eulogistic remarks, feeling that at last the fact Portsmouth was to have a monument is now assured through the generosity of the Eldredge family. The location of the monument will be a very appropriate one, opposite the family residences of our old war governor Goodwin, and our public-spirited Mayor, the author and moving spirit of the enterprise. The lot will need but little outlay to make it a handsome little park, which with its monument in the center will remain a thing of beauty and joy forever."

In April the fund was still about $1,700 short, but various money-raising events were planned. Periodic reports on donations were published in the newspapers, and by May only another thousand was needed. In small amounts, sometimes as little as 15 cents, the money kept coming in. A Boston-based Portsmouthite suggested that former residents be solicited and a committee was named to see what could be raised from such sources.

In July the mayor reported that $5,515 had been donated. Frank Jones alone had put up $1,000. In October the foundation work was completed and the field had been graded up toward the center by seven feet. In December came a tentative description of the proposed monument, and it differed considerably from the original proposal by Marcellus Eldredge. What had been decided was that the memorial would be 36 feet high, 12 feet square at the base, and surmounted by a statue of Liberty eight feet high. The following is a description published in the *Journal* a few days before the dedication on July Fourth and it had been changed:

"The Base is 12 ft. square, 3 ft. 10 inches high. This followed by the Plinth, which is 9 ft. 7 inches square and 4 ft. 7 1/2 inches high; on each side of this section is a buttress which projects 17 3-4 inches. Standing on the front and back buttresses are pyramids of cannon balls, with a life-sized statue of an infantryman at 'parade rest' on the right buttress, and the same statue of a sailor resting his right hand on an anchor . . .

"On the face of the front buttress is the City Seal of Portsmouth, on the right face a stack of muskets, on the left a capstan, and on the back the United States Coat of Arms, all in bold-raised bas-relief. Beneath these and on the face of each side of the plinth are the battle names, Gettysburg, Fredericksburg, Kearsarge and Antietam. The Die, which is octagonal in shape, is 5 ft. 2 1/2 inches in diameter and 7 ft. 4 inches in height. On its front tablet is the dedicatory inscription. On the right tablet is the bas-relief of a mounted Parrot gun, on the left the sinking of Confederate States cruiser Alabama by the United

States ship Kearsarge, and on the back a list of twenty-three battle names, commencing with Williamsburg and ending with Sherman's March to the Sea.

"The Upper Die is also octagonal and is 3 ft. 3 inches in diameter and 6 ft. 6 inches in height. On the front tablet of this section is a medallion of New Hampshire's War Governor Goodwin, on the right tablet the Crossed Swords, on the left the G.A.R. Badge, and on the back a medallion of Abraham Lincoln. Surrounding the top of this section is a beautiful frieze in bold relief. At the top the United States Flag is gracefully festooned. The spire is surmounted by a beautiful floriated Cap which is 3 ft. 8 inches in diameter and 1 ft. 11 inches in height. This section is broken by four raised tablets, upon each of which is a raised five-pointed star. The whole is surmounted by the statue of America, which is 8 ft. 6 inches in height. She is resting her left hand on the United States shield and sheathed sword, and is bestowing a laurel wreath with the right hand. The whole structure is 42 feet 6 1-2 inches in height."

It would be easy to fill a modest book with all the details of the preparations for the dedication of the Soldiers' Monument. Anyone who wasn't on one of the committees must have been a "carpet-bagger," a term in no more repute in Portsmouth, or down South, than it is today. And most of us are "carpet-baggers."

But it's amazing to read the old newspaper files and learn of the concessions the railroads were making to get delegates to come to Portsmouth for the dedication. The railroads agreed to charge only 1 and 1-2 cents a mile to get to Portsmouth. Can you imagine coming from Boston for 75 cents, or Manchester for about 60 cents? More than 40 bands, drum corps, etc., were engaged, and it was planned to have a boat parade on the South Mill Pond as part of the exercises. Before present-day readers start waving red flags, let it be remembered that in those unenlightened days, there was no Junkins Avenue. Even the South Mill Pond was larger—the city had only started using it as a dump.

Andrew P. Preston, the city's leading apothecary, was elected chief marshal for the parade. On June 9, 1888, came the "fullest attended meeting" of the monument committee. With that, much of the nitty-gritty was wiped out, and, most importantly, Chief Marshal Preston was vested with real authority. The details of the parade route were worked out. The local contingents were to form on Pleasant Street, so they could march along Market and Deer Streets to greet the incoming units at the depot. As is so often the case, the best laid plans "gang aft a-gley." The railroads, the predecessors of the airlines in moving people, weren't on schedule, and the parade, and everything else, ran an hour or so behind.

Even the governor of New Hampshire, who had a commitment in Amesbury, was unable to wait out the erratic train arrivals. However, by noon, all the contingents were on hand, and the procession got under way. The surmounting figure of the monument had arrived a few days before from Bridgeport, Conn., where it had been fabricated. On its arrival, throngs had gone to the waterfront to inspect it.

"After the exercises at Goodwin Park, the route was from Goodwin Park to State and Middle to Court Street and collation tent in rear of the Courthouse, where the parade was dismissed. The several organizations are then to be considered in charge of their commanding officers."

In 1888 the courthouse stood where the Central Fire Station stands now. When the fire station was built in 1920, the court house was moved to the general vicinity of the former Home for Aged Women. It burned May 1, 1953. The traditional platoon of police, headed by City Marshal Jefferson Rowe, led the parade of five divisions. The fifth division consisted of all the city and other dignitaries, including those who had headed committees. Soldiers in the Guard of Honor at the monument were William H. Lear, Charles F. Goodwin, James F. Moore, Henry B. Colson, Henry F. Fuller, and Carl Carty. Representing sailors were James A. Snow, Charles Cunningham, James Barr and William Watkins.

The monument was unveiled by the Misses Sadie E. Eldredge and Martha Sophia ("Fie") Sinclair. However, there was a bit of a bad moment. As the veiling was dropping, it caught on one of the figures, but a retired seaman, Boatswain Isaac T. Choate, quickly climbed up and cleared it to the applause of the multitude. Lt. John H. Hutchinson, chairman of the building committee, then presented the monument to Mayor George E. Hodgdon. After that, former Mayor Marcellus ("Cel") Eldredge presented the crowning figure, Miss Liberty. There was no mention of Franklin Pierce.

The *Portsmouth Times*, the *Chronicle* reported, did an eight-page special section on the dedication, including pictures, but, unfortunately, that issue isn't extant, not locally anyway. The formal ceremonies weren't the end of the day's program. In the evening, the boat parade took place on the South Mill Pond. A light breeze interfered with the illumination of the boats, but the situation was saved by the presence of musicians on the boats.

Fireworks were displayed at Langdon Park with no less than 10 set pieces, among them the Shield of Iris, Bands of Orion, Arthursian Fountain, Passion Flower, Rose of Sharon and the Soldiers' Monument. All in all, it was a great day. True, one tragedy took place on Water Street. A teenager named George Herbert was fatally injured when a box of gunpowder blew up in his face. Young Herbert had come in from the Isles of Shoals to enjoy the festivities.

The *Chronicle* was pleased to note that there was "but little drunkenness observable during the day." And that was noteworthy indeed because quite often public celebrations were attended by wild drinking sprees, with the imbibers, including children, passing out on the street.

The Soldiers' Monument stood in all its splendor for 67 years. Memorials to the men and women of other wars were put up in the vicinity, but Miss Liberty dominated the scene, as she still does. However, in 1955 it was determined that the two sections immediately below Miss Liberty were deteriorating. On March 31, 1955, Miss Liberty was lifted off her lofty perch and stored while the two lower sections were removed.

Miss Liberty was then returned to her place of prominence.

V Some Women of Spirit: Madam Knight, Ann Downing, Lucy Stone

Madam Knight

IN THIS DAY WHEN WOMEN orbit the Earth in NASA space vehicles and one New Hampshire woman died in the Challenger mishap, the story of a lady named "Madam Knight" won't seem like much.

But, in 1704, she embarked on a journey that was a marvel for that time. She rode on horseback, alone, from Boston to New York, Her exploit even has some local interest because she probably once lived in Portsmouth.

Madam Knight's story became public in Portsmouth on May 28, 1825, when the *Portsmouth Journal* published a report it had taken from the *New York Statesman* which had been given access to the journal Madam Knight kept while on her hazardous journey. Hiring local guides as necessary, Madam Knight went through Indian country including the Narragansett area. The item said;

"She was obliged to ford rivers, pass the night in log huts, and frequently ride 18 or 20 miles to find a place to bait . . . " That last phrase meant finding fodder for her horse.

The *Journal* was puzzled by one paragraph in the article in the *Statesman*, wondering if anyone "conversant with the early history of this town" could explain it:

"It was supposed on a perusal of this work, that it might be a fiction; but an examination of the manuscript has fully satisfied us that it is genuine . . . It has indeed long been cherished by a family in Hartford as a curious literary relic, without any intention of making it public. Madam Knight was one of the most remarkable women of the age; and there is now a house in Portsmouth, N.H., designated as having once belonged to her, and with which many traditions are associated . . ."

If nothing else, Madam Knight must have been an unusual woman in that she could keep a journal. Women in the early 18th century were given little or no formal schooling, and the keeping of a journal necessitates the ability to read and write. However, the *Portsmouth Journal* wasn't concerned with that kind of trivia. What the *Journal* was curious about was what house was referred to, and it observed:

"The house in Court Street [now the northern end of Pleasant Street], which was formerly called Madam Knight's (now the Farmers' Tavern) we have always supposed derived from a Madam Knight of a later generation—a lady who died not many years ago."

The Farmer's Tavern, along with the Rockingham National Bank building, were demolished in the 1850s to make way for the huge granite pile we now call the Old Federal Building. The Farmer's Tavern became a hotel about 1818, and, from its general appearance, would seem to date well back into the 18th century.

Whoever she was, Madam Knight was a courageous, able woman.

Ann Downing

If Ann Downing were alive today, she would be more than 170 years old.

That being a bit improbable, it can be said that the spirit of Ann Downing still exists in America's women. In fact, Pvt. Ann Downing would undoubtably be delighted to see women wearing the stars of admirals and generals. But Ann Downing came along 140 years too soon because such exalted military ranks were unheard of for the women of her day. Nevertheless, Ann Downing did serve in the Mexican War 16 months.

So who was Ann Downing?

Ann West was born in York, Dec. 15, 1829, the daughter of Mary West Sides. About the age of 14 she came to Portsmouth to live and work. At one time she was in the employ of the famed shipwright George Raynes, working as a domestic in that household on the edge of the North Mill Pond. Where and how Ann West met Havilah F. Downing isn't known. Quite probably he, too, was employed by Raynes, and worked in the shipyard as either a laborer or carpenter. When the war with Mexico began in 1846, the United States was soon forced to start raising troops to do the fighting.

In March, 1847, an advertisement appeared in the *Portsmouth Journal*, seeking recruits for service in the 9th U.S. Infantry Regiment. Applicants had to be between 18 and 35 years of age, and at least five feet-three inches tall. The recruiting officer was Capt Theodore F. Rowe. Two companies were to be raised in New Hampshire; four in Maine; one in Vermont; one in Rhode Island and two in Connecticut. Ft. Constitution was designated as a receiving depot for the New Hampshire volunteers.

Company C, 9th Infantry, was taken out of Portsmouth by First Lt. John H. Jackson, the captain commanding, Stephen Woodman, having gone AWOL. The New England Regiment, eventually was part of a brigade commanded by Brig. Gen. Franklin Pierce, a Concord lawyer. Little did the men and the woman in the regiment imagine that their brigade commander would become president of the United States. The 9th Infantry fought its way through the whole campaign in the Valley of Mexico. And Ann Downing was right there with her man and men.

Jackson, by now a captain, still had Company C. In the fighting around Mexico City, he was hit in the chest by a musket ball, which fell to the ground. The ball had struck a breast pocket in which Jackson was carrying a Bible given him by his sister as he left home for the war. In July, 1848, the 9th began leaving the war theatre and the Massachusetts contingent of volunteers arrived in Boston. The other part of the 9th Regiment was at Ft. Adams, Newport, R.I., by Aug. 15. A news article commented on the fine, fresh appearance of the troops:

"One would not suppose they had seen active service in Mexico, and indeed but very few of them have done so. Out of the whole number of about 600, just arrived, there are but 105 who composed the whole regiment which left the fort a year and a quarter ago . . . The remainder are recruits."

While Mexican bullets took their toll, another insidious enemy was the yellow-fever-bearing mosquito. The winged devils struck all ranks and no doubt Ann Downing did plenty of nursing. In her pension petition, Ann Downing said her husband was separated from the service on Aug. 23, 1848, and this statement was supported by his certificate of discharge. When they came back to Portsmouth, the Downings apparently returned to the employ of George Raynes. In the *1851 City Directory*, Downing is listed as a ship's carpenter. Downing went back to the wars with the 6th New Hampshire in the Civil War. Ann apparently didn't go that time.

It would appear that the Downings had their problems. Havilah was in Municipal Court on June 8, 1874, for stealing 16 pounds of pork. For that offense, he was given 60 days at Brentwood. Added to that was another 60 days for being a "common drunkard." Within five days, the poor devil was dead, and his body was returned to Portsmouth for burial in the North Cemetery.

The Mexican War Pension Act of Jan. 29, 1887, gave Ann Downing the right to apply for benefits. Her petition was approved March 11, 1887, to take effect in May, 1887. She received eight dollars a month. Never to the end of her days would Ann Downing admit to her age. She told the *Herald* that anything under sixty was alright, and the article added:

"Whatever her age, she was as straight-backed as a West Point cadet, and as firm and elastic of step as most women of fifty. For half a century she has been a tower of strength and comfort to many families in distress. With the power of a coal-heaver, the courage of a border trooper, the nerve of an Army surgeon, and the tact and tenderness of a real woman, her presence in the sick room has been a benediction, and the sorrow surrounding many a death bed has been lightened by her administration."

Few of us now living could command such a eulogy. Ann Downing died April 21, 1903. Her grateful government had paid over that span approximately $1,500 in pension rights. But she had served from the "Halls of Montezuma . . . " Today she sleeps in the North Cemetery beside her war-time companion and husband, Havilah Downing.

Recently the writer learned that Ann Downing was one of three women who were enlisted in Company C by Capt. Theodore F. Rowe. They were recruited to serve as laundresses.

A reminisence published in the *Portsmouth Chronicle*, April 5, 1887, gives more details about the raising of Company C. The recruiting officer was on the second floor of a building that stood on the northeast corner of Penhallow and Daniel streets. Capt. Rowe had fifers and drummers marching the streets to stir the populace to patriotic fervor.

"Pretty soon two recruits signed the roll, and then came street parades . . . and all the little boys and girls who dared to play hooky from school followed the pageant on its semi-daily rounds . . . "

Seventy-eight men and three laundresses were with the company when it left Portsmouth. Eighteen of the males were recruited in Portsmouth; 20 from Manchester; 27 from Dover; one each from Rye and Durham; the rest scattered around the state.

Two of the laundresses were sent home from Vera Cruz, but Mrs. Ann Downing, wife of Sgt. Havilah Downing, "remained with the company, entered the city of Mexico with the rest of the soldiers, and returned and was honorably mustered out at the close of the war." Company C arrived in Mexico with 72 men, and only 28 returned to New Hampshire, "one having deserted in Mexico, two having been transferred to another company, and 40 having been returned as killed or missing in the campaign." At the time that was published, only Ann Downing and the first sergeant, Alfred J. Hill, were living in Portsmouth.

In April 1889, Alfred J. Hill joined the company of old soldiers responding to the last "Assembly." He was 84, and had served in both the Mexican and Civil wars. His latter service was with the 3rd NHVR, but didn't last long. He was thrown from a horse, badly injured and was discharged.

Lucy Stone

The emergence of women into all phases of American life makes it difficult to realize how their lot has changed in the past century. Ardent feminists continue to push for more gains, especially in the field of business where women often still find themselves outside the "Old Boy" network. However, no matter how strenuous they find the struggle, what today's feminists face in the way of obstacles is nothing compared to the high walls that Lucy Stone tried to tear down in the last half of the 19th century.

Lucy Stone was born in 1818, and her entire life was dedicated to women's rights. After many headaches and heartaches, she finally graduated from Oberlin College in 1847 and a few weeks later gave her first public address on women's rights. She stumped the country giving lectures, and, as an added burden, took up the Abolitionists' cause as well. Lucy Stone gave a lecture in Exeter in 1855, which occasioned a letter to the editor of the *Chronicle* in the issue of Jan. 23, 1855. Because the letter so typifies the anti-feminism of that day, it will be quoted in full:

"One of the most popular topics of the day, and one which we consider of great importance, is Women's Rights. A number of communications on this subject have already appeared in the Chronicle; and we propose to review the arguments and suggestions contained therein, and add a few of our own. One writer, signing himself 'G.P.,' gives an abstract of a lecture delivered in Exeter, by Lucy Stone, who thinks that because drunkards, foreigners and negroes vote, women should have the same privilege. This is rather poor reasoning; and is equivalent to saying, that because we already have many unfit voters, we might as well have still more by letting women vote.

"There would be some force in the argument, if it were proper for any of the class she names to exercise the privilege they now do; but we hope to see the time when no foreigner, drunkard, or person who cannot read and write, will be allowed to vote. The greater portion of womankind do not wish to vote; and it will be time enough to talk about the matter when they manifest a general desire to do so. Feathers, bracelets, satins, beads, and other gewgaws are all that the majority of women care about; and even the most ambitious are satisfied with a carriage to ride about in, the last new novel, and a liberal sprinkling of balls, parties, etc.

*Early feminist. Lucy Stone was an early champion
of women's rights and was scorched by the media for
her efforts.*

"Of course, besides what we have named, each wants a good smart man. If there are any so unreasonable as not to be satisfied with all these desirable things, we hope it will never be our bad luck to have any dealings with them. A few freaks of nature, in the shape of women, would like to dabble in the dirty waters of politics; but such characters are usually more fit subjects for an insane asylum than for leaders in public affairs. Again Lucy says if politics would have a tendency to make women corrupt, as some contend, men should never meddle with them.

"This does not follow. Men can and do engage in many undertakings without determent to their characters, which would entirely ruin a woman. Think of a female constable, sent out to catch thieves, robbers, murderers, etc., and of what sort of company she would be likely to meet within her search. Most men visit places where they would not like to see their wives or daughters, and yet where it is necessary that somebody should go.

"Men also do many things that are useful and respectable, which at the same time are dirty; for instance—butchering. There is not a civilized butcher in Christendom so brutal as to want his wife or daughter to aid him in his slaughtering. Imagine a lady who had been engaged all day in killing oxen, sheep, calves, and pigs!—what a lovely creature she would be. And yet nobody will deny that this dirty work must be done. Butchering is far more honorable and cleanly business than the wire pulling and log rolling, done by most politicians. That the laws in regard to the property of females, need amending, in every State in the Union, we presume no one will deny; and the sooner it is done, the better. But the property laws, after all, would not benefit the poor sewing woman, for she has no property to lose. Very few women ever get rich by their own exertions; and as long as they are so poorly renumerated for the labor they perform as at present, we don't see how they can. The greatest wonder is, how some of them stay at all, (we cannot think they live) on the miserable pittance they receive.

"This matter of wages, however, is in their own hands; and they can regulate it as well as the men do theirs. It is a notorious fact, that when one woman has occasion to hire a number of others,—as is the case with milliners and dressmakers—she beats them down to the last copper on their wages, and then grumbles when called on to pay at all. This is especially the case in large cities; but we have never yet heard of an instance, even in small towns, where one woman was very liberal towards another in her employ; when we do, we'll make a note of it. Wealthy ladies, too, when they hire girls to work in their kitchens, think one dollar per week good wages, and if two dollars are paid, it is thought enormous. We think if women were paid double what they now are, they would not be overpaid.

"Lucy, like all her tribe, advises the girls not to get married. Perhaps they will heed her teachings in this respect, if nobody asks them; but let a young spark come along that one of them is pleased with, and offer himself to her, and the chances are she will snap him up as quick as powder burns when a coal of fire is touched to it. But even allowing all the principles and arguments laid down in Lucy's lecture to be correct and sound—then we should be opposed to woman's voting and for this reason: Everybody knows that the women far outnumber the male. Let them vote and they can choose officers of their own sex, in spite of all the lords of creation. Now as we detest petticoat government, we decidedly object to letting women have any-thing to do with politics. In our schoolboys days we were under the charge of seven or eight female teachers, at various times, the last of whom—a peppery old maid—seemed determined we should not spoil on account of her sparing the rod. Having got out of her power, we are not anxious or willing to be under the rule of another like her.

"Another correspondent, 'A.,' ridicules the idea of women's voting, but does not give any good reason why they should not. He says the women took part in politics in Harrison's time, when almost every-body drank hard cider. The hard cider made many of the men drunk; and 'A.' insinuates, many of the women, too. What if it did? Women have as much right to drink as men. He thinks the women on election days will wade through the mire, with garments drabbled and muddy for a foot or two.

"He is much mistaken. When the women acquire brass enough to want to vote, they will wear boots and breeches. The former, it would be wise for them to wear in moist weather, like the present; when they attempt to wear the latter, family jars are apt to occur."

As one of the Portsmouth Public Library staff said after reading the letter, "Times have surely changed, haven't they?" Apparently the writer was correct in claiming that Lucy Stone opposed marriage. Yet she did marry within a few months of her Exeter appearance.

She consented to wed Henry B. Blackwell on May Day, 1855, only after he gave a solemn pledge to support her campaign for women's rights. She kept her maiden name, merely changing "Miss" to "Mrs."

Lucy Stone would have relished seeing a woman running for the vice presidency of the United States on the ticket of a major party.

But Lucy probably wouldn't have been surprised to read after Geraldine Ferraro's debate in 1984 with George Bush, the Republican vice presidential candidate, that Bush gallantly made the remark to the media that he had had to "kick a little arse last night."

The feminists of our day may believe that they are pioneers, but really there's nothing new in the movement. More than 130 years ago there was a Women's Rights Convention in Worcester, Mass. It closed its sessions after passing the resolution printed below:

"Whereas, The very concentrated sphere of action for women, arising from an unjust view of her natural capacities and powers, and from the infringement of her just rights as an equal with man, is highly injurious to her physical, mental and moral development:

Therefore -

"Resolved, that we will not cease our endeavors to secure for her political, legal and social equality with man; until her proper sphere is determined by what alone should determine it, her powers and capacities strengthened and refined by an education in accordance with her nature."

Believe it or not, the above was published in the *Portsmouth Journal* on Nov. 2, 1850. Despite Betty Friedan, not much has changed in 150 years. The *Journal* said the principal "actors in the convention were the usual leading spirits, male and female, of the ultra-abolition meetings, viz: William Lloyd Garrison, Wm. H. Channing, Samuel J. May, Frederick Douglass, Parker Pillsbury, Lucretia Mott, Abby Kelly Foster, Sarah J. Kenney, etc. But one of the most delightful sentiments of the convention, and one still echoing down the years, was uttered by Abby Foster:

"Woman is trodden down and crushed by man, and would be justified in rising up and cutting the throats of every man that makes laws opposing them."

Tough stuff? So what else is new?

Well, three years later hangers-on in the vicinity of the Spring Market, at Ceres and Bow streets, were treated to the spectacle of practical enforcement of "Woman's Rights," carried out in a manner that would have delighted Abby Foster. The *Journal* said:

"The attention of buyers and sellers of butter, chickens, berries, beans, peaches and melons, was suddenly arrested by the whistle of a whip lash and its smart swipe, as it wound itself around the unmentionables of a fisherman. It was wielded by one of the weaker sex, who had in some way taken a dislike to the said strong man. The enraged piece of finer fabric stood off at the fair distance and cut him right and left, interlarding the stripes with admonitions for him to be 'be careful how he told his stories' about her in the streets.

"Fortunately the man was a non-resistant—for resistance to such a lash, would have been in vain, as it would have been for the crowd, which witnessed the scene, to have tried to refrain from hearty shouts of laughter. The man finally retreated, leaving his castigatress mistress of the field, amid the applause of the populace. What a noble stand for women rights, (say a correspondent) the right to flog a man publicly, without the right on his part to flog back again."

VI Some Tales of Dentistry

Dr. Sylvester F. A. Pickering

In the course of this now fast-ebbing century, many changes —mostly for the better—have taken place in the health-care professions, but few any more so than the field of dentistry. The photograph accompanying this tale shows what it was like in one Portsmouth dental establishment right around the turn of the century.

Today Portsmouth and its surrounding communities are well served by many fine dentists, and over the years many other dedicated men have also served their communities well—by the standards of a day when you could get a tooth pulled for half a dollar—usually without anesthetic. One such professional set up a practice here a bit more than a hundred years ago, and when Dr. Sylvester F. A. Pickering died in 1945 he had been working longer than any other dentist in New Hampshire. And Dr. Pickering was so highly esteemed by his fellow citizens that he was elected mayor in 1932, serving a one-year term.

Despite his Pickering name, Dr. Pickering wasn't a native, although his family was connected to the long-established Portsmouth clan. He was born in Niantic, Ill., Jan. 1, 1867. When he was seven, his parents returned to the ancestral habitat, and he went to school in Newington and Portsmouth. Those who knew him, and their numbers are still legion in the Portsmouth area, thought highly of him as a man. In physique, the good doctor was a bit over-powering. D. Porter McIntire, one of the city's eminent octagenarians, estimates that he weighed 280 pounds and stood well over six feet.

49

Old-Time Dental Office: Strawbery Banke's photo library lists this picture as the interior of Dr. S. F. Pickering's office on Congress St. However, many former patients are emphatic in contradicting the claim. Photo courtesy of Strawbery Banke.

McIntire also recalled, with a bit of a shudder, "He was a brute when it came to pulling a tooth," but he hastened to amend that observation by emphasizing what a fine man Dr. Pickering was. Another life-long resident, Miss Dorothy G. Pridham, agreed that an extraction by Dr. Pickering was painful, saying, "He did one for my mother once; she never went back."

William H. P. Hopley remembers him with affection, and recalls a day when Dr. Pickering pulled a tooth for him. He said, "it was over so quick that it didn't hurt that much." Hopley said he was excused from class at the old high school by Francis T. "Babe" Malloy to get the tooth taken care of. He returned so quickly that Malloy had to see the tooth before believing he had been to the dentist. Later in life, Hopley and his wife, Dorothea, were neighbors of Dr. Pickering's and Mrs. Hopley, before her marriage, had worked in the doctor's office.

In fact, "Bill" Hopley recalls with glee that on one occasion while his wife was working for Dr. Pickering, a macho type (Yes, they had them, even then.) came into the office to have a tooth pulled. Trying to tease Dorothea Emerson, as she was then, the patient opined that she couldn't pull his tooth; she wasn't strong enough. Miss Emerson said she could, and Dr. Pickering told the patient that if he gave permission he would have her pull the tooth. Caught in his own trap, the patient acquiesced and Dorothea quickly and efficiently extracted the tooth. When the patient tried to pay Dr. Pickering, he made him pay the half-dollar to his helper. She accepted; 50 cents was real money in those days.

Dr. Pickering established his practice in Hampton after getting a license in 1889. Two years later he moved to 32 Congress St. in Portsmouth, a building long since leveled by fire. Dr. Pickering became very active in community life, serving on the 1923 Tricentennial Committee and on the now-obsolete Common Councils. He also served as water commissioner, three terms on the Police Commission, and as chairman of the Planning and Development Committee.

A staunch Republican, he was elected mayor while Portsmouth tried to cope with the onslaught of the Great Depression. In his inaugural, Dr. Pickering took full note of the economic paralysis that stalked the land. In the Portsmouth area, the pinch was heightened by the reduced payrolls at the Navy Yard.

Dr. Pickering, still active in his profession at age 78, died in 1945 from injuries he suffered in a fall while doing a chore at his Pleasant street home.

Dr. Daniel H. Peirce

The little yarn to be spun below is a bit unusual for a community that has many excellent dentists practicing their profession in its midst. Dr. Daniel H. Peirce had only one patient for whom he extracted a tooth, charging the going rate of 25 cents.

Dr. Peirce was born in Portsmouth in 1801, a scion of the well-entrenched Peirce family; the son of John Peirce, the man who built the Peirce mansion that still graces Haymarket Square, albeit it has been moved back 50 feet from its original location. He attended Phillips Exeter, graduated from Harvard, and on his return to Portsmouth studied dentistry under the guidance of Dr. James H. Pierrepont, who was primarily a physician, but the two disciplines worked more closely together in those days. Finishing his training with Dr. Pierrepont, Peirce went to Paris to complete his studies.

As noted above, however, that one extraction constituted his active dental career. For the rest of his life, and he never married, Daniel Peirce, contented himself with study and comradeship at the Portsmouth Athenaeum. On his death on April 26, 1877, he left a fortune of $400,000. Even at today's fee schedules his modern successors will be hard put to amass such a sum in a life-time of work, especially when one tries to figure the purchasing power of a dollar in 1877.

Dr. Samuel Baker

And now a tale about a dentist who was an inventor.

It's hard to imagine, but only 130 years ago, housewives did the family wash with scrub-boards and a lot of elbow grease. Washdays were indeed days of drudgery for a woman. But there were people working on ideas to relieve much of this back-breaking labor. One of them was Samuel Baker, a Portsmouth dentist with an office on Congress street. His home was on Parker street.

In the mid 1850's, Dr. Baker developed a washing machine, and gave it two years of testing before going public with his idea. When a reporter for the *Portsmouth Journal* saw it, he wrote:

"In a box 3 or 4 feet long, twenty inches wide, and 14 inches high, is placed within an inch from the bottom, a board with six half rounds, similar to a hand washing board.—This board slides, and has a horizontal motion of about two inches when in operation On this board the clothes are placed. Over it another similar board is placed, with the half rounds under.

"A weight is placed on it, boiling water is turned in, then covered. By the operation of turning a crank a balance wheel is put in motion, and the two boards operate on the clothes much like rubbing between immense hands, effectively doing the work in a short time, with much less damage to the clothes than by any other process.

"In a net bag, hung like a hammock over the box, the clothes are then put, and by turning a crank at one end, the bag is twisted, and the water much more effectually wrung out than it can be by the hands.

"He is taking measures and intends to secure a patent. We thus see that even a man in good business can turn his leisure moments to good account."

Still hard work. This advertisement for a still well known laundry soap appeared in the Portsmouth Chronicle *50 years after the story on Dr. Baker's washing machine. So it can be seen that automatic washers were far in the future.*

Dr. Edward B. Goodall

No discussion of old-time Portsmouth dentists would be complete without a few words about Dr. Edward B. Goodall. Dr. Goodall was unique, if only because all his life he wanted to teach music, not pull teeth. Not until nearly the very end of his life did he get a chance to do exactly that.

He was one of twin brothers, born in Bath, N. H., on Jan. 4, 1838. His twin, Frank, was in the service of the U.S. Treasury, Washington, D.C., for many years. Edward Goodall trained in dentistry and came to Portsmouth in the early 1860s. The first mention of him in the local newspapers came on March 16, 1864, in the form of a long letter to the editor of the *Portsmouth Chronicle*, in which Dr. Goodall discussed the use of "Nitrous Oxide Gas," which had been "attended with fatal results":

" . . . I will state a few facts in my experience and observation. I only wonder that there have been so few cases reported of fatal results. I fully expect to hear of many more, considering the way in which dentists have rushed into the use (or rather I might say, the abuse) of this popular anaesthetic. In the first place, *I know* that hundreds of dentists have even *dared to administer the Gas without any instructions whatever*, and have constructed their own apparatus to manufacture the gas—not knowing, or caring to observe common prudence, whether they have used a *pure gas* or not . . .

"I manufacture my own gas through *fresh water every time I make it;* and the apparatus I use has been pronounced by the State Chemist of Massachusetts perfectly satisfactory for manufacturing *positively a pure gas* . . . "

Dr. Goodall continued lauding his skills in gassing his patients at some length before concluding:

" . . . I have extracted several thousand teeth during the past few months, under the influence of the gas, and to my knowledge, have met with no injurious or even disagreeable results. It is used in New York and Boston by the best practitioners, and with entire success . . . "

The doctor was never reluctant to promote himself or his skills. On Dec. 17, 1864, the *Chronicle* reported:

"Dr. E.B. Goodall has just received a package of the newly patented 'Pink Dental Rubber' (used as a base for artificial teeth) directly imported from London. He considers this article a great desideratum in dentistry, and he is now prepared to counterfeit nature even more perfectly than heretofore.

"His very extensive apparatus for generating pure Nitrous Oxyd Gas is still in full and successful operation. As this is the only apparatus now in use in this city, Dr. Goodall will endeavor in the future to meet the numerous calls for this popular anaesthetic."

Apparently, Dr. Goodall was ever an innovator in the practice of his profession. On Dec. 19, 1868, he reported that he had obtained "a patent on his improved method of setting false teeth. The improvement, simple as it appears, is said to be a really great invention . . . It consists in so arranging the rubber which supports the teeth that they are firmly held in the mouth by springing into position against the back teeth without the use of the broad plate, which in the common style, supported by suction, covers the roof of the mouth . . . "

Not long ago, the writer's own dentist, who constantly updates himself in techniques, suggested the possibility of having two pivot teeth implanted surgically in the jaw bone. If Dr. Goodall is to be believed, that's really old hat. Goodall claimed in a news item, April 20, 1872, that he had, six years before, successfully re-implanted an extracted tooth for a Portsmouth patient, "who still has the reimplanted tooth."

However, even Dr. Goodall found himself susceptible to the ailments common to mortals. A news item on May 8, 1880, reports he had moved his practice from Congress street ["Where the familiar sign has swung in the winds of twenty years"] to his residence at 36 Islington St., "two doors above Langdon st." Dr. Goodall was afflicted with rheumatism, and practicing in his home would end the necessity of getting out in the "east winds and storms." Most contemporary dentists will shudder at learning his offices hours ran from 7 a.m. to 9 p.m. With the New Year, 1881, Dr. Goodall published a lengthy ad which outlined details of his practice, and what he thought was a modest schedule of prices For example:

"Cavities filled with Goodall's Amalgam (prepared by Dr. Goodall) at reasonable charges, from 75 cents to $3, according to the size of the cavity. Platina and gold fillings, bright and durable for common cavities, only $1. Cavities filled with pure gold from $1.50 to $8, according to size . . . "

On Oct. 10, 1883, the *Chronicle* reported:

"It is well known that Dr. Goodall of this city has an extended reputation as a skillful surgeon in his specialty. For more than 15 years he has used forceps which he especially adapted to the teeth and hand—using curved handles in all cases, which cannot slip from the hand, and curved beaks lock themselves firmly to the teeth. A catalogue just issued by a large business house in Boston contained two pages of cuts illustrating these perfected forceps, which are catalogued 'Goodall Forceps' in honor of their inventor."

Eventually, Dr. Goodall moved his dental practice back into the down-town section, taking up quarters over Grace's Drug Store, 16 Market Square. Apparently he remained there for the rest of his long career.

One of the man's less endearing characteristics was complete lack of modesty about his accomplishments. His self-promotion in dentistry had already been noted, but he was no less aggressive in touting his talents in the field of his avocation: music. A sample of this was found by Richard E. Winslow III in the *Portsmouth Herald* issue of Oct. 5, 1917. When it was published, it was in the form of an ad, nearly a column long, and obviously written by Dr. Goodall. In reading excerpts of his ad, it should be kept in mind that Dr. Goodall was then 79 years old:

"It is a well known fact, that Dr. Goodall has been prominent in musical societies, choirs, cantatas and public concerts and lectures for the past 40 years. He had retained his health and vigor and his robustic baritone and tenor voice is now well developed and full of resonance, so that he offers his services to the public as a leader, director or precentor, to organize and drill choirs and choruses (large or small) for musical societies or public concerts. Dr. Goodall can also be engaged to supply in quartet choirs, either at tenor, baritone or first base [sic], also as a soloist for concert work . . .

"As soon as he sells out his office and dental business, he will devote all his time to music teaching, vocal and voice placing for both ladies and gentlemen, also diaphramatic or deep breathing, which is essential for singers, and is also hygenic and a promoter of health. Call on him now and make appointments for private lessons, day or evening . . . "

The ad continued on for many more lines in which Dr. Goodall extolled his abilities in the musical field, and, because so many ministers had gone off to war, he proclaimed himself the "Singing Evangelist." And he used a final paragraph to say:

"NOTICE CAREFULLY.—Until Dr. Goodall sells out his office and dental business he will attend to all his patrons in dentistry as usual, but it would be well for those patrons to make engagements with him directly or they will lose this opportunity now offered."

On Dec. 16, 1917, one of the great comedians on the American stage, through the last half of the 19th Century, Henry Clay Barnabee, died. Barnabee was a Portsmouth native and widely acclaimed. Dr. Goodall utilized the occasion for a reminiscence in which he took full credit for bringing Barnabee to the local stage around 1865. Dr. Goodall said that at that time he was producing "a series of concerts to be given every fall and winter under the auspices and co-operation of the Portsmouth Philharmonic Society which was organized and established by Warren H. Day, organist and pianist and director; Dr. Goodall, assistant director and capitalist, and Frank Miller, editor of the Chronicle, looked after the advertising and the booming . . . "

The musical dentist said he paid Barnabee $50 for two performances in a cantata, *The Haymakers*. Barnabee played the part of "Snobkins," a city dude. After further discussion of Barnabee's appearance, he told how the Philharmonic Society produced many musical shows in the old Temple and when that was destroyed by fire, the organization used the new Music Hall on the same site. Emma Jones Sinclair, the adopted daughter of brewer Frank Jones, sang the lead of Esther in the cantata of that name. Two nights in the Music Hall netted $1,200, he said.

However, it was not given that Dr. Goodall would long be free of his dental practice. On April 28, 1918, at the age of 80, Dr. Goodall died. The *Herald* published a short obituary on the 29th. Perhaps Fernando W. Hartford, publisher, thought the doctor had sung enough of his own praises over the years to constitute a eulogy. The paper did say, "he was also prominently identified in musical circles in this city, being a well known singer and chorus leader and a musician of ability."

Dr. Goodall's wife, Louisa Bartlett Goodall, preceded him in death, dying on June 16, 1916. None of the couple's children survived them. The doctor's twin, Frank, was the closest survivor.

The Oar House. One local woman was a tad upset when told her hus-
band had gone to the "Oar House." However, she was mollified when
the matter was explained. Author photo.

VII Some Little Tales Are Told

THE HISTORY OF A COMMUNITY IS NEVER completely told by the recital of political and economic chronology. Insight into community character can be gleaned from the many little incidents that never find their place in the books. And, before going forward, credit for many of these little glimpses into Portsmouth's yesterday must go to the late Alvah Card. A genial little gnome of a man, Card accumulated many such items in the course of his life. It's regrettable that he couldn't be persuaded to go on tape. So one rushed home, and made notes before the tale was forgotten. All of this is a belated thank-you to Alvah Card, who, sometime since, went to the bourne from which there's no return.

It's All in the Way It Sounds

Some years ago, when the highly esteemed Oar House restaurant first opened, a prominent businessman sauntered down to Ceres street on his lunch hour to sample the tasty viands.

While he was away from his desk, his wife called and wanted to speak with him. The secretary said, "I'm sorry but he isn't here."

"Well, where is he?"

"He's gone to the Oar House."

There was a long silence, the chill of which began to frost the telephone in the secretary's hand. Suddenly, she realized what the boss's wife thought she had said. After a hasty explanation that the Oar House was a new restaurant on the waterfront, a thaw set in.

Up Jumped the Devil

A generation or two ago, Portsmouth's merchants were accustomed to being simple and direct in their dealings. Their business arrangements were basic, and the modern trend to computers and other electronic gadgetry would have been beyond their ken. One such concern was Dennett and McCarthy, a dry goods house at 64 Market St.

Frank B. McCarthy and George Dennett prospered in their own fashion, enjoying the tranquility of a well ordered business that had the faith of its patrons. Then one day, as in the Garden of Eden, a disturbing, sinister element ended the calm of their days. Mr. McCarthy was at the cash register when a polite, well dressed young man entered and said he was from the Internal Revenue Service. After further courteous exchanges, the man from IRS asked to see the firm's books.

"Books?" Mr. McCarthy asked in a questioning tone, "but we don't have any books."

"You don't have any books!"

"No, sir."

"But you have to have books. How else can you do business?"

"It's simple," replied the merchant of the old school. "Each morning, Mr. Dennett and I each put $20 in the till. We sell only for cash, and we pay cash for what we buy. At the end of the day we count the money, and divide it between us. There's no need for books."

Then the man from Internal Revenue began to explain . . .

A Different Drummer

Over the long years, Portsmouth has had its share of people who marched to the beat of a drum heard by no one else. Few were more independent then those who lived around old Puddle Dock before it was supplanted by Strawbery Banke. Back in the 1930s, when the Banke wasn't even a gleam in the eye of Dorothy M. Vaughan, the woman who inspired the colonial restoration, representatives of the millionaire Prescott sisters began to acquire property in that vicinity.

Their laudable object was the general improvement of the area, which had become badly run down during its century as Portsmouth's Combat Zone. One result of the efforts of the Prescott sisters is still to be seen, ongoing and very much a part of Portsmouth life. Today it's Prescott Park, all of which is located on the water-front side of Marcy street. In the early days of the Prescott project, some houses were acquired in the neighborhood of Jefferson and Liberty streets. In at least one instance, demolition began before the unwilling occupants had moved out. The wreckers tore down one wall, exposing the interior of the house to the view of passers-by. This afforded an intimate view of the family's daily life.

One of the chambers thus opened up was the bathroom, which included the usual fixtures. The necessity of meeting nature's demands on the human body fazed the residents not at all. Everyone has to respond to such needs, or so they reasoned. What did it matter if their chores were done in open air? In fact, the man of the house, ensconced on the throne, quite often would wave and call out cheery greetings to passing neighbors. And, once they became used to the situation, the neighbors simply accepted it as a way of life in Old Puddle Dock. The wreckers merely waited; they knew cold weather would bring about an evacuation—no pun intended—that they hadn't been able to achieve.

Short-Changed

Every politician is well aware of the contrary meanness of voters. They can look a candidate in the eye, even put an arm across his shoulder, and lie like hell. Years ago, in Portsmouth, a veteran politician learned that lesson the hard way. He was Andrew Barrett, better known as "Angie," who had held various ward-heeling posts in old Ward One, the home turf of the late Mary C. Dondero.

On the occasion, "Angie" was running for the Democratic nomination to the State Legislature. When primary time came, Barrett inserted an advertisement in the *Portsmouth Herald*, saying that he would transport workers to the polls free of charge; he owned a taxi-cab, so that part was easy.

On primary day, "Angie" hauled 19 voters to the old Eureka Fire Station, on the southeast corner of North Cemetery, where in those days Ward I voted. It should be mentioned that "Angie" was a Democrat, and being a Democrat—even in old Ward I—wasn't exactly a way of life. In those days Democrats were, and still are in some places, an "endangered species."

But that's all by the way. "Angie" toted 19 to the polls and only got 13 votes. To the end of his days, he wondered who the six ingrates were.

A Matter of Where

Newspaper reporters can be the sources of many tales—some of them true, and this one is.

One weekend afternoon, a boatman on the river informed the Coast Guard that he had seen a "floater"—a some-time deceased person who had finally surfaced—just off the New Castle station. The Coasties went out and retrieved the cadaver and brought it to their dock, an unpleasant task at best, but part of the job. In the meantime a couple of reporters from the *Herald* arrived to inspect the corpus delicti and the general scene. One of them asked the chief petty officer where the human remnant had been found, and that unsuspecting individual replied, "Right over there beyond the state bouy." The reporters had no desire to lose any more of their weekend; the person was obviously dead—the lobsters had seen to that.

So the chief was given a lesson in basic forensic civics. As a past generation knows, Dr. Wendell P. "Cowboy" Clare, so known for his hats, was the medical referee in Rockingham County. His opposite number in Maine was "Charlie" Kinghorn, and it should be said that no love was lost between the two medical experts. It was obvious to the newsmen that where the Coast Guard had recovered the body was on the Maine side of the buoy. With completely selfish motives, their weekend being at stake, the reporters explained to the chief that if he told the truth, he would have to take the remains over to Maine for Dr. Kinghorn's inspection. That would ruin everyone's weekend because of lengthy jurisdictional arguments between the two medics.

The chief and the newsmen gazed on the remains for a few moments before the arrival of Deputy Sheriff Floyd I. Gale of Hampton, who busily asked, "Where did you find him, chief?"

"Right over there, on this side of the state buoy," replied the chief with a straight face. Minutes later, the flamboyant "Cowboy" Clare arrived to claim another of his own.

Just incidentally, it was one of the reporters from the *Portsmouth Herald*, Richard J. Connolly, now retired from the staff of the *Boston Globe*, who told the local police whom the victim might be, and he was right.

Wrong Body

Harrison Workman, better known throughout the waters of Portsmouth Harbor as "Worky," is the source of this anecdote.

Shortly after World War II and the end of his service with the Army's mine planters in Portsmouth Harbor, Workman had gone back to lobstering, and one morning went down to where his boat was tied, ready for another day on the water. As he bent over the stern, he found himself eyeball to eyeball with a dead man whose untidy remains had become entangled in Worky's lines.

Worky did the obvious: he called the appropriate officials. But it was early in the morning, the guy was dead, so no one felt any great urgency. Having recovered a little from the shock of his discovery, Worky waited. Then he did what all GIs over the years have learned to do when nothing was stirring: he laid down for a nap, only a few feet away from where the victim's body still awaited forensic medicine.

Deep in his slumber, Workman at first was only a little disturbed as he felt someone lifting him, but it was enough to make him sit up—to the consternation of the undertaker's crew who apparently thought Workman's was the body they had come to pick up.

Workman said: "The guy on the foot end was so startled that he dropped me." The appropriate body was later removed.

Joe's Place

Eileen D. Foley, the oft-times mayor of Portsmouth, is a woman gifted with the ability to laugh at herself. She told this story on April 29, 1984, at a fund-raising brunch for the Prescott Park Arts Festival.

At the time, Joseph G. Sawtelle, a benevolent real estate developer, owned the building on Marcy street that had formerly housed the Blue Fin Fish Market. On learning that PPAF, Inc., was hoping to find more space for its various activities, Sawtelle offered use of the building until he made other disposal of it.

Mayor Foley, wearing one of her other hats—vice president of PPAF, accepted the offer. The next day, the mayor's husband, John J. Foley, went to the mailbox, and brought back with him a key which he thought she ought to explain because the tag tied to it read:

"The key to Joe's place."

Joe's Place. It's still Mayor Eileen D. Foley's dream that this building, once the Blue Fin Fish Market, will become the city's "Heritage Museum. Author photo.

Time on His Hands

The late Andrew Jarvis was one of Portsmouth's most successful businessmen and politicians. Born in Greece, he came to the United States as a youngster of 13, and, by the dint of hard work, he became a wealthy and influential man.

Jarvis was one of several long-lived brothers, but in the long run he outpaced them all. In his mid-90s, he was still strolling the sidewalks of Market Square, the area where he had founded his fortune with a successful restaurant. He cared greatly for Market Square and for his adopted city.

Meeting him one day on the Square, he was asked, "How goes it with you, Andrew?" His answer showed his keen sense of mortality:

"Marking time!"

As it must to all, death came for Andrew Jarvis in 1991, when he was only six weeks short of his century.

Home Brew Days

Fair warning!

If you have a stomach that would get queasy during a quiet row on the South Mill Pond, or you can't stand gruesome topics, don't read what follows.

In many quarters today, it's agreed that one of the most foolish laws ever enacted in the United States was the Volstead Act—Prohibition, by which the manufacture, sale or consumption of alcoholic beverages were banned. Immediately, otherwise sober, law-abiding citizens sought ways in which to circumvent the law.

One quartet of beer drinkers lived in the vicinity of Marcy and Court streets before the Prescott sisters turned the area into a respectable neighborhood. Each member of the foursome, in turn, brewed a batch of sudsy beverage which might not have equaled the output of the Frank Jones Brewery, but did bring pleasure to the participants. They didn't bother to bottle the produce, simply using a dipper to take out a serving from the crock in which it had been brewed.

One member of the syndicate had a family cat, which became quite fond of beer, lapping up the driblets when they fell on the floor. One day when the merry imbibers gathered, they dipped in the crock, and one said to the brewer:

"Hey, I haven't seen your cat lately!"

To which owner of the crock responded:

"You know, come to think of it neither have I. I don't think I've seen him for two or three days."

There was a general chortle over the caprices of cats, especially their sexual activities. One of the brotherhood dipped into the crock. As the dipper emerged, there were hairs, a cluster, hanging to it. Finally one brave soul put his hand into the crock, and brought forth the remains of a cat.

There was a prompt rush to regurgitate what had been taken in, and, who knows, it may have cured them of beer drinking.

She Did It Her Way

Another great story that shouldn't be lost to the Portsmouth bag of history is of the night that Mary Carey Dondero, the city's first female mayor, was trying to railroad something through the City Council.

In recent years, the world has been treated to the spectacle of a tough-minded woman, Britain's Margaret Thatcher, running roughshod over opposition. On a much smaller scale, Mayor Dondero was cast in that mold.

On that particular night, opposition rose to one of her pet schemes, so she turned to her appointed city solicitor, Charles J. Griffin, who, in late years has become one of the deans of the Portsmouth bar—legal, that is—and asked him for a ruling.

Griffin informed her honor that what she wanted to do was illegal. Without hesitation, Mayor Dondero regally announced:

"That's just one man's opinion."

And so she did it—her way. Of course, she had to get a new city solicitor, as city attorneys were than known.

No Time to Waste

Because the family name is now synonymous with Portsmouth's revitalized waterfront, it would be unfair to cite it here. But the little story that follows offers an insight into the way prohibition was enforced 70 years ago.

One day there was arraigned before Municipal Court Judge Ernest Guptill, a woman who made no pretense: she was a bootlegger. She had pleaded guilty, and Judge Guptill mulled over what to do with her. So he thumbed through the book, trying to determine the fine.

Finally, the admitted bootlegger burst out:

"Come on, Judge, hurry up! I've got a customer waiting!"

Judge Guptill, a realist, quickly obliged, knowing that to the woman his fine was part of the cost of doing business.

Then the willing seller quickly pulled out the bills needed and rushed out to satisfy the wants of her willing buyer.

VIII   Tales of Old Fort Constitution

Fourth of July Explosion

THE FOURTH OF JULY, THE GREAT NATIONAL HOLIDAY, was marked in a far more vigorous fashion in the early days of the Republic. In fact, the "Safe-and-Sane Fourth" concept came into being within comparatively recent times and it's doubtful that there breathes a "boy" in Portsmouth of 70 or more years who doesn't carry on his epidermis some scar tissue derived from too close proximity to exploding firecrackers. But observance of the Fourth wasn't just an affair for youngsters in the early days. Oldsters made a day out of speeches and eating. The political partisanship, so dreaded by George Washington, was manifest in the celebration of the Fourth.

For example, in 1809, the Federalists marched down to Meeting House Hill where they heard an oration by Isaac Lyman. They then marched back uptown and dined at the Assembly House, then on Vaughan street, and razed during the Urban Renewal fad in the 1950s. Their opponents, and mortal political enemies, the Democrat-Republicans, the party of Thomas Jefferson and the incumbent president, James Madison, convened in the old North Church and listened to Joseph Bartlett expound on the virtues of their political faith. However, and on the following hangs this tale, some individuals on July 4, 1809, were invited to visit Ft. Constitution and to dine with Col. John Walbach, the commanding officer.

Walbach Tower—This pen and ink sketch was drawn by then 1st Lt. Victor C. Gilbertson of the 22nd Coast Artillery during World War II.

As remarked at the outset, the Fourth was observed with much noise, and injuries and deaths often ensued. Old Portsmouth newspapers, and those from other towns and cities, frequently carried stories of the personal injuries suffered by celebrants, as well as damage to buildings.

But no Fourth of July tragedy in the Seacoast ever equalled the event at Fort Constitution in 1809. The *New Hampshire Gazette* article on the affair began:

"Would to heaven this day, whose commencement was so auspicious, and to us so joyous, could have been exempt from the melancholy disaster which occurred in our vicinity, which we must here narrate, as concisely as possible . . . "

The "melancholy disaster" was an explosion at Fort Constitution in which seven people died, and a dozen or more were badly injured. Unfortunately, the *Gazette's* account is the only newspaper version of the affair. In his *Rambles*, Charles W. Brewster offers details not found in the *Gazette*. In his Ramble CXV, Brewster recorded that among Walbach's guests were Dr. Lyman Spaulding, Col. Jacob Cutter and officers from the fort, "and a few others." The *Gazette* said:

"In the midst of the joyous hilarity of the 4th inst, between 4 and 5 o'clock, p.m. the following terrible disaster took place at Fort Constitution (in this harbor). Two chests of gunpowder, and a number of loose cartridges, which were placed near, took fire (supposed from the slow match) and in the explosion killed and wounded from 14 to 20 citizens and soldiers, besides doing much other essential damage. The quantity of gunpowder exploded between 3 and 400 weight . . . "

While no longer having blind faith in Brewster, it's probably fairly safe to assume that his information came from the *Oracle of the Day*, the predecessor of Brewster's own paper, the *Portsmouth Journal*. Certainly, Brewster, then only seven years old, could have little personal knowledge of the event. His account reads, in part:

"The company was enjoying the hospitalities of the Colonel [Walbach was actually a captain] in his quarters, and the outside visitors were just collecting on the platform on the north-west corner of the Fort, two of the 24-pounders had been removed to make way for a brass 6-pounder from which it was intended to fire salutes after dinner . . . The company had been at the table about three-quarters of an hour, when a tremendous explosion took place—the sides and ceiling of the room were driven in, the tables upset, and everything on them shivered to atoms!"

More than 300 pounds of gunpowder had detonated, yet no one in the room was seriously hurt. Mrs. Walbach suffered cuts. But when the diners hurried out of the room, a terrible scene of death and injury was in front of them.

" . . . One poor fellow was carried over the roof of the house, and the upper half of his body lodged on the opposite side near the dining room, leaving a hole in the door in the shape of a foot; parts of other bodies were carried nearly a hundred yards from the fatal spot . . . "

When the casualties were counted, it was found three soldiers, one civilian and three young boys were dead, and 14 persons, soldiers and civilians, were injured. It was thought that the blast was caused by a chance spark from a lighted fuse held in a linstock, which had been put in readiness for firing salutes.

The dead included Ephraim Pickering of Newington; James Trefethen and Joseph Mitchell, New Castle boys; a boy from Kittery named Paul; Sgt. Joseph Albertz and Pvts. Peletiah McDaniels and Theodore Witham. The *Gazette* concluded its account with the following:

"No blame whatever can be attached to Capt. Walbach, commander of the Fort. He directed an under officer to attend carefully to the firings that afternoon, while he should enjoy himself with a few selected friends at his house, which was within the fort, and also within thirty feet of the awful explosion! Judge ye of the surprise of this excellent officer, when his house was nearly blown up, with his guests and family with him! —The windows with part of the house bursting in, and everything breaking and crushing around them, so that there was scarcely a pane of glass, or an article that could be broken, but was dashed to atoms."

In the days following the explosion many Portsmouth residents and curiosity seekers traveled down river to the fort to offer their services, to which Captain Walbach made proper response. It may have been the destruction of their quarters that induced the Walbachs to move their residence to Portsmouth, where bad luck continued to follow them: they were burned out in the Great Fire of 1813, and returned to New Castle to live.

Mutiny at Fort Constitution

If the walls of old Fort Constitution had the gift of speech, what tales they could tell, although none would be of real combat because the guns of the centuries-old fortification never fired a shot in anger. However, in that span of years many men have been garrisoned there, and even today a military presence, in the sleek forms of two Coast Guard cutters, serves the country outside the ancient walls.

One story those walls knew well was reported in the *Portsmouth Journal* in 1850—a mutiny of sorts. Immediately, it must be made clear that the U.S. Army of more than 150 years ago bears little resemblance to the TV Army of today: "Be All You Can Be!" It's taken a few wars to shake the U.S. Army down to a point of being as pleasant as military discipline allows.

Early public notice of the case at hand appeared in the *Journal* on Oct. 26, and the report was taken from a competing newspaper, the *Weekly Messenger*. Three men were tried by courts-martial on charges of mutiny. They were James Smith, Michael Kennedy and Henry McMahon, all privates in Company K, 3rd Artillery. The charges had been brought against them by Capt. Henry B. Judd, the unit commander. A Lt. Col. Bolton presided over the court, and found the trio guilty as charged.

According to the *Messenger*, they were sentenced to a year of hard labor by day and solitary confinement by night; "to wear during that time a 24-pound ball attached to their legs by an ox chain weighing some 12 pounds more, and an iron collar weighing seven or eight more pounds, with seven equi-distant spikes seven inches long diverging from it; receive no pay during that period and only such clothing as the commanding officer may direct."

The *Messenger* contended that the men, from the time of their arrest, had been in the guard house, in irons, and had had nothing but bread and water. The paper then asked:

"Is not this sentence disgraceful to the service and the government that upholds it? And yet such a sentence has been passed, here, in democratic New Hampshire, and approved by Major General Wool—and the victims are now undergoing this barbarous punishment. And for what enormous crimes? Their offense has this extent and no more: When commanded to row a party of ladies to some distant point—a service not in the line of their duty, and which the officer had no right to command them to perform—they refused, pleading exhaustion and sickness as a reason for so doing."

The *Journal* commented:

"Such is the statement, as published. If too highly colored, our columns are open for a correct statement—if true as stated, our sympathy for manacled slaves and Algerine captives should be turned to objects nearer home."

The controversy stirred many Portsmouth citizens into protest, and a meeting was held on Nov. 1 in the Temple (where Music Hall now stands) not only to take exception to the situation at Fort Constitution but also to demand reform of military discipline. Actually, Gen. Winfield Scott had already ordered the iron collars stripped off the prisoners, but the Portsmouth citizenry passed a resolution demanding that the rest of their sentences also be remitted in view of the public opinion that the offenses with which the men were charged were, at worst, misdemeanors. U.S. Sen. John P. Hale was invited to the meeting, but couldn't make it, but he forwarded to William Claggett copies of his correspondence with the secretary of war, C. M. Conrad, in which it was made known the collars had been removed.

Claggett, whose grandfather, Wyseman Claggett, had been the prosecutor of the unfortunate Ruth Blay 80 years before, outlined the development of the regulations governing military discipline, from the time the code was formally adopted, Sept. 29, 1789, to conform with the new U.S. Constitution. Claggett strongly attacked the stern, abusive traditions of Europe. He said, in part:

". . . In past time, those who enlisted to peril their lives in battle in defense of their country's rights, have been treated as mere machines, without any other privileges than were allowed them by their command officers. But a soldier is a man. In a civilized community he should be treated as a man, and be allowed to enjoy the rights of a man . . . "

According to Claggett, in 1806 regulations adopted by Congress provided that for 16 different offenses soldiers could be disciplined at the discretion of courts-martial, and for 14 offenses (but not homicide) the death penalty was required. Claggett continued for many more paragraphs, but his theme essentially was that the code of military discipline needed revision and humanizing.

Various other speakers attacked the military code. G.H. Rundlett, publisher of the *New Hampshire Gazette*, observed that he had already announced his dislike of barbarism, and, expressed his "warm sympathy with the suffering soldiers at Fort Constitution."

Another, the Rev. William Lamson, said he had attended the session hoping "to see present some officers from the fort, or some of their friends, who might present the other side of the case—if there was any other side." The last six words were italicized in the ancient *Journal*.

At long last there came a few words on behalf of the commanding officer of Company K, 3rd Artillery. Henry Bethel Judd, graduate of West Point, Class of 1839, was no fly-by-night officer. His serial number was 999, and he retired as disabled in 1861, but had served well in the Mexican War. He came back during the Civil War and breveted as a lieutenant colonel in 1865. Judd died in Delaware Dec. 5, 1892, at the age of 73. Apparently a strong coterie of friends in Portsmouth wanted him to make a strong rebuttal to the wild-flying charges. A letter to the editor of the *Journal* said:

"Capt. Judd bears the highest character, both as a man and as an officer; and it is his greatest pleasure to allow all under his command every privilege and comfort consistent with the regulations of the Army. During his short residence at Fort Constitution, he has made the most favorable impression upon those who have had the pleasure of forming his personal acquaintance.

Capt. Henry Judd told his story in a letter to the *Journal* on Nov. 30, 1850. In order to keep it within reasonable length, the *Journal* set it in four-point type, which taxes bi-focals to great lengths. And, first and foremost, it must be stressed that Capt. Henry B. Judd was dealing with an entirely different type of enlisted man than now being recruited by the U.S. Army. Again, let it be stressed that not even lawyers would reduce their victims to four-point type, only insurance companies.

Captain Judd thanked the *Journal* and denied he had kept the prisoners on bread and water for three weeks before trial:

"I will state, that believing they would remain prisoners for a long period before a court could be assembled for their trial, I gave strict orders to the officer of the day and to the first sergeant of the company to cause to be issued to these and several other men awaiting trial *the entire ration.*"

Capt. Judd lauded both his temporary successors, Brevet Capt. Field, and the first sergeant and expressed belief that his orders were carried out. The captain lashed out at critics who claimed he created special cells in a dungeon for the three men, contending that the guard house was actually in such bad shape that it wasn't a proper place to confine prisoners.

"I regret to be obliged to state that the guard-house was too bad, not only for the proper security and imprisonment of men who were so unfortunate as to be arrested by their non-commissioned officers, whose duty requires them thus to notice all acts of drunkenness, disorderly conduct, absence without leave, neglect of duty, &c.; but that decency, propriety and morality demanded that some change should be made that should separate the good from the bad, and prevent the pernicious and ruinous influences resulting from the mingling together in one common room the depraved with the well-disposed; the insubordinate and mutinous soldier with the well-meaning but erring recruit; the besotted drunkard with the sober but negligent defaulter; the violent and furious madman, impiously raving in his paroxysms of drunken rage, with the penitent old and faithful soldier who may be just returning from attacks of delirium tremens; the shameless and hardened deserter from a foreign service, denouncing and threatening his newly acquired superiors in authority, with the spirited and proud young man who had been driven by misfortune to seek the school of military discipline for reformation, but who may not have been able entirely to resist the temptations of the bottle."

And the above quotation really is one sentence, containing approximately 240 words.

Before concluding the paragraph, Capt. Judd described the cells in which the prisoners were kept, which he said were created by partitioning two larger rooms into individual places of confinement. Judd insisted the men were fed properly and their quarters inspected each day by the officer of the day. Judd also discussed the disciplinary problems of Company K, 3rd Artillery:

"Of the 50 men who have constituted the garrison of this post in the last five months, 29 have been arrested at different times by their non-commissioned officers for offenses that can never be allowed to pass unnoticed in a well-regulated command. Of these, 18 have been confined for drunkenness or offenses arising therefrom (some three, four and five separate times); eight for 'mutiny,' 'insubordinate' or 'unsoldierlike conduct;' three for absence without leave" for one to 10 days . . ."

Judd then discussed the circumstances which led to the arrest and trial of the three soldiers. Because Fort Constitution was a sea-coast installation, three boats were assigned to it, for "the use of the officers and men and their families; and the duty of boating is as important as that of guard or exercise of the guns. During the summer I have allowed two of the boats of this post for the exclusive use of the soldiers and their families for fishing, sailing or recreation, while one has been appointed for the service of the officers and their families but seldom used by me."

A long, convoluted rationale was then offered by Judd as to the arrest of the men. The captain offered use of the boat to the widow of a former Army officer. Her son was Judd's subaltern, and the widow and her daughters wanted to go to an island in the harbor. He added:

" . . . I feel confident that had the misguided men who selected that occasion to set my authority at defiance been aware of the facts, their conduct would have been widely different; insubordinate and mutinous though they have been, I still believe them to be brave."

That apparently was the last word on the matter. As mentioned earlier, the trio had the spiked collars removed but they still were at hard labor with their chain and ball. Late in December, 1850, War Secretary Conrad promised a thorough investigation, but denied the men had been justified in refusing to row the boat.

The several wars over the past 130 years have brought many changes in military discipline. It's still more arbitrary than the civilian code, but no offender today wears a ball and chain while in the stockade, as far as is publicly known.

IX Some Odds and Ends of Local History

The Lost Lot

MANY REALLY ODD-BALL HAPPENINGS have taken place during Portsmouth's 365 years of history. One of the more peculiar was the "lost lot." One would believe that in their zeal to get in every tax dollar available, the city fathers would have found the "lost lot" long before 1925, but they didn't. Actually, the fact that the city owned 250 acres of prime woodland adjacent to the Newington town line was discovered solely by accident.

In the year 1925, the State Forestry Commission was working assiduously to prevent the spread of blister rust among white pines. The inspectors, as part of the job, searched for gooseberry and currant bushes which were seen as part of the ecological pattern in the development of crippling blister rust. However, the work went beyond that. Squads of forestry workers scoured the woodlands looking for infected trees and bringing them to the owners' attention.

In the course of his work, one of the inspectors found a tract of land on the Newington border of which there seemed to be no title holder. The more he looked into the situation, the more the state worker became convinced that the city itself owned the land. The late Orel Dexter was then mayor, and he had the city solicitor do some title work, and, at last, it was realized that the city did indeed own the land.

Jean Pierre Boyer, President of Haiti

Apparently the land had come into the city's possession from someone's estate, the papers were duly shuffled out of sight, and stayed that way for years.

Today, of course, the tract is buried under the concrete ramps and runways of the former Pease Air Force Base.

Carriage for Royalty

Exactly why two relatively obscure Portsmouth mechanics, Alfred M. and Andrew J. Beck, were chosen to build a carriage for royalty is well covered by history's dust. The Becks were brothers and their shop was at what was then 6 and 7 Congress St., and 3 Church St. The carriage was built in 1836 to the order of Jean Pierre Boyer, president, and practically king of Haiti. The carriage was described:

"It resembled a huge square-topped chaise, hung on four C springs weighing 75 pounds, with two wheels, the whole painted red, and with an immense heavy 'boot' hung on hinges in front, like a trap door, and painted crimson on scarlet. The whole weighed 1160 pounds."

The contraption was drawn by three horses, with the driver actually riding the center horse. It was made from a model of a carriage imported from France in the 18th Century by a Portsmouth merchant named Daniel R. Rogers.

When the Becks finished their handiwork, it was shipped to the West Indies in a Portsmouth vessel but neither the vessel nor carriage reached Haiti. A storm wrecked the ship and the carriage went with it. However, before it left Portsmouth, a local coachman, Sam Robinson, drove it around town using a single horse. Robinson exhibited the vehicle in Market Square for the entertainment of townspeople and visiting farmers.

Alfred M. Beck was chief clerk in the post office at the time, and, when Portsmouth became a city in 1849, Andrew J. Beck was the first city marshal. Although he never received his magnificent equippage, Jean Pierre Boyer extended his rule over Haiti until 1843 when he was finally driven out. He died in Paris in 1860.

Pope's Night

Lost in Piscataqua's swirling fogs is an ancient tradition, dating back to the 17th century. It had its start with the Gunpowder Plot of November, 1605, when a silly man named Guy Fawkes planted gunpowder under the then-houses of Parliament. In the United Kingdom, youngsters still run around neighborhoods, trying to "collect a penny for the guy."

Locally, it degenerated into "Pope's Night," then "Beggars' Night." Present-day grandmothers recall "Beggar's Night" as coming before Thanksgiving, and one said "there were times when we needed the donations." In 1891, the *Portsmouth Chronicle* observed:

"This year there has been no divergence from the usual custom that Portsmouth's youngsters annually observe, viz, an occasional bonfire, the sounding of the tin horn and the illumination of the pumpkin lantern! Each succeeding generation celebrates the event as regularly as it does the Fourth of July, but the north-enders no longer long for each other's gore . . . " And, thereby, also hangs a tale of years gone by. Hard as it may be to envisage, all Portsmouth was divided, 150 or more years ago, into two parts, north and south of present-day State Street. With that in mind, it's possible to go forward. The battleground was laid.

Quoting from reminiscence, the *Portsmouth Chronicle* said:

"There is much wind in the small boy of the period, but his valor is quenched by acquired wisdom born of faithful listening to the tear-rending accounts of what his father was accustomed to do in the bloody days (or nights rather) of 1840 . . . "

However, like it or leave it, "Pope Night," "Beggars' Night" have now degenerated into "Trick or Treat Night."

The end result is the same: too much candy and too many cavities for the young.

Rubber Shoes

One of the great discoveries in the early years of the 19th Century was that rubber would keep out water. Although the Indians of Central and South America were using rubber when the Spanish explorers arrived in the 16th century, its value went unappreciated up north for nearly 200 years. In 1811 a rubber factory was established in Vienna and in 1823, Charles Macintosh devised a water-proofing process, and gave his name to waterproof coats. In 1839, Charles Goodyear first vulcanized rubber, and created a whole new industrial world.

And so it was in June, 1836, that experiments were conducted at the Portsmouth Navy Yard involving a bag made of India rubber. There were three experiments:

"1st. A keg of powder, several flannel Cartridges filled with powder, and a quantity (several pounds) of loose powder were placed in the bag; it was then immersed in water nearly up to the top, and remained an entire week in a tank filled with water—at the expiration of this period, it was taken out and examined, the powder was perfectly dry, and no moisture inside the bag.

"N.B. The canvas was so stiff, that the top of the bag could not be turned over and the mouth secured, so as to keep out the water;—this can be corrected by having the mouth piece of more pliant material.

"2d. The bag was filled one week with water; not a particle oozed out that could be perceived, but the water acquired such an unpleasant taste, as to unfit it for drinking; this it is presumed can be corrected by lining the bag with some material well coated with beeswax similar to that used on iron water tanks.

"3d. Filled the bag with Indian meal, and placed it in the barn where there are many oxen, and rats abound, the first week the rats did not touch the bag although the outside of it was sprinkled with meal; the bag was then greased outside and remained a second week in the barn, when it was found the rats had eaten the grease but without injury to the bag."

Within a year of so, Portsmouth merchants were advertising the arrival of India rubber overshoes, as can be seen in the photo copies of their ads. The good burghers of Portsmouth were becoming able to walk the muddy, dung-littered streets of their town without getting their feet wet, and the street slime washed off easily.

Lighting the Clock

No object in downtown Portsmouth is more familiar than the clock in the steeple of the North Church.

Most people are aware that a town clock, thanks to Daniel Pierce, was "set agoing" way back in 1749. One can only speculate as to what determined the hour at which it would be set. Perhaps the town fathers brought a couple of sun dials to The Parade, and, with the ever-present help of senior mariners, determined high noon, and so the clock was set. This is neither the time nor place to mention how much different that clock tower of 1749 was from the present, which was put up in 1854.

Anyway, can anyone remember when the clock face wasn't illuminated at night? In fact, the only time we of today give thought to the clock is when its four dials are unlit. So this is the test for today: When was the town clock first illuminated?

If your answer was that the clock first became visible on the night of Aug. 7, 1893, you're the winner of a traffic-free passage across Market Square—if you're quick enough. However, a lot went into getting the town clock ready to have its face shine forth into the night. The whole works had to be rebuilt, and when it was returned to Portsmouth, the fire alarm superintendent, Wilbur I. Trafton, the city's electrical genius, was put in charge of it. Trafton sounded as worshipful of the clock's inner workings as Capt. Ray Jones, USN, Ret., does of the ship's bell clock on the Portsmouth Naval Shipyard:

"In the adjustment of the escapement, he considers it unsurpassed by any tower clock manufactured, and after it is thoroughly regulated he sees no reason why reliable time cannot be obtained."

It should be observed that only nine years before had the United States finally adopted a standardized time. Before 1884, time was what-

Town clock. Well lighted by fireworks on the night before the Fourth in 1992, the North Church clock's dials were first illuminated nearly a century ago. Photographer Bill Murphy, a superb craftsman, climbed to the roof of the Portsmouth Athenaeum to get this photo. Courtesy of the Portsmouth Herald.

ever any individual community said it was. It could be noon in Portsmouth; 12:15 in Hampton; 12:20 in Exeter; and 12:05 in Kittery, and all would be right, by their town clocks. Trafton, a bit of a mechanical and electrical genius, was made privy to the secrets of the clock by the firm charged with repairing it.

"Mr. Trafton was a careful observer of the most essential parts of the mechanism in their workings, and through the courtesy of Mr. Prescott (the clock rebuilder) was shown and explained the workings of each piece as it was set up. He was the only person instructed how to adjust and care for the clock; wound it up, set and started it, and Mr. Prescott placed him in entire charge of it until he or some other persons should be appointed to take care of it."

Trafton told the *Chronicle* that if he wasn't appointed caretaker of the clock, he would pass on to the appointee all the information he had received as to its care. Under such provisions was the illuminated tower clock set "a-going" on Aug. 7, 1893.

Liquor Controls

From time immemorial abuse of alcohol has been a problem for society. So it's no surprise to find that from early colonial times on there were efforts to regulate the use of alcohol. The New Hampshire General Court, which is really the correct name of our Legislature, in 1717 enacted the following:

" . . . And to prevent Nurseries of vice and Debauchery Be it further Enacted by the Authority aforesaid That there shall be a Limitation of Taverns or Ale houses within the respective Towns or Parishes within the Province. To Say, the Town of Portsmouth six. The town of Hampton three. the town of Dover three, whereof one at Oyster River. The town of Exeter two. The town of New Castle two. The town of Kings-town one. The parish of Newington one.

"And that the Justices of the General Session of the Peace be hereby directed from year to year to License no more than what is above express'd from and after the first of June next."

And the State of New Hampshire, in its finite wisdom, is still trying to control the use of alcohol, but, at the same time, promoting the sale of liquors as a source of revenue.

Old Horseshoe

This little tale is one that brings up the question: "I wonder where it is now?"

New Hampshire's last royal governor, John Wentworth, was one of the more able chief executives to hold the office. He returned to the province in 1767, designated to succeed his uncle, Benning Wentworth, and in the years before the Revolution was highly esteemed, until the political turmoil of the day cost him both his job and his property.

Among his major achievements was opening the middle of the province to development, and his summer place in Wolfeboro was one of the first of its kind in the colony. When he returned to Portsmouth, he had brought with him large English draught horses, which he put to good use on his place in Wolfeboro.

Many years after Gov. Wentworth was driven out of the province in 1775, George Whitton, a farmer, plowed up a large horseshoe, one that had a span of eight inches, and a length of nine from toe to heel. In 1877, 102 years after Wentworth's departure, the shoe was owned by William C. Fox of Wolfeboro, a collector of the "unique and antique," which brings us back to the question: "Where is it now?"

Diphtheria

Those who like to wander occasionally through old-time cemeteries are often startled when then they come across a lot in which several children are buried, with the dates of death often spanning only a few weeks.

Perhaps the passage of time has so eroded the grave markers that such burials in a Stratham cemetery are no longer visible. But 1742 was known in that community as the "Bereavement Year." Between Aug. 18 and Dec. 31 in that year, 77 people, including 70 children died, in an epidemic of "putrid sore throat," as the deadly killer diphtheria was then called.

It its issue of Dec. 23, 1876, the *Portsmouth Journal* said that Deacon Samuel Lane, styled as the "pall keeper," kept a record of the deaths. At the time of the *Journal* items Deacon Lane's record was in the possession of his grandson, Deacon E. J. Lane of Dover.

Greenland in 1897

Early in 1897, the Greenland correspondent of the *Exeter News Letter* informed the paper:

" . . . With less than 800 inhabitants the town can muster 10 blacksmiths, five butchers, 15 carpenters, two carriage makers, three clergymen, seven dress makers, two doctors, three lawyers, two

Iron fence. The wrought iron fence in front of the Stone Church (Unitarian-Universalist) on State Street came from England in 1827, shortly after the church was built. Author photo.

masons, four painters, two printers, six shoe makers, one surveyor—Twelve school teachers, three telegraph operators, and about 159 1/2 farmers.

"There are two churches, three common schoolhouses, one academy with upwards of 40 students, one town hall, one hotel, one Masonic hall, four private boarding houses, one livery stable, three grocery stores, three saw mills, three grist mills, one shingle mill, three cider mills, one gunsmith, two wheelwrights and two stone cutters or stone masons. We have had an eclectic or literary club which is now obsolete; and we have had a temperance reform club."

Stone Church Fence

For more than 160 years the iron fence around three sides of the Stone Church on State street has defied the weather, and seems as substantial today as when it arrived in Portsmouth aboard the ship *Marion*.

The *Marion* was built in a Berwick shipyard by William Hanscom, and her first master was Ichabod Goodwin who later became New Hampshire's first Civil War governor.

A news item in the *Portsmouth Journal* for July 15, 1876, said that the fence was bought in Liverpool by Capt. Goodwin while he was master of the *Marion*.

Goodwin may well have ordered the fence while on a visit to Liverpool, but the commander of the *Marion* when she arrived here in May, 1827, with the fencing, was Nahum Yeaton.

How often that old iron fence has been repainted isn't known, but it was getting a coat of paint at the time of the *Journal* article in 1876.

Tea in Kittery

Cutts Island, out in Kittery Point, has long enjoyed an honored place in the stories and legends about one of Maine's first towns.

One little known tale concerns the drinking of tea.

It seems the pouring of the first cup of tea in Maine took place on the island about 1720. The *Portsmouth Journal* printed that bit of intelligence in October, 1887, offering this following background:

"A daughter of Major Cutts was returning from school in Massachusetts with a daughter of Governor Vaughan. A severe storm detained her at the governor's house at Portsmouth for several days, and at the governor's table she was first offered tea. The young lady followed Miss Vaughan's example, and, adding sugar and cream, carried it to her lips. She afterwards purchased a pound of tea for a guinea [21 shillings], sent to Boston for cups and saucers, and thus introduced the first tea and tea set into Maine."

Anyway, it's a charming little yarn, although it poses a lot of questions. For example, why wouldn't a young sophisticate like Miss Cutts have been served tea in the New England metropolis—Boston?

North Church Vane

Many Portsmouth residents are under the impression that the weather vane which rides high in the sky over Market Square is the original put in place when the tower of the old North Church was erected.

Sadly, it just isn't so.

The Old North was razed in 1854 to make way for the present structure that graces the Square, and probably Benjamin P. Shillaber, Boston newspaper columnist and Portsmouth native, put it best in writing a reminiscence article for the *Portsmouth Journal* on Oct. 15, 1887:

"The old vane still swings on its circuit aloft, and, still vigilant in duty, tells the world the drift of the wind as it did 200 years ago."

However, Lewis G. Brewster, publisher of the *Journal* and son of the "Rambler," Charles W. Brewster, mournfully penned a contradictory note:

"It is too bad to spoil a beautiful flourish by pronouncing it incorrect history. But the fact is, when the edifice was demolished, the old vane after singing its song, through the medium of the pen of the Rambler about Portsmouth, retired to innocuous desuetude in the woodshed of one of the wardens of the parish, where it remained some years, until it finally passed away, no one knows whither . . . "

Had he wished Lewis Brewster could have further heaped flaming coals on Shillaber's head by pointing out that the Old North hadn't stood for two centuries when it was torn down. It was erected about 1714, and the tower even later.

Rye Taxes in 1877

Reading the lists of taxpayers years ago in some of the towns around Portsmouth always amaze in the number of family names still on the tax rolls more than a century later.

Such is the case for Rye in 1877:

E.H. Balch, $37.77; Amos P. Brown, $46.57; Daniel Brown, $36.95; George H. Brown, $29.82: John H. Brown, $27.54; Joseph W. Brown, $54.10; Daniel Dalton, $38.54; Albert Dow, $63.49; Charles A. Drake, $52.59; John O. Foss, $29.31; John Foye, $38.04; Orin L. Foye, $33.21; William E. Chesley, $25.86; Moses Clark, $30.91; Joseph J. Drake, $29.25; Charles Garland, $27.51; Moses Garland, $27.51; Rufus I. Garland, $27.07; John I. Goss, $26.67; Richard T. Goss, $27.54; John Gover, $29.42; Heirs Edward Garland, $42.79; Moses L. Garland, $32.44; William Holmes, $25.02; Alfred G. Jenness, $46.98; David Jenness, $38.55; Emory C. Jenness, $39.57; George W. Jenness, $33.52; Gilman G. Jenness, $32.81; Job Jenness, $40.71; Joseph D. Jenness, $32.47; N.G. Jenness, $29.04; Oliver Jenness, $27.82; O.P.

Jenness, $53.13; Richard Jenness, $35.11; Sheridan Jenness, $51.21; Uri H. Jenness, $49.38; Mary Jenness, $25.99; Maria S. Jones, $29.09; Charles N. Knowles, $25.02; George G. Lougee, $106.05; Joseph Locke, $25.56; Jenness Marden, $29.16; Levi W. Marden, $30.72; Thomas I. Marden, $26.40; Heirs, O.D. Marden, $35.10; C.A. Odiorne, $43.51; Thomas J. Parsons, $79.18; Warren Parsons, $25.80; Abraham Perkins, $90.86; Daniel Philbrick, $54.31; E.B. Philbrick,$93.36; J. Curtis Philbrick, $32.80; J.N. Philbrick, $30.16; G.W. Peirce, $25.63; John R. Poor, $151.84; Heirs J. Philbrick, $229.50; Elvin Rand, $37.14; Henry S. Rand, $36.92; Isaac D. Rand, $33.88; Jedidiah Rand, $60.74; J. Jenness Rand, $30.52; William J. Rand, $29.83; John S. Remick, $48.87; Levi T. Sanborn, $33.07; George H. Seavey, $28.23; Eben L. Seavey, $28.42; Joseph W. Seavey, $29.20; J.P. Trefethen, $26.65; G.L. Trefethen, $25.29; Miss E. A. Walker, $63.76; Widow, J. H. Webster, $27; John Woods, $62.61.

NON-RESIDENTS

Woodbury Seavey, $30.63; T.C. Cummings, $40.50; E.A. Straw, $75.27; heirs J.H. Down, $41.88; William Walker, $27; Direct Cable Co., $27.

An Old Well

Back in 1929, a house stood at the southeast corner of Aldrich road and Islington street. In its glory days, the old house had been occupied by such local luminaries as True M. Ball, merchant and shipping investor, and also High Sheriff Edward D. Coffin.

At the end the house was in the estate of Elizabeth Mooney, and was sold and razed for what has now, finally, developed into a structure occupied by Fleet Bank. While tearing down the house, the workmen also cut down an old elm that had provided shade for the house for generations.

Then, to make more room for the new building, they took out the stump of the elm. When they did they found a large part of stump and its roots were spread over an old well.

"The top of the well was covered with a large, flat stone. The well itself was in a good state of preservation and contained considerable water."

It was speculated the well had been abandoned after Portsmouth Aqueduct Company began operating mains throughout the community.

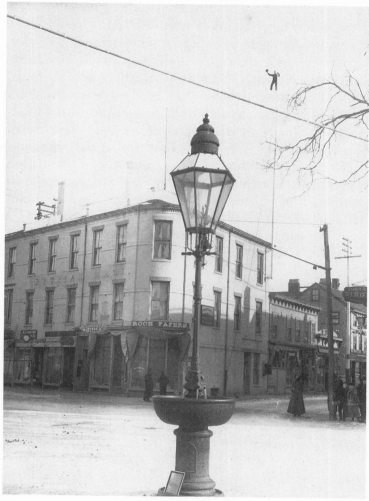

Drinking fountain. This gas-illuminated fountain was a pleasure for both man and beast in the 19th century. Note the steeple jack at the top of the photo. The store for room papers now houses Alie's Jewelry. Strawbery Banke photo.

Drinking Fountain

Market Square today is, of course, a place where motorists enjoy an open season on any pedestrians trying to get from one side to the other. The irony is that those same pedestrians, once seated behind the steering apparatus of their personal juggernauts, become the hunters instead of the hunted. But that's all by the way of recalling a tranquil time when more thought was devoted to providing water for man and beast than to safe crossing for pedestrians.

Back in July, 1885, the city proudly installed a drinking fountain in Market Square. Not only did water become available, but the fountain was also illuminated by gas. They brought water from the 10-inch main on State Street, through Church Street and over to the fountain in the Square. The overflow was vented into an old stone drain.

However, it wouldn't be Portsmouth without someone making complaint. Teamsters contended the fountain was set up too high for equines to quench their thirst, and that it was impossible for horned cattle to drink out of it because they were too used to drinking from brooks. An item in the *Portsmouth Chronicle* on Sept. 17 indicates that the fountain became an accepted Market Square feature:

"Alderman Cook's drinking fountain on the Parade, though considerable fun was made of it at first, owing to the height of the drinking trough from the ground, is really one of the best things the city has procured for some time. Oxen cannot drink from it, it is true, but horses can without being unchecked, and the number of teams that drive up to it daily is very great.

"Alderman [Oliver H.] Cook is entitled to the credit of getting the fountain placed there, for it was mainly owing to his persistent energy that it was done, and he was chairman of the committee under whose supervision the work was performed."

The phasing out of horses in favor of horsepower eventually led to the fountain's removal.

Lost Ring

Some little time ago, the story was told of a ring, lost at the Isles of Shoals, and then found after the owner left the Appledore House.

Then it was lost again, and found years later on the banks of the river at New Castle.

Well, this is the strange story of another lost ring.

It began in 1820, when James B. Rand of Greenland was a boy of nine. His father was a man who believed that a judicious mixture of work and play was the right formula for raising a son. So, one summer day, the father sent son James to the potato field for a day with the hoe. The field was in Rye on Breakfast Hill road.

When you're nine years old, even 15 minutes of handling a hoe can get wearisome, but he had to stay at it. Out there with him was a young miss he called "sister," and her teasing finally, by mid-afternoon, frayed his temper. Reaching down, James Rand caught up a lump of loam to throw at her. Before he could toss it, the lump dissolved in his hand and left behind a gold ring. Inside the band was the date 1747.

How the ring came to be there no one ever knew, but the young boy kept the eagle-inscribed ring into his manhood and it became his wife's wedding ring. But at that, it was twice lost and found again. Once it was lost on the road at Rye, and was found after it had been gone over a winter.

The ring may still exist in the possession of a member of the multitudinous Rand family.

Nothing Changes

For most of the existence of this country, the postmasters supervising mails in the various communities were entirely the creatures of political caprice.

As the Administrations changed, especially if the out-of-office party captured the White House, there would be new postmasters. It didn't matter how efficient the incumbent was; if his party lost, he was out. This happened in 1893, when Grover Cleveland recaptured the White House, after being out of it four years.

The incumbent Portsmouth postmaster was William O. Sides, and he was promptly replaced by a man named Leavitt. Shortly after Sides left the post office, it was learned that his accounts were short. The Postal Dept. sent a draft to Leavitt ordering him to collect from Sides the money that was due.

Sides quickly agreed rather than have a running spat with Washington. He wrote a check for one cent, the amount his accounts were short.

X Tales of Smelting

Smelting as an Industry

ONCE THE FESTIVE HOLIDAY SEASON is safely out of the way and plenty of freezing weather has been noted, there will get under way one of the really ancient tribal rites for many hardy souls who make their homes in the Seacoast. Smelt fishing on Great Bay is as old as the oldest settlements, and what the fishermen can't eat themselves they are able to pass off on neighbors or in the markets.

In its issue of Feb. 4, 1856, the *Portsmouth Chronicle* reported that three young men from the city, fishing between 9 a.m. and 7 p.m. had caught between 90 and 100 dozen smelts. They sold their catch for eight cents a dozen. "We call this a good day's sport." Two days later, the *Chronicle* published an article that is in many ways just as binding today as it was in 1856. Because the *Chronicle* did it so well, much of it will be reproduced here:

" . . . It seems to us that the large and beautiful sheet of water, at the head of Piscataqua River, known as Great Bay, is not sufficiently appreciated. It is in summer one of the most beautiful and picturesque sheets of water, richly wooded along its shores, and affording, except at low tides, uncommonly fine ground for boat sailing. It is many miles in extent, and offers a great variety of delightful scenery to the visitor.

"The filling and emptying of this broad basin, gives the great impetus to the waters of the Piscataqua. Water fowl formerly abounded here, but the too near approach of railroads and other civilizing instrumentalities have made them shy, and at last scarce. But we referred to the Great Bay now, the purpose of giving a brief notice of the great business now being carried on there, in the smelt catching line, or rather by the lines of the smelt catchers . . . "

The next paragraph catches the eye rather than catching smelts:

"Large numbers of smelts were formerly caught from the Creek Bridge in Portsmouth, at the high tide — when the fresh water, drained from above, was deep there. Of late years, however, the railroads have spoilt that fishing ground. . . ." The Creek Bridge, of course, spanned Islington Creek which flowed down from the direction of Pannaway Manor. The Eldredge Brewing Co. had an ice pond a few rods west of Bartlett street. In ancient times, unbelievable as it may be, vessels of fairly deep draft could penetrate deep into the North Mill Pond. But to go on with the *Chronicle's* smelting story:

"Now (1856), the way to catch smelts, is to go to Great Bay, cut a hole, 10 feet by two will accommodate four fishers with their three or four lines each, now three or four feet thick; put up an awning perpendicular to the ice — to keep off, NOT the sun, but the wind, ugh! and then go back into the fish. That is, put your hook, baited with worms, which you can dig only in the salt mud on the shore at the edge of the water, somewhere — we say, put your hook and bait down about five feet into the water, and let 'em bite.

"We were always entirely willing the fish should have a bite at OUR bait, but they never did seem to care much about it. Not so with other's worms, however, for we have known instances here of one man's catching this way, from 20 to 60 dozen smelts in a day. Very many men and boys from all the towns adjoining the Bay, are daily employed in this business; and make good wages, — the fish being sold at from 6 to 10 cents per dozen for shipment to Boston — whither many hundreds of thousands must have been sent during the present season. It was estimated that 300 men were engaged in this business, on Great Bay, some days last week — the number varying according to the INTENSITY of the weather, and the time of the tides."

An indication of how important the smelt fisheries were to the local economy more than a century ago is found in a well written *Portsmouth Journal* article, published on Feb. 13, 1858, at a time when shipbuilding was in the doldrums. The author made clever use of a play on words to get his point across:

"Those who have sought the golden fields of California will look with some interest on the discoveries which have been made in our immediate neighborhood, and the success with which the diggings are now being worked. In the early part of winter, many who were out of employment fitted themselves for the silver mines which have been worked for a year or two past at the mouths of small streams which empty into Great Bay, four or five miles from the centre of Portsmouth.

"They were so successful, that the companies daily became enlarged, until on some days 500 people, men, women and children, might be seen at work at the various excavations, realizing from 50 cents to $3 each, per day, according to their skill and luck in bringing up the shiners. In California the miners are content with digging the ore, but here we go farther—our miners even smelt it. The smelting business has been very successfully conducted. Some have hooked up to 50 dozen shiners in a day.

"These have found purchasers readily on hand, who have paid from 5 to 7 cents a dozen. The products have had circulation, not only in our vicinity, but also in the Boston market, and from Boston, they have been sent abroad to meet the wants of the west, even to Chicago. In this way, thousands of dollars have been realized the present winter by various mechanics and artisans of Portsmouth who otherwise would have had scarcely any employment. The silver smelts vary in size from three to 14 inches, and, like the products of the gold mines are a luxury with which few become satiated."

Fundamentally, smelt fishing hasn't changed much over the decades. Nowadays many smelters get to their favorite spots riding snowmobiles; power tools are used to cut the ice; and portable huts are used to shelter the fisherman from the fury of the northwest winds that still howl down from Canada and out across Great Bay.

There are now stringent limits on the number of fish that can be kept each day, and that's probably a necessity in view of the steadily increasing number of fishermen.

Another change in smelting is the price the markets will pay for Bay smelts. In 1990 at the peak of the season, the Olde Mill at the South Mill Bridge, was selling them at $1.99 a pound. A pound might contain a dozen or so smelts, for which the fishermen 135 years ago would get six to 10 cents.

However, with most smelt fishermen the fun of the game is catching smelts, not how much they can be sold for, and that will be the case in all the winters to come.

More Smelting

For generations a favorite wintertime activity for some hardy souls has been fishing for Great Bay smelts through the ice.

Today, of course, many of the fishermen get to their favorite spots by snowmobile, and have their fishing shanty dragging along behind them, and then use a power augur to get through the ice.

While many years ago, some of these amenities were lacking, the fishermen in 1859 were busy as a story in the *Portsmouth Journal* indicates:

"The business of catching Smelts on Great Bay has been carried on as extensively during the winter just closing, as it was last year. The first catching was about the middle of December. The company of the Bay on some days has been a hundred, and an average of perhaps fifty persons has been kept up to the present time.

"Some tend three or four lines; and while some have caught 80 dozen in a day, others have toiled all day for the first dozen. On some days the catch on the Bay has been known to reach a thousand dozen. The price on the Bay has been four cents per dozen.

"They have usually been purchased by a few, and a large proportion have been forwarded to Boston market. The movable house on the ice has been a convenience to the fishers. Between two and three thousand dollars' worth of smelts have probably been drawn with the hook from the Bay this winter."

From Great Bay to the Courtroom

As the preceding pages show, smelting on Great Bay has been an economic and recreational winter activity for generations of Seacoast residents. The tale that follows offers still another look at this favorite hobby of those who enjoy the blast of northwest winds across Great Bay ice.

Late in January, 1867, one of the worst snowstorms in many a year swept into the area. Railroad traffic, highway use came to a complete halt. Trains couldn't move between Boston and Portsmouth for hours. The cut across Greenland road was filled with snow.

Weather forecasting, being no more of an exact science than it is today failed to warn of the coming storm which hit in Boston hours

before reaching here. So it was inevitable that devoted smelt fishermen were out on the Great Bay ice when the storm struck, and they
compounded their up-coming misery by lingering on the ice until the
storm was well established. Perhaps the smelts were biting savagely
and, like all fishermen, one little party didn't want to give up. But the
snowfall, coupled with the coming of night, forced them to leave Great
Bay and head for their Portsmouth homes.

In an article headed "Inhumanity vs. Hospitality," the *Daily
Morning Chronicle* didn't say how many were in that little party of
smelters, but, in the course of the trial almost a year later, the names
were made public.

Wiley Coleman apparently was the guiding spirit, and his com-
panions were Frederic Smart and two young brothers, Alfred W. and
Woodard Tucker.

Their story of what happened when they tried to get home to
Portsmouth was told to George W. Marston, a proprietor of the
Chronicle, and published by him on Jan. 23, 1867:

" . . . Not being aware of the violence of the storm on the land, the
party of 'smelters' before alluded to, delayed leaving Great Bay for
home, until late in the afternoon, and consequently found the roads
almost impassable, and their progress at every step growing less,
until weary and almost exhausted, they stopped at a farm house, the
residence of Mr. D. R. Ambrose, and requested shelter for their horse
in the barn and for themselves in the house.

"Their request was not granted, the proprietor refusing point
blank to accommodate them or allow them to open the barn.
Expostulation and entreaty were vain, and they were literally turned
away from the doors of this inhospitable christian (?) gentleman, and
again plodded slowly along through the drifting snow, scarcely able to
set one foot before the other.

"They next came to a small shanty and smaller barn owned by an
Irishman (we wish we knew his name), who welcomed them with true
Irish hospitality, inviting them into his dwelling and declaring that he
would take his heifer from the barn and bring it into the house, to
make room for the horse.

"Before a roaring fire the party soon thoroughly thawed out, and
having refreshed the inner man, rested and warmed themselves,
thought they would start for home again, notwithstanding their host
(who positively refused any remuneration for the trouble they had
caused him) and who urged them to stay with him all night, offering

March House. When Clement March lived in this mansion on the old Greenland Road, he was master of all he surveyed in the little town. Author photo.

them the best quarters he could afford. The kind offer was declined because of the necessity of taking the heifer into the house to make room for the horse in the barn . . . "

When the above article was published in the *Portsmouth Herald* the identity of that Irish benefactor wasn't known to the writer. It was an era of bigotry in which persons of Irish extraction were held in deep contempt by the so-called natives. Not even during the trial, in which the Irishman testified, was his name printed. However, since the article appeared, it's been made known that he was Patrick Daley, who lived near the present Pease Golf Course. Paul F. Hughes, Jr., provided the information from files kept by Paul Sr., the Greenland historian. The lower nine of the Pease Golf Club is built partly on what was property owned by Daley. However, to go on with the story:

"And so thanking the kind-hearted Irishman, they started along, but soon found themselves at dark, when the storm was at its height, in an almost impassable drift, though which the horse could not force his way. They were then compelled to shovel a path, through this and other drifts, until they came to the house of Mr. John Tabor, where they were again refused admission, and ordered away; with the owner using harsh language in his refusal . . . ”

By this time, the smelting party had decided that further efforts to reach home were useless, and they would be better off to retrace their steps. In so doing, they finally reached the home of Clement March, one of Greenland's richest men. They were soon given shelter in the house of Jonathan Ladd, a tenant of March's, and the horse was put in March's own stable. The next morning, the storm having abated, the party set out for home where the members were given warm welcome by their anxious families. And there it would be supposed the tale would have its ending. Marston, to show the contrast between the actions of Ambrose and Tabor, did an item about the behavior of John W. Kinnear, a Navy Yard quarterman in the brass foundry.

“Mr. Kinnear, after returning home from work, felt concerned in regard to the whereabouts of a fellow workman, and started for the man's residence, nearly two miles away, for the purpose of ascertaining whether he had arrived home, but finding it impossible to reach the house, was returning home by the way of Freeman's Woods [Freeman's Point area] about 7 P.M. when he accidentally fell in with a Mr. Staples, belonging in Eliot, who had lost his way, become bewildered, and exhausted, and had taken off his shoes,—his stockings being covered with ice and snow to the depth of several inches . . .”

Kinnear brought Staples to his feet, and literally dragging him managed to reach the town where shelter was found for him. Kinnear didn't bother to tell anyone about his feat, and it was only after Staples told the story that Kinnear's family learned of the heroic role he had played.

Exactly who informed the *Chronicle* of the inhumanity of Ambrose and Tabor wasn't made known by the newspaper. However, George Marston wrote the article and Ambrose brought suit for libel, and the case went for trial on Nov. 13, 1868.

Ambrose's daughter was the first witness for the plaintiff. She told the jury of the insults that were showered on the Ambrose residence by smelt fishermen going to and from Great Bay, and that her mother “was unwilling to go to town with her father on account of the insults to which they were subjected,” and they were afraid to have a light on in the mornings when the smelters were going by. Ambrose, in supporting his charges, testified that about 5:30 of the afternoon of the storm, a man called at the house and asked for accommodations for his horse and himself. Ambrose said he replied that the barn was full, and he could see it for himself.

Ambrose testified that when he saw the article in the *Chronicle*, he went to Frank Miller, owner of the paper, and asked him if he didn't think he was "liable" for it. He said Miller replied, "Oh, yes, liable," and turned away. Ambrose claimed he said, "Frank, this won't do." Miller asked, "What do you want?" Ambrose replied, "Justice." Miller said, "then you better get it." Leading witness for the defense was Wiley Coleman, the man who had approached Ambrose for shelter, and he told substantially the story above.

Not only was the case tried in the court, but it also was tried in the columns of the *Chronicle*. Ambrose wrote a long letter to Miller, outlining all the suffering he had undergone as a result of the article in the *Chronicle*. Miller published his rather testy response on Jan. 12, 1868:

"Mr. Ambrose—Sir, In reply to your long, impudent and impotent scrawl, I shall only say now, that so long as I know I have not and never had any enmity against any body, your idle argument to the contrary proves nothing, and troubles me not. I am sorry to say I have always regarded you—as I have no doubt you are generally regarded—as a 'sore-headed' and petulant man in the community; but rather perhaps to be pitied than blamed for that. I am half-minded to demand of you an apology for your foolish note on penalty of exposing you still further to the contempt of the public, but I have more regard for your family than you seem to have, and so may not stir the matter more in public unless you insult me further.

"The smelters shouted at you as they passed your house, before our publication, and would do so if we had never made you famous (or infamous) as you seem to think. And you deserve it all too for rabid inhumanity—notwithstanding your idle pleas in justification. I have had barns and sheds all my life, and never saw one in which I could not store away ten horses out of such a storm as that. But your family troubles I deeply regret and advise you to keep the whole affair out of sight in future—for instead of a verdict (and money) to exonerate your conduct and fill your pocket, you will surely get the contrary.

"Take this only for what it is worth from an interested party (you think), but coming at the same time from one who has always succeeded in all his undertaking (for which he is humble, and never proud) to one whom we never knew to succeed in anything.

"P.S. I shall only add that your letter shows you to be a bigger fool than I had always thought, and no more worthy of the name of Christian (?) than some of the 'sharp-practice' lawyers with whom you fellowship. As to buying Lincoln Hill—it is not for sale—but to do it 'a dozen times over' would cost a round $300,000—more money than all of the name of Ambrose have got in the country. In conclusion, I advise you to 'go to the d—l and shake yourself.'"

In his reference to Lincoln Hill, Frank Miller was speaking of the huge housing development he had under way between Richards avenue, Middle street, Union street and South street, and which will be the subject of a future article. Miller was quite correct in telling Ambrose that his lawsuit would net him nothing.

On Saturday, Nov. 14, W.H.Y. Hackett, chief counsel for the defendants, Miller and Marston, gave his concluding arguments to the jury. He was followed by Albert R. Hatch for Ambrose; the famed Judge Charles Doe charged the jury. The jury took only two hours to find for Miller and Marston. And the *Portsmouth Times*, a bitter political enemy of the *Chronicle*, remarked:

"We are heartily glad of this result, and hope the community will understand that when a newspaper publishes matter of common report, which the editors have reason to believe to be true, is no libel."

Portsmouth Acamdemy. Built in 1806–1808 from designs prepared and executed by a local contractor, James Nutter, the building served as an academy for about 60 years. During that span William C. Harris was the teacher. Today it is Portsmouth's heavily over-burdened public library. Author photo.

XI Some Notable Teachers

William C. Harris

THE OLD MAIN BUILDING OF THE PORTSMOUTH PUBLIC LIBRARY once housed Portsmouth Academy, an educational institution presided over for many years by Master William C. Harris. In the centuries of Portsmouth history hundreds of dedicated teachers have labored to educate the community's young people.

Of them all, and it's in no way disparaging, only one so inspired his students that they erected a monument to him in Harmony Grove Cemetery—William C. Harris.

The academy building was designed and erected by the master joiner, James Nutter, shortly before the War of 1812. The promoters formed a stock company, and, at various times, the building was used for purposes other than schooling. It's not now known when Master Harris first began teaching at the academy. His pedagogical career began in Newington, but before that he had been engaged in commerce, working for his father, Abiel Harris.

Master Harris was often called upon to perform tasks in the community that were outside the immediate educational field. For example, in 1834, he was the marshal for the Fourth of July parade and celebration. On that occasion the parade formed at what is now Temple Israel, heading west. It moved along present-day State street, to Middle, turning right toward Congress, and east on Congress to the North Meeting House.

The exercises in the church included reading of the Declaration of

Independence; then attorney James W. Emery, gave a talk on "The Influence of Public Schools Upon the Permancy of Our Institutions." The exercises over, the participants reassembled outside and marched back to the assembly area for dismissal.

Probably the greatest moment in Harris's career came in 1853, when the "Sons of Portsmouth" staged their first "Return," a grand reunion that might well have been the inspiration for the "Old Home Week" celebrations that were popular a generation or so ago. During the reunion over the Fourth of July, hundreds of men who had been gone from the "Old Town by the Sea" for many years met with Master Harris, and their very presence told the aging teacher that some of the principles he had expounded had been well absorbed.

In the fall of 1853, Master Harris returned to his school, and it was there on Nov. 22, 1853, that he died. He had been listening to recitations, and, as the hour neared noon, he rose, opened the door, turned and put his head down on his desk, then fell to the floor. Quick-thinking students ran for doctors, and found two. They came, but it was too late—Master Harris had heard his last recitation. He was 65.

Some of his former students immediately began plans for a suitable tribute to their teacher. They met the next afternoon, appointing William Simes as chairman, and William H. Sise, secretary. A committee was designated to prepare resolutions. Serving on it were T. G. Senter, William H. Rollins, I. B. Claggett, A. B. Bennett and Edwin F. Mathes.

The committee submitted its report at 2 o'clock on Friday, and the resolutions offered were unanimously adopted:

"Whereas, The intelligence of the sudden death of William C. Harris, while in the midst of his labors, having filled the hearts of us, his pupils, with the deepest sorrow, we regard it fitting, that we should, on this solemn occasion, give expression to our sense of his eminent worth,—therefore,

"Resolved, That in his death the community has sustained the loss of a Teacher, whose fidelity, energy, untiring industry, and eminent tact in educing the talents, imparting instruction and winning the affections of his pupils, are seldom equalled and never have been excelled—a teacher who has done more than any other person to render the Sons of Portsmouth eminent as pioneers in the field of American enterprise.

"Resolved, That we, whose happiness it was to be blessed with his instruction, regard our prosperity and success in life, as mainly attributable to his fidelity in unfolding the latent energies of our minds, infusing within us a love of literature, and teaching us how to study.

"Resolved, That we do, and must ever cherish the memory of the venerable deceased (whose chief delight through life has been to rejoice in our prosperity) with sentiments of the highest regard; and though we deeply mourn his sudden removal while in the actual discharge of his arduous duties, and in the midst of his usefulness, we find consolation in the blessed hope of his being at rest in the bosom of Infinite Love.

"Resolved, That we deeply sympathize with his bereaved family, and in token of our sympathy request the chairman of this meeting to furnish them with a copy of these resolutions.

"Resolved, That the Press be furnished with a copy of these resolutions.

"Resolved, That as a token of our respect, we now proceed to attend the funeral."

Students, past and present, then marched to St. John's Church where the funeral services were held and to the interment in Harmony Grove. Nearly a year later, in November, 1854, a memorial stone for William C. Harris was erected in the cemetery. It was described:

"The Base of the Granite; the Relief Base, Die and Cap are in one piece, of Italian Marble; the Shaft is of Italian Marble; the height of the monument is 7 feet, with a base of 3 feet square.

"On the Cap is carved in raised letters the name William C. Harris, under which, on the Die, is carved a Book, opened near its close, on which is inscribed, so as to fill both pages,

Born March 17, 1788
A
Faithful Teacher
Died November 22, 1853
On the opposite side of the Die is inscribed:
Erected By His Grateful Pupils
The work was designed and executed by Mr. Allen Treat of this city.

That memory of Master William C. Harris stayed green is evidenced by a paragraph in the *Chronicle* on Dec. 1, 1890, noting that the beloved teacher had died in his schoolroom on Nov. 22, 1853.

Edith G. Brewster

Few educational functions in Portsmouth are more highly prized, or more taken for granted, than kindergarten. From infancy to age five, the proud parents of a youngster look eagerly forward until little Mary or little John can be enrolled in this first step in the 13-year process toward a school diploma, and then on into advanced schooling for many of them. Actually, the kindergarten concept was nearly 60 years old before it was introduced in Portsmouth in 1895. Conceived by a German educator, Friedrich Wilhelm August Froedel, in 1837, kindergarten developed slowly in the United States.

By 1895, Portsmouth's Board of Instruction, as the Board of Education was then known, was ready to take the giant step forward. The news reports don't say so, but the feeling is strong that Superintendent of Schools J. Clifford Simpson had prepared the path he wanted the board to follow. In February, 1895, Miss Edith G. Brewster of the Haven School was chosen as the teacher for a kindergarten. Although born in Boston, April 1, 1873, Miss Brewster belonged to the ancient Portsmouth family whose ancestress, Mary Brewster, was scalped by Indians out at the Plains in May, 1696, and lived to tell the tale.

Modesty probably led the editor of the *Portsmouth Journal* to let the *Portsmouth Times* tell the story of the kindergarten experiment. Edith Brewster was his cousin, and she and her sister, Miss Alice L. Brewster, made their home in the Brewster house at 198 Islington St. Miss Brewster apparently came to Portsmouth to live at age 21 after her training in kindergarten work.

Throughout her long, useful life she was active in many aspects of the community, even having a role in the Dover Neighborhood House from 1926 to 1942. From 1943 to 1947 she was resident director of the Portsmouth YWCA. She was a member and deaconess of the North Church; a member of the Piscataqua Pioneers; the Graffort Club; Portsmouth Historical Society; League of New Hampshire Arts and Crafts; and a charter member, Women's City Club. Miss Brewster died March 15, 1960, at the age of 86. Her work with that first kindergarten is her enduring memorial.

Exactly why the *Portsmouth Journal* chose to republish an article that had appeared in the *Portsmouth Times* isn't clear, but after a brief introduction, it began quoting the *Times*:

Monday's Wash Day
A wash tub was the symbol used to teach
Portsmouth's first kindergartners to recognize
Monday on calendars.

"That the introduction of the kindergarten was a move in the right direction is amply shown by the increasing interest therein and the fine results that have already accrued and are constantly developing. Hardly any other outcome could have been expected from so able and thorough a teacher as Miss Brewster, whose love for children, whose easy adaptiveness to the variability of youthful minds, and whose ready comprehensions of the best modes to reach the child have placed her 'just in the niche she was ordained to fill . . . '"

There were 24 youngsters, ranging in age from 3 1/2 to 5 years, in that experimental kindergarten group. Many familiar family names were on the roster, and the grandchildren of those pupils are now well along in years. Class members were: Gertrude Beyer, Laura Belong, Bessie Call, Katherine Chase, Essie Caswell, Lizzie Hall, Marie Kennison, Helen Odiorne, Sophia Pecunies, Ida Pearson, Bella Rose, Flossie Snow, Mabel Somerby, Clara Spinney, Eloise Whittier, Ralph Anderson, Stuart Coleman, Bernard Fitzgerald, Ralph Hamilton, Ellsworth Hoyt, Henry Morrill, John O'Neil, Harvey Smart and Shirley Woods.

The article in the *Times* went into far more discussion of the teaching methods than is permissible here. Today's youngsters, even tots, have been made so sophisticated by their daily dosage of television that some of Miss Brewster's teaching techniques would seem primitive. For example, the *Times* was ecstatic over the manner in which the pupils learned the days of the week:

"One of the happiest among the many valuable instructions which Miss Brewster gives her class of little ones is the calendar work where in the child is daily called upon to register by means of various insignia for weather conditions, the holiday and other adjuncts.

"Then, being unable to read, the tot is taught to know the calendar days by certain household assignments . . . A church for Sunday; washtub, Monday; flatiron, Tuesday; workbasket, Wednesday; letter writing, Thursday; broom, Friday; and a cooking dish, Saturday . . .”

Although those with more than a little white mixed into the grey in their hair can well recall when they knew what a washtub looked like, or a flatiron, today's toddlers know that mother operates a washing machine; and, when she irons, it's with a gadget on the end of a wire. Apparently the success of the Haven School kindergarten persuaded the Board of Instruction to expand the effort to the Cabot Street School.

“ . . . The work accomplished by the children in their little matters is quite remarkable. The training takes early effect, and is enjoyment—not labor—to the little pupils.” Thanks to Miss Brewster, kindergarten became a fixture in the Portsmouth school system, although occasionally a target of budget-cutters as a frill and a luxury.

Today, more than a little appropriately, the Children's Museum occupies the building on Meeting House Hill where Miss Brewster introduced kindergarten to the youngsters of Portsmouth.

Arabella C. Morgan

In the course of its more than 350 years of history, Portsmouth has known many remarkable women, and some not so remarkable. The same can well be said about the masculine side of the war between the sexes, a conflict in which too much fraternization slows the progress of battle. The emphasis here will be on an unusual woman, Arabella C. Morgan. Sadly, few, if any, know who Arabella C. Morgan was, or why she was remarkable.

Perhaps it's easiest to explain that Miss Arabella C. Morgan was the first female in the Portsmouth educational system to lash out against the sexual inequities that prevailed more than a century ago. First public notice of a coming storm appeared in the *Portsmouth Chronicle* on Aug. 30, 1873:

“A change has been made by which Mr. Aurin M. Payson is to be Principal-in-charge of the Boys' and Girls' High School [our former City Hall] at a salary of $1,700; Mr. Stephen W. Clarke and Miss Arabella C. Morgan assistants, with salaries of $1,200 and $700 respectively. Mr. Payson's salary is increased $200, Mr. Clarke's $100.”

It was worth a small paragraph in the *Chronicle* on Sept. 3, 1873,

Girl's school. Arabella C. Morgan had Benjamin F. Webster erect this building for use as a boarding school for young women. Today it is an apartment building. Author photo.

to note "Miss Arabella C. Morgan, Assistant at the High School, returned from a European trip, Thursday." At the first swipe of an eraser across the blackboard, it would appear as though Arabella Morgan was doing quite well on her stipend of $700 annually, if she could afford to go to Europe.

First, who was Arabella Morgan? She was a native of Lowell, Mass., and her Portsmouth connection was her sister, Adelaide Foster. She came to the city "in young womanhood and secured a position as assistant in the Girls' High School." She had been in the city 18 years when her problem became public. Other than a glance at the salary schedule, what more is needed to understand Miss Morgan's discontent? The *Chronicle* reported on Dec. 18, 1873:

"We understand that Miss A.C. Morgan has resigned her position as Assistant in the High School. Miss Morgan has been a successful teacher for 18 years and has many friends among pupils and parents. Had the school committee accorded Miss Morgan justice, her valuable services might have been retained, perhaps. Is it too late?" As always, when a school controversy begins, there are always those who try to cover their tracks. One such was a writer to the editor on Dec. 20, 1873, who put the blame on the High School Committee by quoting the ordinance:

"The sub-committee on the high school shall consist of three members, one of whom shall be from each ward, and selected by the members of their respective wards. Said sub-committee shall have full control of the high school, including the appointment and salaries of the teachers. So the general committee are not responsible unless they may have been unfortunate in their selections. I have no doubt the general committee very much regret the conclusion to which Miss Morgan has arrived and would most heartily endorse any effort to have her withdraw her resignation . . . "

Two days later the real worm in the apple of the Portsmouth school system poked out of the core. First the writer to the Chronicle told how Miss Morgan, out of a salary of $700 had to pay a substitute "to take advantage of a favorable opportunity for visiting Europe. She begged for the chance to go, but was refused until she agreed to pay the substitute."

And then, the letter writer dug into the middle of the Portsmouth educational apple. It seems that the high school committee, ever zealous to have the students able to sound musical notes, hired a music teacher at $800 per annum: The writer noted:

"Miss Franklin has taught music in a portion of the public schools for a few months past, her salary at first being fixed at $600 per year . . . and now it has been raised to $800 a year. This may not be too much to pay for the service rendered by Miss Franklin, the $1,000 per year is far too little to pay for such services as Miss Morgan's." Other letters pounded a similar theme, with one sounding a keynote, "The best is always the cheapest." When Arabella Morgan sounded her swansong at Portsmouth High, the pupils presented her with "a splendid silver card-receiver, gold lined." The students also honored Stephen Clark of the Boys' High, and Auren Payson, the Principal.

At a distance of more than a century it's impossible to understand the political, social and other relationships involved, but, somehow, it has to be thought that the high school committee, at best, was a bit stupid. But Arabella Morgan wasn't long down. In mid-January, 1874, it was reported that Miss Morgan "is soon to open a boarding school for young ladies in the city. Our best wishes are for her success." The next news mention concerning Arabella Morgan said:

"Mr. B.F. Webster is laying the foundation for a building to be used as a young ladies seminary, at the corner of Miller Avenue and a new street north of Lincoln Avenue. It is to be completed and ready for occupancy Sept. 1st." Benjamin F. Webster and Frank Miller were the developers for the tract centered by Miller Avenue in the 1870s. Webster was a master carpenter whose mark is on many of the houses standing today along Union Street, south of Middle.

Rockingham County Deed 0449-0090 in 1874 shows that Arabella Morgan paid Webster $1,250 for a lot of land "beginning on a new street to be called Rockland Street, running easterly to Richards Avenue and then 102 feet southerly along Richards."

This transaction and the construction of a building thereon prompts a question: Where did a $700-a-year female school teacher get the money to undertake such a project?

The answer has to be based on speculation. Arabella Morgan's sister was Mrs. Joseph Hiller Foster, who was the wife of the president of Portsmouth Savings Bank. It's more than probable that Foster advanced the funding in some private family arrangement. Miss Morgan's first advertisement for her school was published on July 20, 1874. The prospectus said:

"Instruction by the best Teachers in all branches of English education as well as in Latin, French, German, Music and Painting. The School Building is new, situated in the pleasantest part of the city, and provided with all conveniences for health and comfort. Early application for admission is desirable, as the number of vacancies is already limited. Refer to Rev. Mr. Peabody, Cambridge; George B. Emerson, Esq., and James T. Fields, Esq., Boston; Gov. Goodwin and Rev. James DeNormandie, Portsmouth."

Those references were men of power and prestige. Goodwin had been New Hampshire's first Civil War governor; James T. Fields was the founder of *Atlantic Magazine*. It's quite probable that one or more of the Goodwin daughters attended the school. Shortly before she opened the school, a news item in the *Chronicle* hailed the enterprise of the "Gas Company in laying pipes down Miller Avenue to light the new Girls' School of Miss Morgan" and the Board of Aldermen drew praise for voting to accept gas lighting for Miller Avenue.

Miss Morgan's school was a success from the start. The Chronicle reported on Sept. 25:

"Miss Morgan's boarding and day school for young ladies opened Thursday under flattering auspices. Accommodations had been prepared for a number of pupils in excess of what were expected to be present on the opening day, but the preparations had to be supplemented."

It's impossible, of course, to learn now who those "young ladies" were. However, Miss Helen Pender, who would become the mother of Wyman Pender Boynton, Esq., was at one time, enrolled in the school. And a news item concerning a Christmas surprise for Miss Morgan gives the name of yet another student, Emma Sise, who apparently was "head girl" in presenting a silver tea service to the principal.

From an ad in August, 1876, it is possible to learn the names of some of the teachers. They included Miss E. Victoria Fournier, "from Paris," a resident teacher of French; Emma Krauss, German teacher, also a resident; Mary E. B. Miller, drawing and painting, non-resident; M. Louise Smalley, piano-forte. What the boarders paid for fees wasn't listed in the ad, but the day students, over 12, paid $100 annually, and under 12 the rate was $75.

In December, 1876, Miss Morgan staged a series of lectures on Natural Science. She engaged Prof. C. A. Pitkin, an instructor at the U.S. Torpedo Station, Newport, R.I., as the lecturer. A limited number of tickets at one dollar for the four lectures were available. In another series of lectures, she presented James T. Fields, the noted editor and writer. He was the chief attraction at her school exhibition in June, 1877.

Pages could be devoted to the innovativeness of Miss Morgan's program which "combines at once pleasure and profit, instilling in her pupils an enthusiasm for their work, which assumes more than the character of an exhilarating intellectual entertainment, than of a task."

Again the name of another student is learned through an item in which the *Franklin* (N.H.) *Journal* is quoted as saying that "Miss Emma Blanchard recently graduated at Miss A. C. Morgan's select school at Portsmouth. She will return next term as one of the teachers at the school."

Also in 1877, among the graduates were listed Lena Hanscom and Addie Doane of Portsmouth; Mary Chase of South Dennis, Mass.; and Fannie B. Peterson, daughter of Edwin A. Peterson of Greenland. In truth, Arabella Morgan brought to Portsmouth an intellectual excitement seldom seen in the community. In May 1878, long before TV's "French Chef" starring Julia Child, Miss Morgan was featuring a series of lectures by Miss M. Parloa, the ex-chef at the Appledore

House, Isles of Shoals, "author of the Appledore Cook-Book." The *Chronicle* gave part of a column to her lectures.

However, one of the greatest features of Arabella Morgan's educational system was her summer tours of Europe. Year after year, she went abroad, taking with her any daughters the affluent were willing to send. In June, 1881, for example, it was reported that Miss Morgan, on July 2, would sail on the steamer *Furnessia*, "Captain Small for Glasgow, Scotland, and with some of her pupils and friends will spend the summer in a tour of Europe." That party, under her guidance, consisted of more than 20 individuals.

In 1893 she scheduled an 81-day tour, via the Red Star Line, visiting Germany, Italy, Switzerland, England and Scotland, for a per-person cost of $600. And that's the way she spent her creative years, perhaps one of the greatest educators Portsmouth has ever had.

Arabella C. Morgan died on June 22, 1894. Her property was left to her sister, Adelaide Foster. The school continued for a few years, but without the inspired leadership of Arabella Morgan it went down. Today the structure that housed it is known as the Rockland Apartments.

But Arabella Morgan must be ranked among the greatest of Portsmouth women, an educator of distinction, and, miraculously, for her day, a woman who realized that there were two sexes, and, under controlled conditions, she let them meet.

Robert Morrison

Today's educators are not unlike their predecessors in having to deal with problem students.

For example, on Oct. 8, 1881, the *Portsmouth Journal* published a letter of reminiscence written by a Portsmouth native who had memories of school days long gone—by 50 years. True, today, even the street where an old wooden one-story school stood has vanished under the hardtop of urban renewal. There probably are a few of those schools still standing, although not in the Seacoast. Some persons still living may have had their early schooling in them.

The writer to the *Journal* a bit over 110 years ago reminisced over his days in the old building on School Street. That building disappeared in 1839, so the writer, admittedly was dipping deeply into the well of memory.

". . . . In the old building, fifty years ago, Robert Morrison was the teacher of what today would be called the grammar school of the district, and many a pupil of that time cherishes the grateful memories of his kind carefulness in conducting the early steps of their education. Mr. Morrison was a lightweight physically, but this deficiency was more than made up by the energy of a firm purpose and strong will, backed with a wiry nervous force which gave him a feline quickness in his movements.

"On the average there has undoubtedly been a great advance in the general conduct and character of the boys who make up the common school of today over those of fifty years ago. A general diffusion of knowledge among parents, and the results of a better home culture, have rendered the task of the teacher far less onerous than it was a half a century ago. The gross profanity and beastly language which was then common among the rougher class of boys are seldom heard from the lips of the lowest of our grammar school boys of today. There is much less of the brutal element, which led to frequent and sanguinary fights in the school yard.

"Nor do we hear of insubordination and positive rebellion on the part of the older and more belligerent pupils, which was far too common at the period of which we speak. An instance of the latter class comes to mind under the administration of Mr. Morrison in School Street.

"The tallest, oldest and heaviest boy in the school was disposed to utterly ignore the rules against whispering in school hours. He had the gruff voice that characterizes entrance upon manhood, and frequently his low rumbling tones were heard in violation of school law. The teacher's patience had long and often been taxed, until at last he could endure the insolence no longer.

"In a sudden, sharp, incisive tone he spoke to the offender, whose seat was in a remote corner farthest from the desk. Calling him by name, he said: 'Do you want a flogging?' The reply came back in low sullen tones, 'Yes, if you can do it.' 'I'll try,' said the master, as he quickly rose from his chair. Buttoning the bright buttons of his blue dress coat over his slim figure, and seizing his cowhide, he stepped down upon the clear space in front of his desk saying, 'Come on!'

"The lumbering giant, who was taller and heavier than the master, came swinging his way down the inclined floor, pulling off his coat with an air of braggadocio worthy of a better cause, until he stood before the wiry little man, who, by this time was full of electricity, who, seizing him by the collar with his left hand, applied the cowhide with a rapidity which almost took away the breath of the lubber, who vainly strove to catch the weapon, and succeeded only by his heavier weight in pushing the master around in a circle, all the time smarting under the lashes so well laid on, until by a sudden movement, quick as lightning the master tripped him, and he fell heavily to the floor, crying 'murder' under the severe lashing now raining upon him in his defenseless position.

"Upon this cry he was permitted to get up. The school door was opened and he was thrust outside in disgrace. We expected to see him no more, but through subsequent humble apologies and promises of better conduct, he was after a week or two admitted to the school again, where he proved a most exemplary and well behaved pupil, until he left to go to sea."

The letter writer added that "such scenes were not frequent." After they had taken place, they were usually followed "by a long season of good order and strict obedience."

Robert Morrison was a popular man in Portsmouth, so much so that he was elected mayor in 1857 and served two terms.

And he was just a tough as mayor as in the schoolroom. On one occasion, after a drunken riot in old Water (Marcy) Street, he closed the bars over the howling protests of the mob.

Morrison later moved to Northwood and died there.

In Command—John Christie was a highly respected chief clerk at the Portsmouth Naval Shipyard, serving on two occasions and after retirement, worked in a Portsmouth bank. Photo courtesy of Strawbery Banke.

XII Some Men of Character

John Christie

FEW MEN HAVE EVER ACHIEVED greater respect and affection in Portsmouth than John Christie. Yet he was the victim of one of the weirdest maneuvers ever pulled off by a Portsmouth Navy Yard commander, and one that couldn't be duplicated today.

By the first of June, 1856, John Christie had been employed on the Portsmouth Navy Yard for 31 years, and much of that service was in the post of clerk to the commandant. It was, obviously, an administrative position, one which maintained the continuity of operations as Yard commanders came and went because of the Navy's constant shuffle of personnel. When John Christie went to work on Saturday, May 31, he had little idea of what was in store for him when he opened a letter from the commandant, Commodore John Thomas Newton. It was a letter of dismissal—just that brutal, after 31 years of service. On Sunday, Christie showed the letter to the Rev. Tobias Miller, editor of the *Portsmouth Chronicle* and "Uncle Toby" the next day published it:

"Allow me on this occasion to express my sincere thanks for your services, which have been most faithfully and diligently performed since our association, and to assure you that under no circumstances other than my son's wish to be with me, would ever have induced me to part with you. You carry with you, dear sir, my good wishes for your future welfare and happiness, which, believe me, will be a pleasure to me to promote."

The young man that nepotism of the worst order put in Christie's place was Gordon M. Newton. The removal apparently stirred no editorial ire. Naval officers in those days, both British and American, were arrogant despots who ruled their ships or their commands as they desired. Gordon Newton held the post during his father's tenure at the Portsmouth Navy Yard. The elder Newton in March, 1857, was detailed to temporary duty on a Court of Inquiry in Washington. Shortly after the court adjourned on July 28, Commodore Newton was fatally stricken.

The *Chronicle* commented that Commodore Newton was the first commandant of PNY to die while holding office. It added that as of that time, only two former commanders were still alive. Commodores John D. Sloat and George Washington Storer. Diplomatically, the newspaper added that Commodore Newton had been "efficient and popular officer." His son, the commandant's clerk, went to Washington to take charge of his father's remains. On Aug. 16, the *Chronicle* published an item that started an editorial tempest with the *New Hampshire Gazette*.

"We learn that John Christie, Esq., has the offer of his old position as clerk to the Commandant of this Naval Station. Mr. Christie had occupied this clerkship for upwards of 30 years, previous to the appointment of Gordon Newton, Esq., of the office, and consequent return to become one of our citizens, would be a subject of congratulations to a very large circle of friends and the public generally. Mr. C. has been in Kansas City for the last few months; but has probably started on his return journey ere this."

There can be no doubt that John Christie had a wide circle of friends. He was one of the state's leading Masons, in a day when that fraternity was at the height of its influence. Details of his Masonic activities won't be dwelt on here, other than to say, he had been master of St. John's Lodge, No. 1, 1832 to 1836; grand master of New Hampshire, 1847 to 1851. While serving as grand master, he served in a lowly official capacity in St. Andrew's Lodge, No. 56, and became master of that lodge, created in 1846, after ending his service with the grand lodge. During the Civil War, he again was master of St. Andrew's. A few days after the *Chronicle* had reported the proposed return of John Christie, the *Gazette* remarked, or so the *Chronicle* said:

"We observe that some of the newspapers in this city, have been trying to impress upon Commodore Pope the urgent necessity of Mr.

Christie's appointment whether on national or personal grounds, we are not aware."

Whereupon, the *Chronicle* riposted savagely:

"Most impertinent and groundless assumption! The commodore had already done his business in his own way, without any outside pressure whatsoever; by offering the clerkship to the old clerk, who knew the duties and who he was sure would perform them faithfully as he ever had done. Some newspapers thereupon congratulated whom—? Not the Commodore, who needed nothing of the kind—but the immediate friends and the public generally—that by this appointment a worthy man and a good citizen might be induced to stay among us, though otherwise he would probably leave us to seek a livelihood elsewhere. Thereupon the mean man interferes with the commodore's business, and pitches, in a pitiful bumbling way, into the clerk and the newspapers."

Of course, the political nuances among the Portsmouth newspapers are important. The publisher of the *Gazette* was from the interior of New Hampshire, and his political course was long under fire from the entrenched journals. On Aug. 24, the *Chronicle* went after the *Gazette* again:

"We have not for a long time, seen a more pitiful article than the one which just now falls under our eye in a neighboring paper, in which a foolish attack is made on the new Commodore, for appointing a clerk on the Navy Yard to suit himself;—on the clerk, who is absent, for being an independent man; and on the abolition papers of this city, for saying something which really they have not said! About 10 days ago, it was within our knowledge that the post of Commodore's clerk on the Navy Yard, at this station, had been offered to Mr. Christie, in the most honorable and proper manner, by the commandant, Com. Pope, and under the recommendation of other high officers . . ."

The *Chronicle* then summarized the journalistic response to the proposal, and found it generally favorable. Apparently, however, the *Gazette* chose to take another tack:

"It is said that John Christie, Esq., has been invited to resume his position at this navy yard; and that he has accepted the office and is on his way home from Kansas, where he has been a squatter for a few months; and the abolition papers of this city speak of the universal satisfaction which this appointment will give."

In the 1850s the issue of slavery tinted the public discussion of everything. The "abolitionists" were under constant fire from those not wanting to upset the status quo. Slavery, as such, was virtually non-existent in New Hampshire long before 1850, yet it was still a hot political issue. And why this had anything to do with the re-appointment of John Christie defies common sense, but there it was. The *Chronicle* carefully explained that Gordon Newton, the incumbent, his boss, his father, being deceased, was leaving the clerkship.

"Com. Pope writes for a first-rate clerk,—and knowing Mr. C.'s long service and accurate performance of duty, with his high reputation among officers of the navy, he has offered to reinstate Mr. Christie in his old post . . ."

As is done today, the newspapers kept on hacking the silly issue to death. The *Gazette* responded:

'Uncle Toby' shall have his say. We cannot blame him for fighting hard for his relative; but from his desperate attacks upon the *Gazette* for the expression of a modest hint, (1) we are confirmed in our belief that his project to arrange matters for Com. Pope, is not so successful as he might wish. (2) We cannot with self-respect bandy terms for such an old sinner..&c."

As might be expected, "Uncle Toby" didn't let that comment pass unanswered, his tirade ran for a few paragraphs, and he never did answer the charge of the *Gazette* about taking care of a relative. The degree of Christie's relationship to Tobias Miller isn't known to the writer, and hardly worth finding out.

John Christie did accept Commodore John Pope's invitation to return, and served both Pope, and two of his successors as commandant's clerk. He left the Navy Yard after the Civil War and became a private accountant. Subsequently, he became cashier of the Rockingham Ten Cent Savings Bank. After the bank failed, Christie was employed by the Piscataqua Savings Bank where he was working at the time of his death at the age of 86.

Israel Kimball

It would be unthinkable today for the principal of Portsmouth Senior High School to go to the chairman of the Portsmouth School Board and ask to have the opening of school deferred for five days because he had a personal matter to take care of. Yet it happened on Aug. 31, 1853.

The principal—and teacher—of the Boys High School, Israel

Kimball, went to William H. Rollins, chairman of the High School Committee, and requested that he be permitted to dismiss the school from Sept. 1 to Sept. 5. Before going on, it should be said that the Boys High School was in a two-story brick building located in the vicinity of the Fahnestock offices on State Street. Grammar school boys were on the ground floor, and the high schoolers on the second.

What about the girls? Oh, they had a high school of their own—of course. It was located in the dank basement of the old court house which was on the site of the present-day Central Fire Station. Now back to the running story:

Kimball's reason for the request was that a friend from a western state would be in town and he wanted to spend time with him. Actually the whole contretemps began early in the summer when the Boys High ended its academic year. After the final "examination" of the school by the committee, it was announced that classes would resume on Sept. 1. This was greeted by a loud hiss from the student body. That angered the school committee, and the members became adamant in insisting that the Sept. 1 date be met.

Principal Kimball protested the decision, saying that the opening date was inconvenient for him as he wanted to attend the commencement at Bowdoin College. He was told in no uncertain terms by the committee that school would begin on Sept. 1, and that after the hissing by the students there would be no change. Bowing to the committee's dictate, Kimball then proceeded to get his own way by setting a different tack which he took on Sept. 1, sending a note to the High School Committee:

"Gentlemen—According to your order at the close of examination, I have met my school and organized, assigning to each class their lessons, and then I adjourned over until Monday, the 5th of September."

The High School Committee lost no time in responding to what it obviously considered defiance:

"Mr. Israel Kimball—Sir—Your letter of this date (Sept. 1) informing us of your having adjourned the Boys High School until Monday next, without consulting the Committee, has been received by us with much surprise; and we shall consider a repetition of such a course on your part a matter which we shall be compelled to notice in a manner less agreeable than the present.

The note was signed by Rollins, Jonathan M. Tredick and Samuel Storer, members of the committee. Kimball answered it immediately, making the reader wonder who the messenger was who scuttled back and forth between the adversaries:

"Gentlemen—Your note of this day (Sept. 1) expressing surprise at my having adjourned the Boys High School till Monday next has been received and excites in my mind corresponding surprise. My note to you this morning informing you what I had done, of itself, aside from the statement of reasons made verbally to the chairman of the committee yesterday, I thought sufficient. I shall at all times hold myself responsible for my doings or misdoings connected with the Boys High School; but that the committee may rest in no uncertainty in this respect, I will assure them that I shall act in the future as I have for 10 years past independently in matter so nearly personal. The threat at the close of your note I deem as derogatory for the committee to make it as insulting for me to receive it."

Kimball's truculent and pedagogical tone must have stunned the committee because it didn't respond until the next day:

"Mr. Israel Kimball—Sir—Your second communication of yesterday had been received by the committee with very great surprise. I am directed to inform you that you are at liberty to withdraw it at any time today, and unless it is withdrawn it will be placed on the files of the committee."

Not hearing from Kimball, the High School Committee met on Sept. 3, and voted to have an arbiter study the correspondence and then suggest the proper course. The man chosen was the Rev. Charles Burroughs, rector of St. John's Church, who was the dean of the local clergy. A copy of the vote was sent to Kimball to allow him to put his part of the correspondence in Dr. Burrough's hands. On Monday, Sept. 5, Kimball made a lengthy reply to the committee's suggestion. In the course of it he fervently denied any intent to defy the committee, but simply that his reasons for adjourning the Boys High School were "entirely personal and affecting me alone." Kimball added:

"I regret as much as the committee possibly can any breach of the good feeling subsisting up to this time between myself and the committee, and I am willing to meet them on the ground of a mutual withdrawal of the entire correspondence on both sides." Kimball proposed a plan for the exchange of the correspondence by neutral parties, and, then served what amounted to an ultimatum:

"If this proposition is not satisfactory to the committee, I am prepared to place my resignation in their hands to take effect immediately . . . only asking . . . a reasonable notice. I shall be in school at 9 o'clock this A.M. [Sept. 5] ready to receive any communication the committee may wish to make." Kimball, who shines through the whole correspondence as a bit on the arrogant side, must have suffered a mild shock when he read the committee's reply, in which the board said it had no desire to have the note of censure withdrawn or destroyed, adding:

"We therefore are of the opinion that the proper regulation and government of the school will be best promoted by the resignation of your trust to our hands, to take effect at as early a day as will be convenient for you." With his retreat blocked by the committee, Kimball wrote on Sept. 6:

". . . I therefore cheerfully comply with the suggestion of the committee, and hereby resign to your hands the office of the teacher of the Boys High School, to take effect from this date." The next day Kimball sent a note:

"Gentlemen—I am now ready to dismiss the Boys High School, and shall do so in 15 minutes from this time, unless otherwise ordered by you."

That, of course, wasn't the end of the matter. On Sept. 30, the *Chronicle* reported that it was expected that "Mr. K." will resume his duties as Teacher of the High School on his return, probably the first of next week—Rev. Dr. Burroughs having effected an adjustment of the difficulty between the Committee and Mr. Kimball.

Kimball, accompanied by two of his former students, Edward A. Rand and Joshua J. Laighton, had gone to Brunswick to assist the youths in getting entrance into Bowdoin College. However, the reconciliation proved illusory. On Oct. 12 two news items appeared in the *Chronicle*. The first said:

"Mr. Kimball commences a Private School for Boys this morning, in one of the Temple vestries—we understand with quite a large number of scholars."

The second announced the appointment of a new teacher at the Boys High School:

"We understand that Aurin M. Payson, A.M., Preceptor of Berwick Academy, has been appointed Principal of the High School for Boys in this city, and has accepted the appointment. Mr. Payson is a graduate of Dartmouth College, and has won and sustained an excellent reputation as a teacher in the seminary which he now leaves to take up his residence among us. He is a brother of Mr. John P. Payson, who had long been a successful teacher of boys in this city."

However, Kimball managed to get in the last word. He wrote to the editor of the *Rockingham Messenger* in regard to an item published. The introduction by the *Chronicle* suggests that the High School Committee was tacitly admitting that Kimball had been treated unjustly. Kimball's letter read:

"Mr. Editor—The notice in your paper of the 12 inst (October) concerning the High School, so far as related to myself and the referees to whom the pending difficulties between the high school committee and myself were submitted, requires this brief notice from me, in order to prevent any misunderstanding as to my own position in the matter. First. So far as I am concerned, there was no advance made toward the committee in view of a reappointment to the office of high school teacher. The committee voluntarily made the proposition to me, and asked me on what terms I would resume the school. Second. In regard to the matter of salary, which was one of my terms, it is necessary to say, in order to prevent any wrong impressions, that inasmuch as the committee had tacitly disclaimed their former action toward me, through which I was subjected to much inconvenience and loss of time, it seemed to me but right that the cost of the mistake should be with those that made it. Third. Concerning the correspondence between the referees, which is asked for publication, I would say that, as the chairman of the high school committee now disclaims the correspondence as in any wise belonging to or involving the committee, it is withheld from the public as a simple act of courtesy to one of the referees who is absent from the city. I would, however, add that, had I known there was no authority in the correspondence so far as the committee are concerned, there would have been saved much time, writing and anxiety."

So it would appear that Israel Kimball marched off the field into the pages of Portsmouth history with his banner flying high. What probably happened is that the newspaper exposure of the correspondence between Kimball and the committee stirred the citizenry to wrath. More than 30 years of reporting and commenting on the doings of public officials seems to justify the conclusion that the Kimball affair became a hotter potato than the high school committee cared to handle.

However, that wasn't the last ever heard about Israel Kimball in Portsmouth. For a year or two, he conducted a private school in the city, but then he drifted on to more lucrative pursuits, although he maintained a residence at what was then 111 Islington Street until his death.

Israel Kimball. Probably Kimball's dour expression was encouraged by the fact he had to sit absolutely motionless for a period of time so the picture could be made. Photo courtesy of Strawbery Banke Inc.

Lewis G. Brewster, then editor of the *Portsmouth Journal*, offered in 1888 some insight into Kimball's highly successful subsequent career, thanks to an article borrowed from the *Tobacco Journal*.

"The subject of this sketch, Mr. Israel Kimball, may very appropriately be termed the Father of the Internal Revenue system of the United States. It is nearly 20 years since he was appointed to a position in the Internal Revenue department, which he has occupied uninterruptedly up to the present day. Mr. Kimball, like many other of our public men of eminence, comes of New England stock. He was born in Wells, York County, Maine. As a boy he was noted for his studious habits and modest and retiring disposition, qualities which characterize him even to the present day.

"Applying himself with great ardor and intense but subdued enthusiasm to his studies, almost unaided he fitted himself for Bowdoin College, which he entered and from which he graduated with honors in 1839. He then began to read law, but never engaged in actual practice. Mr. Kimball preferred the schoolmaster's desk to the bar, as between 1840 and 1852 he was principal of several classical institutions of learning. In the latter year he was principal of the Portsmouth, N.H., Academy.

"It was in 1862 that the Internal Revenue Bureau was organized by Governor Boutwell of Massachusetts. Mr. Kimball was one of the first to whom a position was tendered. Afterward, when the Bureau was reorganized, he was the first Chief of Division to be designated, having in his charge all manufactures except whiskey. During the earlier years of his connection with the Department, a large portion of Mr. Kimball's time was taken up in visiting various sections of the country for the purpose of explaining the workings of the internal revenue system and instructing collectors and assessors in their duties. In fact, it may be said that Mr. Kimball had as much, if not more, to do with organizing the system than any other person.

"In 1878, the German Government, having some idea of establishing an internal revenue system similar to our own, formally requested that our Government send some one connected with the Internal Revenue Department to Germany to assist in organizing such a system, and explain the laws for its government. The Secretary of the Treasury and the Commissioner of Internal Revenue at once selected Mr. Kimball and tendered him the desired leave of absence, with pay, if he desired to accept the honor. Mr. Kimball, however, after some consideration declined it. Shortly thereafter a commission composed of four gentlemen was sent to this country by the German Government to examine and study our internal revenue system. Upon their arrival in Washington the commissioners were introduced to Mr. Kimball and spent several weeks visiting his office and receiving instructions there three or four hours each day.

"All the laws in their operations to the (most) minute detail were explained by Mr. Kimball. Upon the departure of the commissioners, the German minister at Washington tendered to Mr. Kimball the thanks of his Government for his valuable services. In the fall of 1878 the Russian Government made a somewhat similar request, and Mr. Kimball prepared a complete digest of our internal revenue laws and their operations, which was highly complimented and pronounced a very able and exhaustive document, and again he was the recipient of hearty thanks from a foreign government. . . ."

Israel Kimball continued his ascendancy over Internal Revenue until his death, Dec. 11, 1890. The *Journal* said:

". . . He has always retained a residence here, which has been occupied as a summer home by the family, and has maintained an active interest in the welfare of our city and its various institutions. At the time of his death he was the oldest chief of division in the internal revenue department, and was regarded at the capital as one of the most trustworthy and capable of the government's public servants. Mr. Kimball leaves a wife, four daughters and one son, a younger son having died a few years ago. The remains were brought here for interment on Saturday and were buried in the family lot in Proprietors' cemetery. . . ."

Despite Kimball's service with Internal Revenue, don't blame him for your miseries at income tax time. All he was trying to do was assess and collect the levies due on manufactured goods like tobacco.

Some of those problems aren't fully resolved even in the Computer Age.

John McClintock

In the course of her long history, Portsmouth has known many distinguished citizens who, far into their evening years, were still active in community service. The following is by no means an effort to start a competition for longevity honors, but it might be reasonable to claim the record for Capt. John McClintock, who died on Nov. 13, 1855, in his 95th year, while still on active duty as naval officer in the Port of Portsmouth.

"Naval officer" was, of course, a quasi-military post long since abandoned, but in the early years of the country, it was an office of great importance, the incumbent serving as purchasing agent for naval installations such as the Portsmouth Navy Yard in Kittery. Not only was John McClintock providing his country with useful service at the time of his death, but he was one of the last links Portsmouth had with the days and men of the American Revolution.

Captain McClintock was born Aug. 28, 1760, one of four sons of the Rev. Samuel McClintock of Greenland who won immortality in local lore by serving as a chaplain at the Battle of Bunker Hill. All four of Rev. McClintock's sons served in the armed forces of the United Colonies. One, Nathaniel, was in his last year of college at the time of Bunker Hill, but he went into the army, and died after attaining the rank of major. Another son also died in the army service. John McClintock went to sea in the privateer *Alexander*, 20 guns, under Capt. Thomas Simpson, who later commanded the Continental sloop-of-war *Ranger*. Young McClintock quickly became master's mate and commanded a prize vessel that was sent into the West Indies.

After the war, McClintock continued following the sea, and before the close of the century was both master and owner of a vessel. In 1797, he suffered losses exceeding $10,000 at the hands of French privateers who preyed on American vessels in the Caribbean. In one of the most scandalous incidents in American history, mariners like McClintock were never compensated for their losses, although the French government paid the United States for damages done to shipping. Once he left the sea, McClintock went into merchandising in Portsmouth. Records of the Portsmouth Marine Society, then a charitable organization devoted to helping distressed mariners and their families, indicate that he was often granted funds in the latter years of his life. He had served the society as president for 30 years.

Today the Portsmouth Marine Society, reactivated some years ago by Joseph G. Sawtelle and the late Joseph P. Copley, is an organization devoted to publishing books on Portsmouth history and nearly 20 different works have been brought out.

McClintock's friends gained him an appointment as naval officer during President John Tyler's administration in the early 1840s. He was reappointed to his last term in 1854 by President Franklin Pierce.

Charles W. Brewster, editor of the *Portsmouth Journal*, in Captain McClintock's obituary, wrote:

"We met him in the Athenaeum on one morning in that week, perusing, as was his custom, the papers of the day. Speaking of his appointment, he said—'Some may regard me as old and worn out, and the office given to me as a mere sinecure, but such is not the case. For five years I have never been absent from attending to the duties of office but one day, winter or summer'."

Brewster added that the old gentleman had been kept away from his office that one day by a severe snowstorm—and not by illness.

Although the *Portsmouth Journal* did well by Captain McClintock in its obituary, some months later it offered an even better insight into the man when it published the man's own sketch of his life, written a year before his death.

"I was born in Greenland, N.H., 1760, August 28th day. Four years in the Revolutionary war, cruising in ships-of-war against the enemies of our country: in two 20-gun ships from Portsmouth and two 20-gun ships from Salem. Offices held by me on board said ships: Sailing Master's Mate, Prize Master and Lieutenant.

"After peace was made, 12 years I commanded ships in the merchant trade. Ships and cargoes consigned to myself—voyages to the West Indies and Europe. Never met with any loss or damage by sea; owners of ships or cargoes had no claim on insurance for one dollar. Never lost a man at sea during all my voyages.

"When I quit the sea, established myself in business on shore as a merchant, I was appointed or elected to the following offices: Justice of the Peace 50 years; one of the three General Commissioners of Bankruptcy for the state of New Hampshire by President Jefferson; one of the founders and Directors of the Aqueduct; Director and agent of Piscataqua Bridge; President of the Portsmouth Marine Society; Naval Officer of the District of Portsmouth, N.H. I never had a law suit in my life, or a court of reference; nor was ever confined by sickness from attending to my business . . . I was never absent from public worship one Sabbath for forty years. In all the offices I have held I have endeavored to act with the strictest integrity and morality. If in private life I have committed any error, folly or sin, I have a firm trust that my Heavenly Father, who has wonderfully protected and preserved me to my present age, will forgive me.

The Rev. Joseph Buckminster

Perusal of the accepted sources seemingly establish that the Rev. Joseph Buckminster was a real prig, but actually he wasn't. The man even practiced the Christianity which he frequently expounded from the pulpit of the first North Church. Admittedly, the edifice we know today as the North Church is a newcomer to the Market Square scene.

The church, graced by Dr. Buckminster 180 years ago, was ripped down in 1854 after a bitter parochial feud. So we go back to the earlier edifice, one erected in the years 1713-1718, and one in which George Washington sat as a rapt listener to the eloquence of Joseph Buckminster. That was on Nov. 1, 1789.

Exactly when the following incident took place isn't known, but it is part of the North Church's grand tradition. On the Sunday it hap-

Reverend Joseph Buckminster

pened, Dr. Buckminster was reading from the second chapter of James, and it was reportedly on a fine Sunday in summer.

"Just as he had read the second verse, 'and there come in also a poor man in vile raiment,'—an old man, imbecile and feeble, in mean and patched attire, tottered in at the front door and crept up the broad aisle through the most numerous and dressy congregation in the place. No pew doors were opened; perhaps no one observed him in season, as he made no noise; at all events he ascended to part of the pulpit stairs, and took a seat about half-way up, just as the Doctor [Buckminster] had finished the third and fourth verses, which speak of the respect paid to men in gay clothing, while men say to the poor 'stand thou there, or sit here under my footstool'."

Buckminster House. The Rev. Joseph Buckminster married the widow of Eliphalet Ladd. The Ladds were the parents of the "Apostle of Peace," William Ladd, and they built the house, but it's Buckminster's name that is tagged to it. Author photo.

Contemporary accounts leave no doubt that the fine and polished members of Portsmouth's North Church aristocracy saw him, but they didn't disturb the service. While the old man lingered halfway between the pulpit and the congregation, Dr. Buckminster read on. At the finish of the chapter, Buckminster read:

"For as the body without spirit is dead, so faith without works is dead also."

So saying Dr. Buckminster stepped down from the high pulpit that dominated the old churches, "opened the pulpit door, bowed the poor old man in with one of his best bows, and gave him the seat at his right hand, which the old man took as silently, if not as gracefully, as it had been offered . . ."

William Ladd
Apostle of Peace

Everyone, the world around, has heard of the "Prince of Peace," a title conferred on Jesus Christ by practitioners of Christian doctrine. Unfortunately, of far less renown is the man who was known as the "Apostle of Peace." He was William Ladd, a native of Exeter, and a one-time Portsmouth sea captain.

William Ladd's labors in the rocky garden of world peace were the forerunners of the many on-going efforts toward establishing peace as a way of life in the world. Today a simple white shaft marks his grave in Portsmouth's South Cemetery. It should be clearly understood from the outset that William Ladd was no dreamy-eyed idealist with no concept of the reality of life. In his early years, he was very much a man of the world—a sea captain, and there are few more tough-minded realists than shipmasters. As will be seen, he wasn't above a bit of lawbreaking himself.

William Ladd was born in Exeter on May 10, 1778, the son of Eliphalet Ladd, one of the leading merchants, ship builders and political leaders in the Seacoast of New Hampshire. Young Ladd was educated at Phillips Exeter and Harvard College. But, for all his educational advantages, he had a strong yen to go to sea. When one's father owns ships, this isn't hard to accomplish. Before he reached man's estate, William Ladd was captain of the ship *Eliza*, sailing in the West Indian trade. Like most shipmasters of his day, Ladd was often engaged in efforts to avoid paying custom duties.

One such venture led, ultimately, to the impeachment and removal of a U.S. District Court judge, the first in United States history. It came about in this way:

Captain Ladd brought the *Eliza* into the Port of Portsmouth from West Indies. Ladd had bought a new hawser while in the Indies, but declared it as used. The Ladds, father and son, paid the necessary duties on the cargo, but not on the new hawser. An informant tipped off the customs collector, Joseph Whipple, who had the District Court issue an attachment. When it came time for the U.S. District Court judge, John Pickering, to hear the case, he was too drunk, by his own admission, to preside over the proceedings.

Pickering adjourned the court, promising to be sober the next day, and then threw the case out of court, without any justification. Whipple complained to Albert Gallatin, secretary of the Treasury, and Gallatin persuaded the U.S. House to begin impeachment proceedings.

To sum it up quickly: Pickering was impeached, although he was obviously a sick man. The Senate, voting along party lines convicted him, and removed him from office. In the long run, it was largely a political maneuver. Pickering was a Federalist, appointed in 1796 by George Washington. The collector and the U.S. attorney, John Sherburne, were Jeffersonian Democrats. The removal of Pickering gave President Jefferson a judgeship to fill. So Pickering's prosecutor, Sherburne, became a U.S. justice, and one of the key witnesses against Pickering became the U.S. attorney.

Captain Ladd continued to follow the sea until the War of 1812 put an end to American trading. And perhaps it was this circumstance that gave initial impetus to his zealousness in the cause of peace.

After his retirement from the sea, William Ladd moved to Minot, Maine, near Lewiston, and began farming on a large tract of land owned by the Ladd family. He bought the property from the family, and raised sheep. At one time, he had more than 600 sheep on his acres. The early decades of the 19th Century saw many religious revivals and "awakenings," probably like the "born again" phenomenon of our day. During one of these times, William Ladd underwent spiritual change.

Bill Caldwell, a columnist for the Portland papers, once wrote that it was a visit to the Rev. Jesse Appleton, president of Bowdoin College, that was the inspiration for the founding of a peace society. What Ladd envisioned was a Congress of Nations, and this was a century before the League of Nations came into being. He began the work as a one-man crusade for peace and understanding among the peoples of the earth. Ladd was tireless in serving his cause and in 1828 the American Peace Society was founded with him as its first president.

During his sea-going years, Ladd had met and married an Englishwoman, Sophia Ann Stidolph, who died in 1856 at the age of 75. Mrs. Ladd worked just as tirelessly for the cause of peace as did her husband. The couple had no children. In 1832 he published his "Dissertation on the Congress of Nations." Previously, in addition to editing a peace magazine, in 1824, he had published an address he had made to the Peace Society of Maine, and the next year an address to the Peace Society of Massachusetts.

Final resting place. A restless man in his constant drive for world peace, the bones of William Ladd, "The Apostle of Peace," are here in South Cemetery, about a hundred yards from the entrance on Richards avenue.

William Ladd traveled far afield in furthering the cause of peace, and he journeyed in a day when transportation was usually by foot or horseback. It was from such a journey that he came to Portsmouth in April of 1841, to spend a few days resting with his family.

On April 17, the *Portsmouth Journal* reported his death:

"In this town on Friday evening last, William Ladd, aged 63, the well-known and highly esteemed Friend of Peace. Mr. Ladd was one of the most eminent Philanthropists of our age and country; and his name will be held in lasting remembrance by all the friends of humanity. He was in early life a shipmaster, and in that capacity was highly esteemed; but for 15 or 20 years past, having declined all mercantile business, he devoted himself to the promotion of various benevolent projects, and more especially to that of permanent and universal peace.

"His private character and Christian deportment were well known to the people of this place, by whom he was greatly beloved,—and it affords us mournful satisfaction that his remains rest in our midst. He died suddenly, having arrived in the cars [train] at half past 7, and dying before midnight.—He had been absent on a lecturing tour for six months, and was on his way to his summer seat at Minot, Maine.—He paused at the house which was the home of his youth, and where his lady had boarded during his absence,—and thence his spirit took its flight to the mansions of rest above. To him may be applied in its full force that beatitude of the Saviour, 'Blessed are the Peace-makers, for they shall be called the children of God'."

The next week the *Journal* published a lengthy eulogy in which it quoted newspapers and clergymen. The *Exeter Newsletter*, after noting the death of a native son, said:

". . . He has often traveled over this country, in its length and its breadth, and in most of our cities and very many of our villages, has he spoken in fullness of his heart on the Angel's theme—'glory to God in the highest and on earth Peace and good will unto men.' Wherever he went he made himself loved and reverenced; and his influence extended far beyond the circle of his journeyings, or the limits of his native land. He has been the correspondent of Kings; and kings and kingdoms will be the better for his labors, if by those labors they shall be induced to beat their swords into ploughshares and their spears into pruning hooks, and learn war no more. One or two centuries hence, such men as Mr. Ladd—such a spirit as he has exhibited—and such principles as he has advocated, will be better understood and appreciated than by the present generation . . ."

One hundred and fifty years have passed since the death of William Ladd. In the course of those years, two major world wars were fought, and numerous neighborhood affairs, such as in the Middle East and in Central America, have blazed. And it wasn't because William Ladd's cause was speedily forgotten as are many such idealistic efforts. The American Peace Society, at a session that came after the adjournment of its annual meeting, elected Samuel Elliott Coues of Portsmouth to the presidency. One of the directors elected was Charles Sumner, later a U.S. senator from Massachusetts. In his will, William Ladd left his property to the American Peace Society, with his widow having a lifetime interest. To that end, the farm in Minot was sold in 1845 by Samuel Coues and the other trustees.

Coues himself was an interesting character, and will probably be the subject of one of these sketches at a later date. Trained to mercantile pursuits, he was the senior partner in Coues & Goodwin, the Goodwin being Ichabod, New Hampshire's first Civil War governor.

Coues might well be described as an "intellectual." He held some unusual views in the field of physics, including the belief that the moon had nothing to do with tidal action. He published several scientific papers, and was a devoted leader of the American Peace Society until he went to Washington in 1853 to take a job in the patent office. In March, 1842, some people in Portsmouth met to consider founding a Portsmouth Peace Society, and Coues was one of the leaders in that movement. The meeting adopted a constitution in which it was declared that those signing the document esteemed "the principles of international war at variance with the doctrine of the Christian Scriptures. . . ."

The London Peace Society took cognizance of William Ladd's death, and sent a letter of condolence to Mrs. Ladd, saying, "We consider the removal of your dear husband as an irreparable loss to you, and indeed a great loss to us, and to the whole human family."

It is more than a little ironic that only a year before the First World War began, the New Hampshire Peace Society, with the cooperation of the Chicago branch, decided to have exercises in memory of William Ladd to be held on Peace Day, May 18, 1913. One of the features was an essay contest for Portsmouth high schoolers. It was won by Lucius Ellsworth Thayer, son of the pastor of the North Church, Lucius H. Thayer.

Two memorial exercises were held, one in the afternoon at the grave and the second in the evening in the North Church. In its account of the exercises, the *Portsmouth Herald* found it "passing strange" that the observance had been brought about by people from outside Ladd's home city, and that they had arranged for the "care and preservation of his grave."

A Portsmouth historical writer, Joseph Foster, had commented in 1906 on the poor condition of the memorial stone that had been put up by the American Peace Society, and the generally rundown appearance of the lot. Foster observed, "Mr. Ladd left no descendants to care for his grave, and it is greatly regretted that it should be wholly neglected by the American Peace Society, to which he bequeathed his entire fortune of many thousands of dollars, although the attention of its officers has been called to the condition of the monument more than once during the last few years."

The society must have made some arrangements for care of the lot because it's in fairly decent shape today. Probably the First World War dampened the ardor of the peace enthusiasts. There doesn't appear to have been any more exercises at the graveside. Not even when the Russo-Japanese Peace Treaty was being negotiated at the Portsmouth Naval Shipyard was there any demonstration.

In April, 1927, Miss Hannah Fernald, director of the Portsmouth Public Library, received a document from Washington which was a memorial to the 26th Congress, asking the establishment of a Congress of Nations. It was dated Feb. 14, 1840, and signed by Samuel Coues and others.

Two great international congresses have been created in this century. The first was the League of Nations, which the United States didn't join because radical conservatives in the U.S. Senate refused to ratify the proposal.

Today the United Nations exists but somehow the great powers go their own way in matters of international politics. The American Peace Society also still exists. Its official address is 4000 Albemarle St. NW, Washington, D.C. 20016.

NEW CARRIAGE MANUFACTORY,

G. B. & S. W. CAME,

Manufacturers and Dealers in

CARRIAGES AND SLEIGHS

OF EVERY DESCRIPTION.

No. 15 Hanover Street,

PORTSMOUTH.

Having constructed a large building expressly for the Carriage Business, and having first-class workmen in all its branches, we are prepared to take orders for

ANY STYLE OF CARRIAGES,

LIGHT OR HEAVY, OPEN OR COVERED.

Carriages of Every Description on Hand for Sale.

CALL AND EXAMINE BEFORE PURCHASING ELSEWHERE.

☞ **Particular Attention given to REPAIRING in all its branches.**

STYLISH CARRIAGE - The Came brothers placed this ad in the 1871 Portsmouth City Directory.

XIII *Industrial Revolution*

Steam Power

THE INDUSTRIAL REVOLUTION CAME SLOWLY to Portsmouth. It was a town that imported its necessities, either by water, or from the interior by way of the New Hampshire Turnpike. In October, 1845, the *Portsmouth Journal* reported on the proliferation of steam-generated power:

"Within a few years, steam power has been introduced into Portsmouth, and applied to a variety of purposes. There are now in operation and putting up in our town no less than ten steam engines. The first set up was that of the Portsmouth Iron Foundry, Bow Street, of 12 horse power. This establishment has been purchased by Samuel Gookin, Esq., who is adding it to the facilities of a machine shop, and is about to complete some contracts for machinery for the new Steam Factory in this town. It gives employment to 30 or 40 hands.

"The Stocking Factory of Mr. Hosea Crane, head of Islington Creek, is put in operation by a steam engine of 12 horse power, and the Stocking Factory of Mr. Jasper C. Crane, Bow street, by an engine of 8 horse power. The first establishment gives employment to more than 150 hands, and the latter to about 70. They manufacture from 50,000 to 60,000 lbs. of wool annually into drawers, shirts, yarn shawls, comforters, gloves, mittens and other articles so well prepared that the demand is greater than can readily be supplied.

"The Franklin Foundry, Mechanic St., has a steam engine of 10 horse power. It is now operated by Messers. Baker, Huntoon &

Anderson, and gives employment to about 20 hands. A planeing machine, belonging to Messers. Barnes and Pendexter, is operated by the same engine.

"The Marlboro Street Foundry, owned by Mr. Ira Haselton, employs an engine of 5 horse power. It gives employment to about a dozen hands. In the past year about a thousand castings have been made here, and a quantity of the Lever Windlass, which are in use in many of the Boston and New York shops, and highly approved.

"A steam engine of 6 horse power is used by Mr. David Libbey and Mr. Joshua Brooks, Parker st., to perform the laborious part of their business at their Tanneries, which adjoin each other. Messers S. Gerrish & Co., Brass founder, Bow street, have an engine of 4 horse power, used for turning, drilling, &c. One of the firm informs us that it can be kept in operation for about 45 cents per day, which is getting the day's labor of a horse for about 11 cents. There is such a demand for machinery at the present time, that in connection with their present business they purpose to attend to the manufactory of lathes and other tools.

"Mr. Ira Winn has just put in operation, in the building adjoining the former residence of the late Deacon Day, in Bow street, an engine of 5 horse power for a Sash factory where the sawing, planeing, grooving, &c are all performed by the engine. Mr. Parker has power from the same to put in operation his lathe for working iron, &c. When completed, they will give employment to 15 or 20 hands.

"Arrangements are making for erecting at the North-End, another Planeing Machine to go by steam. The tenth steam-engine will be that of the Portsmouth Steam Factory, which will speak for itself next year.

Came Brothers

Although the purpose here isn't to wax philosophical, spending half a life-time in this fair city prompts wondering why so many are always ready to knock any enterprise others may show. So it was in the case of the Came brothers, George B. and Samuel W., when they came to town in 1869 and founded a carriage-making firm.

Portsmouth wasn't very strong in manufacturing then, with local focus on the Portsmouth Navy Yard, the civilian shipyards and a few small industries. Oh, Frank Jones's brewery was successful, along with Eldredge's, but more were needed for the city's future.

The Came brothers were young; Samuel was still in his minority, yet they came here from York County "possessing only a little cash, but having an inexhaustible capital of pluck and energy." They apparently had learned their trade in Maine, but sought wider horizons. Even as they went about the business of erecting a plant, some of the pessimists flatly warned them they couldn't succeed.

"Amid the ice and snow of winter, they laid the foundations of their first building on Hanover street. A plain shop, 30 by 50 feet with three stories and a basement for their blacksmith shop, was soon filled with workmen. They began operations, determined always to make the best work which skilled mechanics could turn out. A few handsome specimens were built, but for six months not a customer did they find."

This observation leads inevitably to belief that someone with more than a bit of capital was financing the venture. Certainly, two young men with what was described as "little cash capital," couldn't have continued meeting payrolls and the cost of supplies. The account of the progress of the Came business in the *Portsmouth Times* added:

"A score of citizens who could not but acknowledge the superior quality of their (the Cames) carriages went elsewhere and purchased, and it may be interesting to know that some of them had their new purchases in the repair shop of Messers. Came within a very few weeks. But at the end of six or seven months, after our enterprising young friends were almost inclined to believe the croakers would drive them out of the city, the 'ice broke,' and since then a flood of business has come in upon them . . ."

As is often the case, recognition of the value of the product being turned out by the Came brothers first came from a place far removed from Portsmouth, the full width of the continent away.

A native of Portsmouth, Oliver F. Gerrish, then living in Port Townsend, Washington Territory, placed an order. What inspired Gerrish to do so is now lost from sight, perhaps he was a relative, or had visited Portsmouth and had seen their work. Whatever brought it about, the Cames were on their way. Demand for their carriages of various models soon exceeded supply, and they were forced to expand their plant.

"Another three story, 24 by 79 feet, went up, fronting on High street, which is connected to their first building on Hanover street by watertight platforms which have a surface of 2,000 square feet. In the

basement of the first building they put in an engine and boiler and
made more room for their blacksmith work. Messers. Cames now turn
out carriages by the score of every pattern the market demands. They
give employment to nearly 40 men, most of whom have families and
have become permanent residents of this city. Their expenses are
about $150 a day, the larger part of which is paid for labor. In the var-
ious rooms of this extensive establishment are now made all the parts
of a carriage with the exception of articles of iron, such as springs.
They make all the wheels, and on this part of the work strive to excel
and can thus guarantee strength and durability. In finish of their
work, both iron and wood, they have succeeded in distancing all competitors. . . ."

And there were a few other concerns engaged in making carriages, but apparently on a much smaller scale than the Came brothers. The *Times* added to the descriptive report:

"The woodwork is given 16 coats of paint, and the iron and running gear eight. All varnish used is subjected to four months test
before being given to the painters. In their Repository, which opens
upon High street, may be seen the varieties of carriages made in this
establishment, and if any of our readers have not visited Messers.
Came, we advise them to do so. They will find our young friends glad
to show them through their manufactory and also to exhibit their
pony phaetons, cutunder carioles and phaetons, Goodard's jump seat
carriages, their coupees, rockaways, barouches, express and grocery
wagons., &c. &c—sold at prices ranging from $100 to $1,000.

"Messers. Came have exhibited their productions at various State
and county fairs and have invariably taken the first premiums. At the
New England fair this year beauty of their work attracted general
attention and brought them a large number of heavy orders from different cities . . ."

To show the progress the Cames were making, the present writer,
in his biography of Frank Jones, the brewer, said:

"Jones himself was the proud possessor of a Came brothers product, which is mentioned to show that as early as 1871 some people in
Portsmouth were coming to appreciate the man (Jones). Came brothers entered an undertop buggy as an exhibit in the State Fair where it
won a blue ribbon. After the exposition Jones's friends bought the
vehicle through a popular subscription in which no one was allowed to
give more than $10. The donors gathered on Oct. 3, in the early hours
of darkness. Led by the Portsmouth Cornet Band, they marched to

Jones's residence on Woodbury Avenue with their gift and made formal presentation."

Flourishing as they were, the Cames also benefitted their suppliers. In the course of the year 1870, they used 60,000 linear feet of lumber, many hundreds of yards of enameled cloth, broadcloth and plush. The *Times* noted:

". . . They are now finishing six to 10 carriages each week, besides doing a vast amount of repairing. In this branch of their business they do all things thoroughly, their rule being to do everything well, no matter how small the job. . ."

Not too surprisingly, the Cames were also manufacturing sleighs. As we all know, winter is a familiar visitor to the Seacoast, and it was the same in the 1870s. As the trite old saying goes: "Nothing succeeds like success," and the Cames were successful. So much so, that by early summer in 1872, they moved their operation to Rockingham Mills, a long-gone structure on McDonough street. They had barely completed the moving process on July 12 when disaster struck. The Portsmouth *Chronicle* reported on the 13th: "About 7 o'clock on Friday evening, Messers. George B. and Samuel W. Came, well-known carriage builders, heard an explosion in the paintroom while they were sitting in the office of their new manufactory on McDonough street into which they had just finished removing their stock. Hardly had they reached the door when the building seemed all aflame and they dashed in opposite directions to escape. Each succeeded in getting into the street, singed, half-suffocated and terribly exhausted, and each thought the other must have perished, until they met outside the burning building, which in five minutes after the explosion, was a mass of flames."

The fire department, largely volunteer, responded quickly, but could do nothing to control the fire. "Two carriages in the building were saved: nothing else, and the entire building with its contents, 30 carriages, a large amount of stock and tools were consumed . . ."

So hot were the flames, the Eastern Railroad rails running on the north side of the building, expanded and trains were delayed in arrivals. It was reported that the Cames had paid $10,000 for the building and it was insured for that amount only. Their total insurance was $32,500, and the total loss was estimated at $40,000. At the time, it was said the Cames would rebuild and not move back to their old plant at High and Hanover streets. That structure had been put up for sale a week or more before the fire.

Tradition has it that two men lost their lives in the blaze that destroyed the Came carriage works, but contemporary news accounts make no mention of the fact. However, in a deeper sense, the tradition is probably right in that two men did lose their lives, partly in direct consequence of that fire. The two were the Came brothers, who died within two years after the fire that ruined their business. When George B. Came died in November, 1874, at the age of 29, his younger brother was already deceased, and the obituary in the *Portsmouth Journal* said that George's health "had been somewhat impaired" ever since the fire.

Perhaps it's far fetched, but it can be speculated that Samuel and George Came, as young as they were, might well have been in the forefront of manufacturing automobiles when that industry developed early in the 20th Century.

After all, Amesbury, Mass., prospered for years in the manufacture of the Essex, which was a fine "horseless carriage" in its day.

Church Organs

Over the course of its existence, Portsmouth has often provided the base for the manufacture of various products.

Previously was discussed the successful operation of a carriage manufactory, Came Brothers, destroyed by fire in the 1870s. Brewing was another prosperous industry in the town, with three major breweries in operation until prohibition laws put them out of business. There were shoe companies, stocking companies, mast and spar makers, etc.

Another notable industry was Morley Button. The buildings still stand on Islington street, occupied by various companies, but none now associated with the making of buttons. Morley Button, in the days of calf-high shoes, fastened by buttons, was the largest manufacturer of buttons in the world. But the high-button shoe went out of style with the end of World War I, and women came to enjoy greater freedom in dress.

In the mid-1840s, a company, Barton, Cobb & Norwood, was engaged in the manufacture of organs, and the *Portsmouth Journal* in 1844 reported the company had just installed one of its products in the Universalist Church. The church stood in the lot now dominated by the First N.H. Bank building. It burned in 1896, and a successor structure burned in January, 1947. In reporting the installation of the organ the *Journal* also said:

"Since the Organ and Piano-Forte Manufactory has been in operation in this town, it has kept at home and secured to us from the adjoining towns a considerable amount of capital, that would have gone the way that everything else goes, to Boston."

Charles W. Brewster, editor of the *Journal*, often gave vent to the feelings of inferiority that Portsmouth nurtured toward Boston. From the earliest days, the populace tended to consider that goods and services obtained in Boston were superior to anything that could be obtained on the Piscataqua. The *Journal* further commented:

"Having no competitors but the prejudice of those who think nothing is well done, unless it possesses the charm of being 'Boston-made,' they have endeavored to make one instrument a sufficient recommendation for another. . . . As we have but one establishment of this kind among us, we wish it success, remembering that the reputation which our mechanics earn for themselves abroad, by excelling in any branch of business, becomes public property at home. The town is benefited as well as the individual."

Barton, Cobb & Norwood had already built a smaller instrument for the Baptist Church on Pleasant street. That building is now an apartment house at Livermore and Pleasant streets. They also made an organ for the Baptist Church at the corner of Middle and State streets, a site now occupied by Louis Dow's service station, and a large organ for the Camenaeum, a former church, converted to an assembly hall, standing in the middle of the present Bridge street parking lot. The organ in the North Church, a structure razed in 1854, was built by a Newburyport firm, as was the one in the vestry of the Court Street Church. The organs in St. John's Church and chapel were of English origin, while the one in the Stone Church was built in Boston. The *Journal* said of the organ makers:

"Messers. Barton, Cobb & Norwood are skillful and faithful workmen, and have had fair success here, in the manufacture and sale of organs and Piano-Fortes, amid strong competitors. They need only to be more widely known, to have an increase of orders from abroad."

Portsmouth Steam Mill

As it sits quietly, gracefully on one of Portsmouth's many side streets, the passer-by is hard put to realize that the structure has passed through more misadventures than most of the city's buildings. One might even ask: How many Portsmouth buildings have lost their top five stories and still stand? It might even be asked how many Portsmouth buildings have passed through fires, tornadoes and modern "progress" and still stand? And there it is, a well-renovated building at Pearl and Hanover streets, presently occupied by JSA Architects, but they were preceded by many others.

Well, let's get back to the beginning. First on the site was the home of Nathaniel Adams, the famed author, and rightly so, of *The Annals of Portsmouth*. In Adams' day, his front yard extended out to Islington street. Around 1845 the property was bought by a syndicate of capitalists for the purpose of establishing a steam factory for the manufacture of cotton goods. Heading the syndicate was Ichabod Goodwin, a South Berwick native and former ship's captain. The *Portsmouth Journal* reported on April 26, 1845:

"The Portsmouth Steam Mill—So great is the interest taken by our citizens to stir the wheels of enterprise in this town that in three days of the past week over 50,000 dollars in stock was subscribed by the middling interest, for a cotton mill in this town; one individual subscribing $2,000, no others over $1,000. A like amount of stock has been subscribed for by our more wealthy citizens, and probably much more will be subscribed. These are the preliminary movements; nothing will be matured until the meeting of the corporation."

Almost a year later, the *Journal* reported that work was moving rapidly on the Portsmouth Steam Factory; that machinery was expected any day; and that the smokestack for the steam plant was "going up fast," and will be "twice as tall as the mill." The mill was to be lighted by gas, and a gasometer was being installed as the chimney was being built. Editorially, the *Journal* proudly commented that a new factory near Philadelphia is "the only one in the United States lit by gas."

On June 6, 1846, the *Journal* reported that "the completion of the chimney of the Portsmouth Steam Factory, 150 feet high, was announced to the citizens of Portsmouth by the discharge of a few rockets from the top of it, on Thursday evening (June 4). The fireworks were very judiciously deferred until the concert closed, thus giving to all who wished, the pleasure of witnessing both."

A week later, however, fireworks of a different kind visited the Portsmouth Steam Factory when a fire extended to the main building, badly damaging the machinery. Two-thirds of the damage was insured, and the engine and boilers were only slightly damaged. It was expected that steam could be produced within two weeks. By September, 1846, 5,000 spindles were in operation. "They spin 81 skeins to a pound. As there are 840 yards to a skein, a pound of cotton will give a thread over 30 miles long and a bale of 800 pounds will give thread long enough to go round the world and tie a handsome beau-knot at the tall chimney." So, for a year, the Portsmouth Steam Mill flourished. Then came Oct. 1, 1847. For the *Journal* it was a "stop-press bulletin:"

"We stop the press to announce an unusual disaster. At 5 o'clock, P.M., a sudden gust of wind from the north-west, of great power, passed over our town. It struck the Portsmouth Steam Factory and removed almost the entire roof in one body! carried it over the counting room without damage and did not strike until it reached the brick barn of Robert Rice, Esq., about 300 feet distant. The force of the blow completely demolished the upper story of the barn, and also entered the house opposite on Parker street, occupied by Mrs. Seavey. A gentleman who witnessed the first movement said that the whole roof except about 20 feet of the east end, rose together about 10 feet, and then in a body sailed to the south-east until it struck the above buildings. The length of the roof is 200 feet—the breadth about 60. Although several hundred were at work in the mill at the time, and some in the attic, no one was seriously injured."

In those days of journalistic innocence, the *Journal* could give an instant replay to the story a week later:

"In part of our edition last week, we gave a short account of the unroofing of the Portsmouth Steam Factory by the tornado which passed over our town at 5 o'clock on Friday afternoon, Oct. 1. Since the gale of 1815, we have not experienced so violent a gust. We have not been able to ascertain its whole route, but learn that on the highlands of Deerfield there was on that afternoon a severe thundershower—that the gust came in a narrow channel through Madbury and Durham, prostrating trees in its course. In Durham, there was a considerable fall of hail. A gentleman from that town says that the gust appeared to keep on whirling in a perpendicular direction, here and there striking the earth with greater force than in the intervals. It did some injury to a barn north of the town farm in Portsmouth, passed a little east of the alms house, marking its course in the trees—and as it passed over the mill-pond to the Factory put the water in commotion and raised the spray to a great height.

"Extending from the back of the Factory at both ends are Ls, two stories in height. The whole force of the gale, after passing unobstructed across the pond, seemed to strike the Factory between these two additions, and the course of the pent-up blast was at once inclined upwards with a fury which nothing could withstand. The copper spout of the addition on the east end, which did not project more than 10 or 12 inches, and was firmly fastened with irons to the roof, offered such resistance that the roof in that part was raised high enough for those inside to look out, and then sunk again to its place—the spout however was turned over upon the roof. The spout and caving of the main building project three feet four inches. It was this coping that received the full force of the blast—and in a moment the whole of the roof between the projecting additions being about 160 feet (about 20 feet on each end of the factory remained in place) was raised in the air and dividing into three sections were borne upon the blast like feathers!

"Some estimate of the power of the wind may be formed from the weight of that portion of the roof which was carried off. The weight of the tin was 10,000 pounds. 106 rafters, 39 feet long, 3 inches by 12, weighing about 240 pounds each, would weigh 25,000 pounds. The nails, spouts, lathing, plastering &c would add probably 10,000 pounds more—making the weight of that part of the roof removed not less than 70,000 pounds!: When raised in the air, the roof divided into three sections. A portion of that on the south side fell into the yard within a hundred feet of the factory. The rafters, coming down endwise, were buried four feet into the solid hard ground, within 30 feet of the counting room. Another section fell about 200 feet in front of the factory. A third section was whirled by the wind directly over the counting room, and then, by another current borne in a southerly direction, it struck the brick barn of Mr. Rice (300 feet distant) in the second story, unroofed it, and demolished that story. The ground on which this barn is situated is about 15 feet higher than the site of the factory, and as the place where it struck was more than 10 feet from the ground—this large section of the roof, weighing perhaps 30,000 pounds, did not descend more than 50 feet from its original position in going 300 feet.

"A providential hand was remarkably displayed in the whole movement. No person was seriously hurt in the factory, although in the room which in a moment was left as open as the deck of a vessel, about 30 males and females were at work. In one house in the neighborhood, a lady had left the room not more than three minutes before the whole end was stove in and the room heaped up with ruins. In the next house some fragments entered a room where an invalid lady was reclining on a sofa, and a piece of timber weighing about 30 pounds fell between her back and the sofa, pushing her from it, but so gently as to inflict no injury. Some chimneys were blown down at the Navy Yard. A person whose name we did not learn, was outside the Shoals, in a whale-boat, which the gale turned bottom up. Understanding his business pretty well, he sat quietly on the bottom of the boat till the gale was over, then managed to put the boat right side up, and was industriously bailing her out when another boat fortunately appeared and took him from the perilous situation of being at sea without oars or sail. The Factory was unroofed in the gale on Friday evening: and on the next Wednesday night the roof was again boarded and ready for tinning. This expedition is remarkable when the fact is known that all of the 106 new rafters were in the log or in living trees when the gale took place, and were sawed a dozen miles from Portsmouth."

It would be good, solid chamber-of-commerce type reporting to be able to say that once the roof was nailed back down the Portsmouth Steam Factory flourished. And it did for awhile. In a meeting of the directors, in February, 1849, it was reported:

"During the past year 2.3 million yards of lawns have been manufactured at the mill. The product of October, November and December was about 675,000 yards, which is the rate of 2.7 million a year.

However, many vicissitudes were suffered by the building, not the least of which was a major fire on Dec. 4, 1880, when it was called the Kearsarge Mills. An article, Dec. 6, in the *Portsmouth Chronicle* gave the details:

"On Saturday morning last the Kearsarge Mills took fire in the southeast corner of the fifth story, and before the flames were under control the buildings were almost wholly destroyed. The mill was built for the Portsmouth Steam Factory in 1845-46. The main building was 204 feet long and 70 feet wide, six stories high, with two ells each 100 feet by thirty, and two stories high. It originally contained 21,250 spindles, but many changes were made in its subsequent operations.

Between the ells at the rear of the main building, were the boiler house and a low storehouse. East of the eastern ell was the machine shop, a wooden building; and east of the latter the cloth hall, also built of wood.

"The main building, eastern ell, machine shop and storehouse between the ells, were destroyed, and the cloth hall ruined. The western ell, containing the engine room and picker room, was badly damaged, and the roof of the boiler house burned. The two engines, of 200 and 300 horsepower respectively, were saved in a damaged condition, and the four huge boilers are apparently unhurt. The baled cotton and manufactured cloth on hand were saved. The western wall of the main building appears to be still good, and the opinion is expressed that all the walls would have stood had it not been for the granite trimmings, which crumbled away with the heat and thus weakened the brickwork.

"The Kearsarge Mills were incorporated July 31st, 1866, after the failure of the Portsmouth Steam Factory. The capital stock allowed by the charter was one million of dollars; the actual amount of capital was $800,000 but it was too large to afford any but the smallest amount of dividends. It was owned largely by non-residents. The stock owned in this city was held in the estates of Wm. P. Jones, A.L. Jones and Wm. Simes, and by Mark H. Wentworth, John Stavers, Wm. D. Fernald, Wm. Sterns, William H. Hackett and a few others. The insurance amounted to $411,000 of which $373,000 was on the mill, and $38,000 on the cloth hall and store-house. The establishment has at different times employed as many as 480 operatives. At the time of the fire the mill was giving employment to 320 persons, and should it not be rebuilt, the fire of Saturday may be set down as one of heaviest blows to the city's prosperity since the great fire of 1813."

Old photographs, reproduced in the *Herald* on March 19, 1925, show the building in before and after views. In the after-the-fire photo, the structure was down to the first story with the chimney a stark finger pointing skyward.

The Portsmouth Machine Company was the next occupant. The proprietors were Edward S. Fay, president; Charles W. Badger, general manager; Charles H. Mendum, treasurer; and Joseph L. Hayden, superintendent. Then came Portsmouth Forge in 1908 with C. Herbert Morton as manager. In 1912 Ellery Drill and Tool was using the building.

So it went over the years. In February, 1939, Brooks Motor Sales, a Ford agency, was occupying the premises. In fact, right after World War II, to approach Brooks Ford, one took off one's hat and stood in an obeisant position to hear a Brooks salesman decree that "we won't want to take in leprosy Pontiacs." But that's another story. When fire again struck the old building on Feb. 20, 1939, Brooks would have been happy to have lost only a few "leprosy Pontiacs." The blaze started in the Diamond Match store next door, and swept the Brooks garage. The *Herald* said:

"In the wake of the destructive fire that caused an estimated damage of $175,000, only a few fire-baked brick walls stood, wire and pipes were twisted into a maze of steel and 15 automobiles were left charred and mangled in the ashes." That fire was probably the work of a young arsonist, but that's also another story.

Frank E. Brooks came back from the disaster, and ran his garage until he sold out to Arthur F. Brady Jr., a recent arrival in the city, and one who was soon so well liked that he was elected mayor in 1971, and served as host to Britain's Prince Charles during the city's 350th anniversary in 1973.

Brady moved the agency out to the Spaulding Turnpike, and it was owned by several different firms after he sold out and retired. In 1991, the Ford agency, caught in the throes of the Reagan-Bush Depression, closed. Brady himself died in 1989.

XIV Some Presidential Visits

James Monroe

IT'S OFTEN BEEN NOTED THAT NOTHING excites a community more than a presidential visit. Such occasions are, without regard to party, usually ceremonious, and often joyful.

In October, 1989, Portsmouth marked the 200th anniversary of the visit by the First President of the United States—George Washington. He arrived on Oct. 31, 1789, toward dusk, and spent four nights in the old town, longer than any other incumbent president has ever done. Washington came because he was well aware that few people knew what he looked like and he admitted his own needs to get out among the people. That visit by President Washington was well told 50 years ago by Judge Elwyn Page in his *Washington in New Hampshire*, a work republished on the occasion of the 200th anniversary by the Portsmouth Marine Society.

Familiar as that story is to most Seacoast residents, few know who the next presidential visitor was. James Monroe, the fifth president came in July, 1817. President Monroe, like the first President, had decided on a leisurely "progress" through the northeastern states. He reached Portsmouth about 7 p.m. on Saturday, July 12. The *Portsmouth Journal* reported: "He was met at Greenland by the committee of arrangement and a numerous cavalcade of citizens on horseback and in carriages, and the company of cavalry belonging to the 35th regiment. When he passed the lines of the town, it was announced by a national salute from the Artillery Company under

Capt. Currier, stationed on the Plains; and on the arrival of the
President at that place, he reviewed the First Regiment, under the
command of Col. Walker, which was ordered out for his reception.
When passing Wibird's hill he was again welcomed by a national
salute from the company of Sea Fencibles, under Capt. Brown, and by
the ringing of the bells; after which he was escorted into town,
through lines formed by the scholars of the several public and private
schools in this place, who were arranged on each side of Middle Road,
extending from Mr. Rundlett's to Maj. Larkin's house. Their numbers
were considerably over a thousand, they were in neat uniforms, and
furnished an interesting and pleasing spectacle. The windows on the
streets through which the President passed were crowded with the
fair, and the streets lined with spectators, anxious to view the man
who had been raised to the highest possible honor, that of being the
Chief Magistrate of a free people."

The presidential entourage moved up Congress Street to Market
Square. The entrance to Market Street was spanned by a floral arch
that had been put together by the women of the town. A band provided music as he traveled along Market Street to Frost's Hotel. That
structure, long since gone, had a balcony over its front door and the
President was escorted into the hotel and out onto the balcony where
he faced the people jamming the street below. To the great lawyer,
Jeremiah Mason, went the honor of making the official speech of welcome. It was printed by the *Journal*:

"Sir—the presence of the Chief Magistrate, selected for his eminent virtues and public services, to preside over and direct the councils of a great nation, must always excite feelings of the highest interest. The inhabitants of the town of Portsmouth, remote from the seat
of the general government, can expect few opportunities of witnessing
such a gratifying scene. We therefore, eagerly embrace this fortunate
occasion to present our ardent and sincere congratulations. Engaged
chiefly in the business of commerce and navigation, we know our des-
tinies are, in a peculiar manner, dependent on the measures of that
government, to which the protection of those important objects, is
exclusively confided. These enterprising pursuits, which have always
been greatly contributory to the general welfare, are now suffering
under a temporary depression. But we have entire confidence, that
the wisdom and justice of government, will extend to them all the protection and support, that shall be in its power.

"To superintend and conduct the national concerns has always, in free governments, been the favorite employment of the best and greatest men. By no other means can an individual of distinguished talents so eminently promote the public good. The successful performance of such duties must, at all times, constitute a sure claim to the gratitude of a generous people. This, Sir, is the arduous and honorable service, which is entrusted to you, by the citizens of the United States. Sensible how greatly the national prosperity depends on the due administration of the government, we recall to our recollection with much satisfaction, the numerous pledges of attachment to the public interest, furnished by the history of your past life. It is our earnest and confident hope that your administration, by perfecting our valuable institutions, and by uniting public sentiment, and wisely directing it to proper national objects, may fulfill the present happy anticipations, and thus establish on a firm basis your own and your country's happiness, honor and glory."

Monroe replied to the welcome in gracious phrases. At his conclusion the Portsmouth regiment of militia passed in review. With that ceremony concluded, the President was escorted to his lodgings on what was then called Jaffery Street, but known to us as Court Street. Many years ago, then Librarian Dorothy Vaughan discovered that the building where Monroe stayed was the Folsom-Salter House.

It was managed at the time of Monroe's visit by a man named Wentworth, and has, of course, been moved from its original site to one further west and on the opposite side. For some years, it was the law office of the late Thomas E. Flynn and his associates. In a later day it has served as a restaurant. The next day of his visit being Sunday, President Monroe had to undergo two church services. As Washington had done before him, he attended St. John's in the morning and the North Church in the afternoon. The St. John's of Washington's day burned in 1806, and the North was torn down in 1854 to make way for the present edifice.

Monroe also visited with John Langdon, then in the last year of his life. Their acquaintance went back many years. Monday the President toured the harbor, the forts and the Portsmouth Navy Yard over in the District of Maine. That evening he had to attend a concert in Jefferson Hall presented by the Social Harmonic Society. Given his "druthers," the President might have preferred going to the theater where a five-act production, "Abellino, the Great Bandit," was playing. The next morning, Tuesday, President Monroe left Portsmouth "for the eastward."

James K. Polk

Thirty years passed before another president graced the streets of the old city. President James Polk ran into some antipathy in the course of his visit. It was his lot to be presiding over an unpopular war, the one with Mexico in 1846-47. Some hint of the problems President Polk faced is contained in an item in the *Portsmouth Journal of Literature and Politics* on June 26th, 1847:

"BUENA VISTA"

"This according to the *New Hampshire Gazette* is to be the watch-word for the Polk War Party at the coming election. This is well. Let it be understood, then that we are not called upon to decide between a federalist and some other 'ist', but to vote for or against Mr. Polk's war—for conquest and slavery. Those who are fond of war and blood-shed, those who approve of extravagance and waste and great loans and burdensome taxes, will vote for a representative who will act as Mr. Polk pleases.

"But those who are opposed to war, who do not approve of slavery, who are not anxious for conquest, and who deem our present debt and present taxes large enough, will vote for a representative whose views agree with their own. Let the issues in this contest be War and Slavery on the one side—Peace and Freedom on the other."

As indicated in the item, an election for seats in the National Congress was brewing, and in June, 1847, President Polk took to the road to campaign for his policies. In the same issue of the *Journal* was a brief item from Baltimore in which President Polk reportedly said in a speech that he wouldn't be a candidate for re-election under any circumstances.

The *Journal* gave the *Boston Post* as the source for the President's itinerary. He was heading toward Boston, via New York, and due there on June 29th. The next day he planned to move on to Lowell, and then July 1st he was to be in Concord, N.H. The next day he would go to Portland. The *Journal* added:

"Letters have been received in this town, stating the President may make a short visit to Portsmouth, probably after visiting Maine. No certain arrangement, however, has yet been made."

However, it didn't take Portsmouth long to get up a full head of steam in planning to receive the 11th President. First in the program was a proper reception on the Portsmouth Bridge where his escort from the Pine Tree State would turn him over to his new hosts, headed by Ichabod Bartlett. With all the fraternal and temperance organizations in the parade, plus federal officers, the Portsmouth Greys, the Hampton Artillery, the procession wound its way up Market Street. Twenty-nine guns were fired by the Portsmouth Artillery as a salute, and the parade passed through several streets, ending at Congress Hall on Congress Street, on the site of the present-day Jarvis Block.

A balcony had been hastily constructed on the southern side of Congress Hall. From its eminence, the Portsmouth multitude was introduced to President Polk on July 5, 1847. In contradictory terms, the July 10, 1847, issue of the *Journal* informs that:

"The president was conducted to a large platform, erected in front of Congress Hall, where he and his suite, the committee of arrangements, and some others were accommodated with seats . . ."

When the multitude below had shuffled into proper positions of reverence, U.S. Supreme Court Judge Levi Woodbury addressed the President, unmatched in civility:

"Allow me, in behalf of my fellow citizens of the ancient town of Portsmouth, New Hampshire, to welcome you to its hospitalities. Interchanges of personal civility between a people and their chief magistrate are usually attended by the happiest influences. We know and are now better by being face to face and heart to heart . . . We greet you, therefore, sir, to our hearths and altars, as the highest administrator of that power for more than 20 millions of free and prosperous people. . . .

Judge Woodbury's welcome continued in the same flowery vein for several more paragraphs. In the course of it, he called attention to the importance of the Navy Yard, and the key location of Ft. Constitution. At the time of President Polk's visit to the town, Congress had just authorized a dry dock for the Navy Yard after years of agitation for it and Woodbury dwelt on the matter:

"We look anxiously toward the means of public usefulness increased here by the Dry Dock which has been happily authorized under your administration; cherishing as we do as strong conviction that such expenditures tend to render imperishable that great principle, now embodied into the American code of public law—'Millions for defence, but not one cent for tribute'." When the dry dock came into being, nearly five years later, it was of the floating variety, and was built on Pierce Island and then floated to the Navy Yard."

The *Journal's* reporter found himself in the sad position, for a newsman, of not being able to hear the President's reply to Woodbury's speech. The *Journal* was strongly anti-Polk, anti-slavery and anti-war, but its coverage of the event was fair. When Polk finished speaking, he was taken inside the building and there introduced to local citizens, and members of his suite were introduced. Among these was James Buchanan, then secretary of state, but who would become the 15th president.

From Congress Hall, the party rode out to Judge Woodbury's mansion at Elm Place, just off present-day Woodbury Avenue. The fine old house is gone, razed to make way for the Woodbury Manor housing project. After enjoying the judge's hospitality, the party returned in town and went to the Rockingham House for a lunch prepared by the owner, Thomas Coburn. That structure, too, is gone, destroyed by fire in 1884. By one o'clock, the President left Portsmouth for Newburyport, where he arrived at 1:45.

Nowhere in the *Journal's* coverage is there any mention of the fact that a gang of youths really had the town jumping in the early hours of the Fourth. The tale is told in the writer's book *They Came to Fish*, and needn't be recapitulated here. What had brought about the wild night was the usual ineptness of public officials. They had ordained that there would be no Fourth of July celebration because of President Polk's visit on Monday the 5th. Portsmouth youths then and now are not easily intimidated, and the police had a pretty rough night on the Fourth.

Ironically, despite the welcome extended President Polk, both in Portsmouth and Concord, the opposing political party, the Whigs, elected two of the four representatives in Congress, to which New Hampshire was then entitled.

Franklin Pierce

Who was the first president to take a sea voyage on a naval warship? Also, who was the first president to send American troops into Nicaragua? And who was the only president ever elected from New Hampshire?

If your answers were "Franklin Pierce" you were correct. Further, let it be known that President Pierce, a former Portsmouth resident, started his ocean journey from the Navy Yard landing at the foot of Daniel street. It all came about in this way:

Franklin Pierce, a desperation choice by the Democrats for the 1852 presidential nomination, won the election, and served a term that is frequently seen by historians as a major step toward the Civil War. Nearing the end of his term in 1856, with James Buchanan the Democratic choice to succeed him, President Pierce visited his home in Concord. He arrived in the state capital on Oct. 3, and thousands thronged the streets to welcome him. The *Chronicle* reported:

"The President was dressed in black—though he stated, in answer to many friendly inquiries, that his health was good, he looked pale, but seemed highly gratified by the reception he had received . . ."

Portsmouth on Oct. 6 and 7 was staging a celebration of a century of printing in New Hampshire, and the president had been belatedly invited. However, he found he couldn't fit it into his schedule, but said he would try to come to the Seacoast city before returning to Washington. A telegram was received by the city government on Oct. 7 that President Pierce would come from Concord on Wednesday, Oct. 8. Mayor Richard Jenness immediately sent a committee of three, headed by Alderman G.H. Rundlett, to Concord to accompany the president to Portsmouth.

The presidential train pulled into the depot at 1 p.m., and was escorted to a hastily erected platform by Mayor Jenness. "A very large number of our citizens, ladies as well as gentlemen, collected to greet the president, not-withstanding the fact hardly any public notice had been given of the time of his visit. A salute of 21 guns was fired as the president ascended to the platform, in front of which a quasi-military outfit, the Buchanan Guards, had been drawn up and came to present arms." Unlike modern practices in which the person introducing the president says only: "Ladies and Gentlemen, the President of the United States," Mayor Jenness gave a speech of welcome. It was mercifully brief in a day when oratory was a favorite indoor and outdoor sport. And Mayor Jenness deserves full marks for being able to note that the administration had been controversial, yet not slip into denigration. The key lines were:

"Whatever differences of opinion there may have been in regard to some of the measures of your administration, none will deny that it has been distinguished for industry, economy and a marked and successful foreign policy, as well as fidelity to the great fundamental principle that lies at the base of this government, the right of the people to govern themselves. Strike from the fair fabric of this union this foundation principle, and the beauty and symmetry of the whole procedure is gone forever . . ."

Mayor Jenness went on for another minute or two, expressing the hope that when the passions of the hour had abated, the Pierce administration would find its proper place. Before going any further it should be emphasized that Franklin Pierce was the only president of the United States who actually ever lived in Portsmouth—even though it was only a short span of years. His acquaintance with the town had begun after his graduation from Bowdoin College in 1824. He came to Portsmouth to read law, as was the custom then. Upon being admitted to the bar, he returned to the Concord area from whence he had come. So, in his brief remarks, the president was able to touch on the familiar.

In its account the *Chronicle* used the third person, saying that the president "felt he must come to Portsmouth if he visited no other place. It was here that he spent some of the most agreeable years of his life, with that great and good man, of statesman-like ability, and national reputation, Levi Woodbury." The president was justified in extolling Levi Woodbury because it's quite probable that but for his untimely death in 1851, Woodbury might have been elected president, and not Pierce. The *Chronicle* added:

The president alluded in feeling terms to Portsmouth as the home of (John) Langdon, Col. (William) Gardner, Capts. (Thomas) Manning and Elijah Hall, true patriots and noble men. He spoke of his early acquaintance with Col. Gardner, whose lessons of wisdom and patriotism he could never forget. "The old gentleman was a devoted friend of the Union and when he spoke of it, his black eyes always sparkled with animation. He often had heard him (Gardner) predict that for our future that remarkable prosperity and progress which we have thus far realized and will continue if the spirit of these patriots is revived and kept alive in our hearts . . ."

Pierce said Mayor Jenness had acquiesced to his request that his visit to Portsmouth be kept as quiet and private as possible; that he most wished to meet with old friends. With the formalities of the welcome out of the way, the presidential party left the depot area and escorted by the Buchanan Guards, went to the Rockingham House. There's a little irony in the services of the Buchanan Guards as escort, in that James Buchanan, who had been in the Pierce Cabinet, was one of the officials who broke with the president over the possible absorption of Cuba. Buchanan wanted to capture it, Pierce didn't.

Dinner was served at the Rockingham and afterward the president held the reception for old friends that he had desired to see. In the evening, there was a ball at the Navy Yard with Commodore Newton as host, which "was graced by the presence of many officers of the Navy and ladies and gentlemen of this city." Pierce returned to the Rockingham about midnight and was the last president to spend a night in Portsmouth until Harry S Truman came in October, 1952, and slept in his private railroad car down at the depot where Pierce had spoken nearly a century before.

In the morning, the president, Mayor Jenness, and friends of the president went to the Navy Yard landing, where they boarded Commodore Newton's boat for the trip down river to the frigate *Wabash*. President Pierce didn't visit the Navy Yard, but as the boat was passing the presidential salute was fired. The yards and rigging of the *USS Wabash* were fully manned, and the frigate and Ft. Constitution exchanged salutes, with Sgt. Davidson doing the honors for the fort.

Then, as now, no occasion was a success unless food was served, and so the captain of the *Wabash* served a collation to the presidential party, then the president inspected the vessel and with that, Mayor Jenness and his party paid final respects to the president and came back up the river. The *Chronicle* said:

"The Wabash weighed anchor and set sail about 5 o'clock p.m. She was heartily cheered by a large number of people who had collected on or about Ft. Constitution to witness her departure. The cheers were responded to by the sailors from the rigging of the frigate and salutes were exchanged between the Fort and the frigate. The President expressed much gratitude at his reception here, which indeed was a cordial one, and doubtless agreeable to all parties."

The summer after he left the presidency, Franklin Pierce and his wife came to Portsmouth and put up at the Rockingham. The couple planned to spend only the month of August, but were still here in October when the Rockingham County Agricultural Fair was held on Auburn Street (Richards Avenue). Ex-President Pierce took part in the fair parade, which prompted an acid remark from the *American Ballot* as quoted by the *Chronicle*:

"Dignity in Carriages—It was an amusing sight to see our city officials riding in carriages in the procession Thursday last, while officers of the Agricultural Society and the ex-President of the United States were content to go the short route on foot. The expense to the citizens of this demonstration, is probably not far from a hundred dollars—an expense incurred, we understand, on the motion of Alderman

[Nathaniel K.] Raynes, one of the great sticklers for democratic economy. The old adage in regard to 'a beggar on horseback' applies well
here."

The *Chronicle* commented:

"We presume the ex-President and others mentioned walked
because they chose to and the City Government rode for the same reason. For ourselves, though not afraid to walk a couple of miles—we
dislike to march in a procession in which there are also carriages and
teams—the oxen and the horses may run you down, and certainly will
kick up dust enough to 'choke a fellow,' unless the streets are too
damp to walk in comfort."

In the years before his death, Oct. 8, 1869, ex-President Pierce
was a fairly frequent visitor to Portsmouth and the Seacoast. The
Civil War angered him as he saw it as a direct blow against his ideas
of States Rights.

Ulysses S. Grant

As is still often the case, presidential visits to Portsmouth are "whistle
stops" as the chief executive moves on into Maine, or leaves Maine on
his way back to the nation's capital. And so it was when, President
Ulysses S. Grant passed through the city in 1871.

On Oct. 17th President Grant was heading to the opening ceremonies for the European and North American Railroad, and an item
in the *Chronicle* said he would be passing through the city during the
forenoon. Members of the city government, headed by Mayor Joseph
B. Adams, were asked to meet at the City Building [where the Fleet
Bank is now] at 9:30, then to proceed to the depot to meet the chief
executive. Traveling with the president were Mrs. Grant, his daughter, Nellie, Postmaster General Creswell and wife, General Porter,
Congressman Twitchell, Speaker James G. Blaine, Mrs. Jonathan
Cresswell and niece, Miss M. B. McIntyre, Secretary Boutwell and
others. In all, more than 200 persons were in the official party.

The train was made up of two Pullmans, a smoking car, a baggage car, a passenger car. This equippage was drawn by the "splendid
engine America." Surprisingly, neither of the two daily papers, the
Chronicle and *Portsmouth Times*, devoted much space to the event,
and it's from the *Journal* of Oct. 21 that most of the story comes.
Shortly after 10 a.m., the special train puffed into the station, and the

Marine Band played "Hail to the Chief." Grant appeared on the rear platform of the last car to a roar of applause from the assembled citizenry.

Mayor Adams and his fellows were then received, and it was the mayor's proud moment to introduce President Grant. After that there were five more minutes of hand shaking. The *Journal* let its cup run over describing the makeup of the train:

"Aside from the other fine decorations of the cars the salon, which the presidential party occupied, was fitted up in the most magnificent and captivating style. It had the appearance of a perfect bed of roses. Festoons of bunting hung pendant in the most artistic manner, blending the red, white and blue, from the center of the salon, while large bouquets of choice flowers hung in the apex. Also trailing vines dotted with tuberoses and rose buds gracefully looped, encircled the mirrors and the air itself was heavy with the breath of choice blossoms.

"Those who had the privilege of a close inspection of the chief magistrate must have been convinced that his was the face of a man of simple honesty and sincerity, yet with all that subtlety of power and reticence which simple but strong natures oftimes possess. Admirers of republican simplicity of manners ought to be content with the president, for there seems to be no want of quiet dignity and gravity about him, and those accustomed to study human nature will readily see him to be a man of remarkable will, strength of character and compactness of brain. His face is one of the best answers to the calumnies and detractions which his Democratic opponents frequently bring against him." Additional guests in the party included:

"Among the official guests were besides the president and Secretaries Belknap and Robeson, Generals Ingalls, Babcock, and Porter. Senators Wilson, Battell, Buckingham and Sawyer. Speaker Blaine, General Burt, Colonel R. G. Usher, Mr. Mullett and Colonel Hurlburt of the Treasury Department, Generals Underwood, Cunningham and Bates of Governor Claflin's staff, Hon. Oliver Warner, Hon. George B. Loring, Hon. Harvey Jewell and many others. Among the railroad men present were president Jewett of the European and North American, president Lyon of Boston, Concord and Montreal, president Browne and superintendent Prescott of the Eastern, and a large number of invited guests out of New England. The party were joined here by ex-Governor Goodwin, Commodore Pennock and a delegation of officials from the Navy Yard and elsewhere. As the train struck Portsmouth bridge a salute was fired from the battery. At Kittery, the president was welcomed to the state by General James A. Hall, in behalf of the Governor of Maine and Senator Hamlin tendered the hospitalities of the city of Bangor.

"General Hall said, 'I have been directed by the Governor of Maine to meet you at the border of the commonwealth and to say that he is now in waiting at the state capital, where he will be happy to extend to your Excellency a most cordial welcome in behalf of all the people of the old Pine Tree State.'

"Between this city and Portland dinner was served in the forward car for the general company, while an elegant repast was served for the president and his suite in his private car. The only stopping place was Berwick Junction. Conductor George Batchelder was in charge of the train from Boston to Portland."

Of course, neither the *Times* nor the *Chronicle* ignored the visitation completely. Politics were politics in those days, too, and the *Times,* a completely unreconstructed Democratic paper, let loose a jibe or two. And even by the low standards set by George Bush in the 1988 presidential campaign, the *Times* was a little rough:

"However unworthy of respect and veneration U.S. Grant may be as a man, we are sorry that any should fail to pay proper respect to the President of the United States. Hence we regret that any persons were provoked by his stupid appearance as he stood on the platform of the car at the depot, to make insulting remarks in his hearing. If Grant does look as though he had been drunk for a week, and act, in a surly, cold and indifferent manner toward the people who throng to see him, still it is wrong to treat him as other men should be treated for such conduct. Remember that he is president, and properly regard his high office."

The *Chronicle,* being a staunch pillar of Republicanism, couldn't let that diatribe pass unanswered:

"The President's cigar-stump appears to have scorched the local Democratic organ, judging from its dismal moanings over it. We should fantasy that the possessor of so exquisitely sensitive a cuticle would be a little more cautious about trying to scalp less vulnerable people, but then it's not often that a newspaper squib hurts so, you know."

Not loath to join the fray, the *Times* riposted: "Another display of wit (?) in the *Chronicle.* It is absolutely crushing, scathing and overwhelming. The editors must have interviewed some boot-black (beg pardon of the boot-blacks) and gathered their original ideas. After replying in their usual 'brilliant and interesting' style to our comments upon Grant's appearance at the depot yesterday, they say—'We hear it suggested that the Democratic organ would have shown less ill temper had its editor managed to secure one of the President's cigar-stumps. That ought to annihilate us. It is the heaviest blow we have had from that quarter. We fear that such herculean efforts will exhaust our contemporary. We recommend a glass of ale.'"

President Grant came back through the city three days later but that time it wasn't even a whistle-stop. However, on Aug. 16, 1873, Grant again whistle-stopped in Portsmouth.

"President Grant and party, consisting of Miss Nellie Grant, (who was dressed in a plain black traveling suit), Ulysses and Jesse, General Babcock, Hon. G. S. Boutwell, Mr. Postmaster Burt, Gov. Pernham of Maine and Speaker Blaine passed through this city Tuesday forenoon in a special train at 11:29 for Augusta, Maine, where the president and his children are to be the guests of Speaker Blaine.

"The train which conveyed the distinguished company was in charge of Mr. Bennett and consisted of Engine No. 73, a baggage car and the new and elegant Pullman car, Mystic, which was superbly decorated. At the rear of the drawing room rested a massive basket of flowers, while the drapery and hangings were so arranged as to produce a fine effect. This car was in charge of Mr. J. R. Nute. The arrival of the train here, which made the passage from Boston in the quick time of one hour and 26 minutes was greeted with cheers by the crowd assembled, the President appearing on the platform and bowing his acknowledgement." General Butler who joined the party at Salem left the train here. Secretary Robeson, who came on board at Newburyport, left at North Hampton for the beach.

"Ex-Governor Goodwin acted as the medium of communication between the chief magistrate and our people. The train arrived at Augusta at precisely 17 minutes past 4 o'clock."

Benjamin Harrison

Benjamin Harrison, 23rd president, in August of 1889 made a vacation visit to Bar Harbor, and it was on his return toward Washington that he paid a fleeting visit to Portsmouth. The president's special

train left Portland at 5:35 and arrived in Portsmouth at 6:48, a run of
an hour and 13 minutes, and one of the best on record. The *Journal*
said:

"The train consisted of two elegant vestibule Pullman parlor cars,
the Mignon and the Maritana, and a baggage car, and was drawn by
engine Tippecanoe, Engineer Lander: The genial and popular conductor of the Flying Yankee, L. O. Lunt, had charge of the train. The
engine was handsomely decorated with bunting and flags, having in
front a handsome picture of President Harrison."

A little recollection of American history helps to realize that the
locomotive's name was of special significance. The president's grandfather, William Henry Harrison, the ninth president, was the hero of a
battle with the Indians known in history as Tippecanoe. During his
campaign for the presidency, William Henry Harrison's slogan had
been "Tippecanoe and Tyler Too." The latter being John Tyler, the vice
presidential candidate. William Henry Harrison contracted a cold during his inaugural; it turned into pneumonia and he died a month after
taking office.

Benjamin Harrison defeated Grover Cleveland in 1888 when the
latter was seeking re-election, Cleveland gained revenge in 1892 when
he stopped Harrison's re-election bid. But that was in the future on
Aug. 14 when President Harrison's train came into Portsmouth. The
crowd began to assemble long before the presidential special left
Portland, and by the time it arrived, the depot area was the proverbial sea of people. A century ago, despite two assassinations, presi-
dents weren't surrounded by Secret Service personnel, so the crowd
surged around the train after it stopped. And Portsmouth's Col.
William H. Sise came out of the parlor car to introduce President
Harrison:

"Fellow citizens of Portsmouth, I have the honor to introduce to
you the president of the United States, Benjamin Harrison."

The train was in the depot for 12 minutes, long enough to switch
the "Tippecanoe" off and replace it with a Portsmouth and Concord
Railroad engine, the "S. M. Bell." Also attached was the special car
carrying the New Hampshire dignitaries who had come to welcome
the chief executive and escort him to Manchester. The conductor for
the P&C said he would make the run of 38 miles in one hour. Coming
the other way, the 1952 campaign train of President Harry S Truman
took a lot more than an hour to traverse the track between
Portsmouth and Manchester. It was in such poor shape that the

Secret Service kept the last presidential campaign train to enter Portsmouth slowed to a snail's pace.

Incidentally, before returning to the *Chronicle*'s thoughts on the Harrison visit, it should be said that Harry S Truman was the last president to spend a night in Portsmouth, albeit he did his sleeping in his special Pullman. And he was also the last president to stroll downtown Portsmouth's streets around dawn.

The *Chronicle* observed:

"We did not notice in the presidential car, nor among the throng which crowded about the train and jammed itself into the narrow space there, any representatives of the city government, or officers of the Navy Yard. Col. Sides (the postmaster) was there but like many others who would have liked to present their respects to the president, he found it impossible to force a way through the dense mass of humanity. It was rumored that quite a number of gentlemen desirous of securing official positions were in the crowd, with their papers in their pockets already for the presentation, but none of them got near enough to that rear platform to even throw their documents at the chief magistrate."

This was a bit more than a century ago. Can anyone today imagine making personal pleas to the president of the United States for appointment as postmaster at Rockingham Junction? Yet that was the way things were then done, and it was what caused the assassination of James A. Garfield. The *Chronicle* went on:

"There was no mishap at the depot, nobody hurt, so far reported, although the ladies and children in the crowd—and there were quite a number of both—must have had rather a hard time of it. When the Concord cars and engine were connected with the Boston and Maine train, the latter was suddenly driven back several feet, and for a moment it appeared that injury must result to a number of persons, but no one was harmed."

That little sidelight is reminiscent of an episode that may have cost New York's Gov. Thomas E. Dewey the 1948 election. At some whistle stop, the engineer jerked Dewey's campaign train around, and the candidate's comment on the engineer's lack of skill quickly spread through all the nation's organized labor.

Other Presidential Visits

Chester K. Arthur: Succeeding James Garfield after the later died from an assassin's bullet, President Arthur came to Portsmouth on Sept. 9, 1882, largely as the guest of the brewer, Frank Jones, and his visit is recorded in the book, *Frank Jones, King of the Alemakers.*

William Howard Taft: Came to the city on Oct. 23, 1912, as part of his campaign for re-election, a bid that failed because of Theodore Roosevelt's Bull Moose movement. Taft did visit the former Elks Home at Pleasant and Court streets, signing the register.

Franklin Delano Roosevelt: As assistant secretary of the Navy, Roosevelt was here quite often. His last official visit to the city and the Navy Yard was on Aug. 10, 1940. During his presidency he had been here twice before.

Harry S Truman: Came in October, 1952, to campaign for Adlai Stevenson, who lost to Dwight D. Eisenhower.

Gerald R. Ford: The only non-elected president, came to Portsmouth twice. Once he campaigned for U.S. Rep. Louis C. Wyman, in the latter's contest for the U.S. Senate, and the second time he campaigned for himself against Jimmy Carter in the 1976 election.

Jimmy Carter: Made a speech at Portsmouth High School and a little girl, Paloma Kressmann, asked him a question that earned her a visit to the White House, to visit with his daughter, Amy, a girl her age.

George Herbert Walker Bush—During his administration President Bush frequently brought Air Force One into the former Pease Air Force Base while en route to his vacation home at Kennebunkport. On arrivals at Pease, he was met by a gaggle of Marine Corps helicopters which conveyed him and party to Kennebunkport. Before his presidency, Bush campaigned in Portsmouth against Ronald Reagan in 1980, and later became Reagan's vice president. In 1992, he campaigned in the city in the months of January and February before the state's Presidential Preferential Primary. On one appearance, he was the guest of the Portsmouth Rotary. The President won a narrow victory in the February 18th primary over Patrick Buchanan, an ultra conservative journalist.

Brewery champs. The five men in white uniforms did the honors for the Frank Jones Brewery in competition with rival breweries in the city. The Herald *didn't identify them, but the man in street clothes is James Whitman, the manager of Jones team. Strawbery Banke photo.*

XV *Sports in Portsmouth Long Ago*

Tug-of-War

BACK IN THOSE BAD OLD DAYS, before television stole the public's will to think and do for itself, people provided their own entertainment in many different ways.

Sports were participated in and watched with eagerness right here in Portsmouth and many games have disappeared into the limbo of foggy memory. For instance, cricket, the famed old English game, was played on a "pitch" where the Morley building now stands. Cricket is, of course, a monument to the artistry of slow play, with "innings" in classic matches often running a day or two. Perhaps that as much as anything killed cricket with Americans—it simply moved too slowly.

Walking matches, either against the clock or a competitor, were often staged in old Franklin Hall. Inter-city spelling matches were held between teams from Portsmouth and Dover, with the newspapers vociferously supporting the representatives of their communities.

Early in the 1900s, a popular form of sport was a tug-of-war, and in 1906 the city champions were the strong men from the Frank Jones Brewing Co. Whether they trained on the nut brown ale from the brewery isn't known, but the quintet on the team prevailed against the other breweries. On Sept. 6, the Frank Jones team won the title from the Eldredge Brewing Co. entry. It had defeated the Portsmouth

Brewing Co. entry three weeks earlier to get a chance at the Eldredge squad. The *Herald* reported:

"The victory was clean-cut and decisive, although it was gained only by the hardest kind of work. The first pull went to the Eldredge team, but the Jones men proved their right to the championship title by taking the next two . . ."

The match was staged in Peirce Hall, where so many social and athletic events were held in the first 30 years of this century. The *Herald's* report continued:

"The crowd in the galleries and on the floor showed the wildest enthusiasm and the cheers were positively deafening. It was impossible to hear the decisions of the judges and most of the people in the hall had to depend upon themselves to decide which team had won. As it happened, there was no chance for doubt in regard to the second and third pulls. The first was so close that many thought it was a tie. When the anchors dropped at the beginning of the initial pull, the Eldredge men brought the knot over to their side. The men on the other team pulled desperately and regained much of what they had lost, but when the allotted two minutes were up, the Eldredge team still had the advantage by the narrow margin of one-eighth of an inch.

"The second pull was a bit one-sided. The Jones team gained at once and, despite the efforts of their rivals to pull the knot back, steadily increased their advantage. They won by two and one-quarter inches. The third pull was a dandy. When the anchors went down, the knot hardly moved and for half a minute it remained practically stationary. Then it moved over to the Eldredge side, only to travel back again. At one time the Eldredge representatives looked like the winners, but the Jones men were good finishers and gradually gained, finally winning the pull and the match by exactly one inch. . . ."

The *Herald* credited the anchor man for the Jones Team, Theodore Eck, with being the key to the victory, and added that it was Eck who had been responsible for the win over Portsmouth Brewing. Other members of the Jones squad were the captain Edward Keefe, at No. 1; Morris Leary, No. 2 and Jeremiah Reagan, No. 3. John Murphy was anchor for the Eldredge team; Patrick F. Harnedy, No. 1; John Crowley, No. 2, Ira A. Newick, captain and No. 3. The latter's daughter, Mrs. Betty Critchley, lives in York, and she was a noted golfer at Portsmouth Country Club in her college days.

Officials for the event were Joseph P. Conner, Sherman T. Newton and J. T. Harrett, judges; William P. Robinson and Daniel P.

Mahaney, timekeepers. James T. Whitman, who served as a city assessor in the late 1940s, coached the Jones club and Frank F. Newick had the Eldredges.

There was music between the pulls, provided by Hoyt and Parker's orchestra. After the match, the teams and officials, 24 in number, went to the Hotel Langdon, at the corner of Congress and Vaughan streets, for a supper.

Women's Basketball

No sport ever caught on as fast as basketball. First devised by Dr. James Naismith at Springfield College in 1891, within a few years it was being played throughout New England. On Jan. 15, 1900, the Portsmouth High School girls organized a team. They played and practiced in the main hall of the old courthouse structure that stood on the site of the present-day Central Fire Station.

The old courthouse was moved off the site to Parrott avenue to make room for the fire station in 1920. The Veterans of Foreign Wars used it as a headquarters until May 1, 1953, when it was destroyed by fire. The Home for Aged Women—now closed—was built partially on the site. The news report about girls' basketball said:

"As soon as the team has a little practice several games will be arranged with a team composed of young ladies of this city and the Navy Yard."

For reasons not understood, that was the end of public commentary on girls' basketball until late in April, when it was announced that a basketball game would be played in Peirce Hall on May 2 "between the high school girls and the young ladies of the Slappan club. The friends and admirers of both teams will be there.

"Mrs. Henry E. Hovey, [wife of the rector of St. John's], who is in general charge . . . is trying to arrange another game of young ladies the same afternoon. The other games will be between a picked team from the Strawberry Bank B.B.C., and a team of the Longwood club of Brookline, Mass. The game will probably be held at Peirce Hall about the middle of May, and will be an invitation affair. Miss Kate Bradford, who was elected captain of the picked team, is at present making arrangements for the game with Miss Olive Halliday, who captains the Longwoods. The young ladies of the visiting team will be the guests of the Strawberry Bank club."

A week later it was confirmed there would be a basketball game in the afternoon between two teams of high school girls, and the winners were to play the Slappan club in the evening. "A large crowd will probably attend, as this is the first public exhibition game of basketball given by ladies in this city." The *Herald* also had a bit of a chauvinistic report on the game:

"A good many people witnessed for the first time last evening, an exhibition of the game of basketball as played by the young ladies, and not a few of these people were considerably surprised to see a game, so different in almost every important detail, from the basketball to which they had become accustomed. The girls play a game, which to one who has followed the livelier games as played by the men, seems rather slow, although it is by no means lacking in elements of interest, and at times even becomes exciting."

Unfortunately neither the *Chronicle* nor the *Journal* chose to give the first names of the players. The game between the high school players was won by the Green team, 25 to 19. In the evening, the Slappan club lost to a picked team of PHS girls, 17 to 4. A comment said "the Slappans good point is their passing. They are weak in both their forwards and backs, while these are the strong points of the High schools."

Some long familiar Portsmouth family names were on the roster of the teams. For instance the Green high school team included girls named Borthwick, Pike, Pierce, Dutton and Horton. Miss Borthwick might have been Susan E. and Miss Pike could have been Etta Grace. The Pinks had girls named Foote, Keefe, Foster, Byer and Davis. Miss Foote might have been Ida May. For the Slappans there were girls named Pickett, Randall, Foster, Hill and Woods. One wonders if Miss Woods might have been a sister to the famed Woods Brothers, a dominant local team in that era.

In their game with the Slappans, the PHS team had players not named in the intra-squad game. For instance there was a Miss Bennett, Miss Russell, Miss Badger and Miss Goldsmith.

It is mildly interesting to note that in the beginning there were only five players on a team in girls' basketball: a center, two backs and two forwards.

A generation or so ago, there were six players, playing in limited zones. Today women play by "boys' rules," and their college games today are often on TV.

Old Time Baseball

Whether it's baseball season or not, now's a good time to tell the story of the rose-wood bat, which is one of the treasures in the John Paul Jones House, the home of the Portsmouth Historical Society.

First, as a bit of background, let it be said that Portsmouth has had a fair share of excellent athletes. For example, a couple of generations ago there was Walter Woods, a player in what were then the major baseball leagues about 1900. In more contemporary years, and well-known because of television, there was Jane Blalock, one of the country's leading golfers in the 1960s and 1970s. And, because this piece has a baseball theme, let it be known "Janie," as she was then known, was a pretty fair baseball player, but girls weren't allowed in Little League in those days. Former Mayor Peter G. Weeks, who grew up in Jane's neighborhood, claims she was "the best pitcher in our crowd."

Of course there were legions of others whose fame didn't carry far beyond the immediate horizon. One such person was James H. Dow, a fine baseball player in the years right after the Civil War, at a time when baseball was beginning to catch on as the national pastime. Dow was a stellar center fielder, and a strong-armed pitcher. But his real forte was in swinging a bat. Some of his hitting feats have lived in legend long after him. Tradition has it that one ball field then in use had its home plate near the brick school house at the Plains, and Jim Dow would often drive a ball deep into the area now occupied by Calvary Cemetery. And that was before the era of the "Rabbit Ball."

Neighboring towns provided competition, and, in Portsmouth there were two or three different clubs by the summer of 1866. Late in August, Jim Dow's nine, the Rockinghams, played the Whipple club of Kittery out at the Plains. In an advance item on the game, it was reported that seats would be provided for ladies, and that a large passenger wagon, or barge, would leave Haymarket Square carrying "ladies having invitations." Several hundred fans were on hand for the game which was won by the Rockinghams with a score of 58 to 25. Scoring was far different 125 years ago, as the final tally strongly suggests. The *Chronicle* commented:

"Though great skill is required in playing baseball, there is yet a great deal in having a run of good luck. One of the finest players on the field Friday was peculiarly unfortunate in his scoring and yet played with skill while his side was out . . ."

Even in those days the games were played over nine innings, and there were three outs to the inning. Dow pitched for the Rockinghams, made four putouts on fly balls and took part in a double play. However, he hit no home runs that day; Hackett, the catcher for the Rockinghams, belted one and J. R. Philbrick, first baseman for the Whipples, hit one. But the big event of the 1866 season was announced on Sept. 1. The Rockingham club accepted a home-and-home challenge from the Kearsarge team of Concord, which was to be played on Sept. 5 at the Plains. The Kearsarge team came in from Concord on the 10 o'clock train, and brought with it a delegation of fans. The running account of the game was published on Sept. 7:

"The match game of baseball, Wednesday afternoon, at the Plains, was witnessed by a large assemblage, notwithstanding the threatening weather. The Rockingham nine went to bat first, and were put out after four runs, while the Kearsarge nine made 11 . . . After the first inning the game was a closely contested one, although we think the play of the Rockingham Club was not up to their usual mark, being inferior to that displayed in late match with the Whipple Club, of Kittery. After the third inning, the Rockinghams appeared to realize that their opponents were worthy of their best endeavors, and pluckily went into the contest fighting for success . . ."

Hard as they apparently tried, the Rockinghams never quite caught up; they closed the gap to three runs, 28 to 25, but lost by 31 to 26.

After the ball game, the Rockinghams, appropriately, entertained the visitors at dinner in the Rockingham house, and accepted a challenge to play in Concord on Sept. 11. The *Chronicle* reported on Sept. 10 that "it is the intention of a gentleman of this city to present a beautiful rosewood bat, heavily mounted with silver to the member of the Rockingham nine making the best score on the occasion. May he win it by a long one . . ."

As scheduled, the two clubs played their match on Sept. 11, "on the inter vale across the Merrimack River " from the City of Concord. Oddly, not even the score of the match was reported in the Portsmouth newspapers. However, a brief account appeared in the *Concord Daily Monitor* that evening and a lengthy report was published on the 12th.

Sadly, again it wasn't the Rockinghams' day. The match went only five innings because of rain, and when called, the Concord team was leading, 32 to 19. The players adjourned to the Eagle Hotel and sat down to dinner at 7:30, after which there were the inevitable speeches. The first event was presentation of the "game ball" by the losing nine to the winners. Captain Hayes of the Rockinghams made the presentation with an apology. He did not have the ball used in the game; some one had stolen it. But his team had brought along a second ball, and that he presented to Captain Gage of the Kearsarges.

In his acceptance remarks, Captain Gage noted the historic significance of the occasion, the matches being the first ever played by teams from two different New Hampshire communities. Through that influence, Gage said he hoped the game would continue to spread. Later, in fact, the Kearsarges did travel to Hanover to play Dartmouth College, and lost 39 to 7.

Among the guests present at the dinner was ex-President Franklin Pierce, who expressed pleasure because baseball was being played. Pierce said he thought people had too little exercise in open air, too few holidays, not too many.

Judge Ira A. Eastman was another speaker, and his remarks are in direct conflict with the widely-held traditional view that Abner Doubleday invented baseball in 1839.

Judge Eastman said that 50 years earlier [1816] he had witnessed a game of ball in which his father was one of the players. He said the game was played differently then, and the rule called for the pitcher to put the ball where the batter could hit it. Eastman said he noticed that in the game that afternoon the pitchers threw the ball too high or too low, and wondered if that was fair.

Now comes a sad moment in this little tale: the tradition that ex-President Pierce presented a rosewood bat to James H. Dow for his outstanding performance in the game simply isn't true. It will make the writer about as popular around the John Paul Jones House as the proverbial skunk at a lawn party, but the *Concord Daily Monitor*'s account contradicts the legend. What happened was this: Dr. A. P. Stevens of Portsmouth, an avid baseball fan, had the bat made with the idea of honoring the highest scorer on the Rockinghams. The *Monitor* reported the day after the game (Sept. 12):

"This morning, an elegant rosewood bat was presented by Dr. A. P. Stevens, of Portsmouth, through Fred L. Dodge, Secretary of the Rockingham Club, to James H. Dow, of the same Club, for the best score in the match yesterday. The presentation took place in the parlor of the Eagle Hotel. The bat bears the following inscription:

"Presented to the member of the Rockingham Nine making the

best score in the second match between the Kearsarge Club, of Concord, and the Rockingham Club, of Portsmouth; Sept. 11, 1866."

"Two members of the Club had the same score—Dow and Barstow—and the ownership of the bat was decided by lot. Dr. Stevens has taken great interest in the Club, ill health preventing him from being an active member . . ."

The match in Concord didn't end baseball for the 1866 season in Portsmouth. Well into October there were reports of games. Many of those games were played on a ball field now covered by Miller avenue, the Masonic Temple and the Masonic parking lot across the street. It was known as Rundlett's Field, for the original owner of the Rundlett-May House across Middle street. Frank Miller and Benjamin Webster began the development of Rundlett's Field and all the adjacent land in the 1870s, but that's a story for another day.

James H. Dow, born on Feb. 7, 1840, lived until Feb. 27, 1918. At one time he operated a fancy goods store at 13 Market St., and then later went to work for George B. French in the latter's Market Street store. Apparently it didn't matter to Dow who had presented the rosewood bat; it was one of his prized possessions all his life, and is now a treasure in the John Paul Jones House, a memento of a day when America was "a kinder and gentler" place.

While we're on the subject of baseball, let it be said that it still isn't exactly clear why Abner Doubleday is credited as the inventor of the game in 1839

But one thing for sure, the business people in Cooperstown enjoy their daily trips to the bank because the Baseball Hall of Fame has proved a lodestone.

Over the years, however, it's become more or less accepted that baseball evolved from an English game called "rounders." The writer played in a game of rounders on Newmarket Heath in England, back in 1928, and was amazed to observe how much baseball was like it in principle.

John W. Whiteman, managing editor of the *Herald*, played rounders many times in his youth in England, and is convinced that baseball stemmed from it. Whiteman makes it sound much like the way American kids pick up sides for a game of "scrub." All of the above was brought about by a letter to the editor of the *Herald* on May 5, 1905, in which the writer, J. A. Mendum, claimed to have played baseball in 1830, and acceptable authorities contend a variety of the game was being played in the New York area in the 1820s.

The *Herald*, in April, 1905, had published a statement by A. G. Spalding, later of sporting goods fame, in which Spalding ridiculed the idea that baseball derived from rounders. This flew in the face of contentions by Henry Chadwick, that rounders was the foundation. Spalding dated the origin to 1845.

Mendum said in his letter:

"The recent article in the *Herald* credited to A. G. Spalding and referring to the origin and age of baseball, carries me back many years and awakens many pleasant memories. The article states that the game dates its birth from the organization of the Knickerbocker Baseball Club of New York on Sept. 23, 1845. I will add that 15 years before that date, I with other pupils of the grammar school on School Street, Portsmouth, found this game one of our favorite pastimes on Wednesday and Saturday afternoons and during the regular summer vacation.

"The writer is inclined to credit Mr. Chadwick's statement that the game of baseball is of English origin and that its age is greater than that of any person now living. While conversing with an old friend recently (an Englishman), on the popularity of the game, I asked him how far back in the history of the game he could go. He replied, "sixty years." He also said that his grandfather when living would frequently present him with a handsome bat, and tell him about the game, especially how he used to play it when a boy. This statement is all in Mr. Chadwick's favor.

"If Robert Morrison and Mr. Hoyt were now living, both teachers at the old wooden schoolhouse on School Street, they would hold up both hands and testify to my statement that baseball was very popular in their day. Many a ball and bat did they capture from the boys, while the lads were displaying the articles during school hours. They would always relent, however, as Wednesday approached and the implements were returned to the owners."

Well, if nothing else, Mendum's letter gives us a peek at a phase of a Portsmouth boyhood 160 years ago. It wasn't all work, as some would have us believe.

But, in the light of the Doubleday myth, it's odd that neither Spalding nor Chadwick gave any time to Abner Doubleday, so often credited as the founder. And Mendum didn't mention him either. However, the good burghers of Cooperstown couldn't care less; they have a small gold mine with an endless mother vein.

And no matter its beginnings, baseball is baseball and is fun for kids of all ages. And there's no more fun than for a father to take his Little League son or daughter to Cooperstown, unless it's a grandfather doing it.

Bicycling in 1899

The coming of fine weather always brings with it the sudden crowding of our streets with bicycles, with riders ranging in age from four or five years to those 20 times that number. Bicycles have long been part of Portsmouth's traffic problems and erratic, careless riding of them seems to increase each year. Apparently, it has always been thus.

In May, 1899, the *Portsmouth Herald* published a list of "Rules of the Road." Some of the suggestions will produce only amusement today, but others are still highly applicable:

1. In meeting riders, pedestrians and vehicles, keep to the right. In overtaking and passing them, keep to the left.
2. In turning corners to the left, always keep to the outside of the street.
3. In turning corners to the right, keep as far out as possible without trespassing on the left side of the road.
4. Never expect pedestrians to get out of the way, find a way around them.
5. Never ride rapidly past an electric car standing to unload passengers.
6. Never coast down a hill having crossed streets along the way.
7. Never ring your bell, except to give notice of your approach.
8. In meeting riders ascending a hill, where there is only one path, always yield the right of way to the up riders.
9. Bear in mind that a rider meeting an electric car carrying a strong headlight is unable to see beyond the light; keep out of his way.
10. When riding straight ahead, never vary your course suddenly to the right or the left without first assuring yourself that no other rider is close in on your rear or on the side which you turn.
11. Always ring your bell when overtaking riders and pedestrians, to give warning of your approach. This does not mean they are to get out of your way.
12. Do not ride too close to a novice, and in meeting a novice give plenty of room.

DON'T TALK TO ME

About your $15.27 bicycle. A NATIONAL is good enough for me. I paid more, but "what I get for my money is as important as the amount I pay." I bought my NATIONAL of

F. B. PARSHLEY & CO.,
16 CONGRESS ST.

SPORTING LIFE - Bicycling was all the rage in 1899 when this ad was published in the Portsmouth Herald. The automobile, whose advent revolutionized American life, was still a few years down the road, and a bike offered quick, easy transportation.

Peter the Cat

XVI   *Some Animal Stories*

Peter the Cat

THIS IS GOING TO BE A TALE ABOUT PETER THE CAT.

It's being told simply because there are those who believe that cats have supernatural powers, and lack only the ability to talk human, in order to take their proper place in society. Peter's story appeared in the *Portsmouth Herald* on Nov. 13, 1909. At that time, he was approaching the age of twenty, and was believed to be the oldest cat in the city and perhaps the state. The *Herald* opined that "his extended age was due to the good care given him by his mistress.

"He looks for his bath every week, and, should the family fail to carry out the custom, he will make it known in quick order and there is nothing like peace in the house until he is given his plunge. . . ."

The people Peter owned were Mr. and Mrs. James S. Plaisted, and he let them make a home for him at 303 Thornton St. The master of the house spent most of his life in the cabs of the Boston & Maine Railroad locomotives, first as fireman and later as an engineer. Peter was early to rise, and, when he felt the time appropriate would devote himself to rousing his servants from their bed; a crying cat is a far better alarm than any mechanical contrivance. The *Herald* story continued, saying:

"In addition to his bath, he takes Doan's pills as a health regulator, and the family has never seen the day when he could be called a sick cat.

"When Mrs. Plaisted wants the butcher, fishman, iceman or grocer, she informs the cat of her want, and he immediately takes his place at the window with a good view of the street. When any of the men wanted comes into sight, he hurries to Mrs. Plaisted to whom he makes the fact known by his cries and a constant pulling at her clothing. His diet is composed mainly of sweet stuff and he can make a meal any time on all kinds of pie. . . ."

And such for all the anti-sweets doctrine professed by the dentists of this world because it was reported that "another remarkable feature is the condition of his teeth that are as good today as they were the first year he was on earth. . . ." Not only did Peter have good teeth but he was also a bit of a neighborhood snob, having no truck with any of the other felines in his vicinity.

Peter was described as being of the tiger species, and he weighed in at twenty pounds.

Later search may disclose how old he was when he passed on to the mouse-filled heaven that is the destiny of cats.

However, when the other man in the house, James S. Plaisted, went to toot train whistles in the sky, Peter wasn't listed among the survivors.

Greenland Steer

Farming is no longer one of the major occupations in the seacoast of New Hampshire. Much of the land once subject to the cutting edge of a plow has been, or is being, turned into housing developments or super malls.

For instance, land that was once an integral part of one of the earliest farms in New Hampshire is now the playground of the Portsmouth Country Club. More than three centuries ago Francis Champernown cultivated the lush acres where divots are now the largest crop. That land was also farmed by Thomas Packer, the high sheriff of New Hampshire who hanged Ruth Blay in 1768 rather than be late for dinner. After Packer came the Peirce family which held the land for more than a century, and farmed it well.

Greenland still has a few farms, but back in 1827 it had a lot more, and the Packer-Peirce farm produced a steer that drew much local acclaim. In February, 1827, this gigantic ox was put on exhibit at the Bell Tavern in Portsmouth. It might not have been the equal of Paul Bunyan's big blue ox, Babe, but it was a big one.

Peirce Farm. In view of the fact that photography had yet to be invented in 1827, this picture of live stock at the famed Peirce Farm in Greenland doesn't show the giant steer told about in the accompanying article.

In those long ago days, the taverns were places where curiosities of all kinds were often put on display, usually for a small admission fee. The Bell was one of Portsmouth's more popular taverns, located on Congress Street, near High. The *Portsmouth Journal* said of the big Greenland steer:

"He is probably the largest animal of his species ever raised in this country and it will probably be a long time before any of us will be able to look upon his like again. His weight 13 months ago was 3,038 lbs., being then not quite six years old; it is estimated that he has increased since then about 500 lbs.—His proportions are very good, the fat being well distributed, and he walks without any difficulty. The following are the dimensions of this noble animal, who it may be well to remark is of our common New England breed. He features 9 feet 10 inches in girth; 11 feet in length; 6 feet in height at the hips and 2 feet 11 inches and a half in width across the hips."

All in all, it had to be conceded that animal was an awful lot of beef. One wonders what happened to him.

Did he go down the road to the abattoir in Brighton, Mass., or was he taken out present-day Richards Avenue to the local slaughter-house?

Winnicummett

Is Winnicummett the Turtle still alive? Or has he gone to that final resting place appointed for venerable reptiles?

Winnicummett, of course, took the name from the ancient name given to this town, and, if he still lives, is well into his third century. In 1906, on one of the several occasions in which Winnicummett was in human hands, he was taken to Boston for examination by expert naturalists, but more of that later.

Peter E. Randall, in his fine history of Hampton, published in 1989, mentioned Winnicummett, but was unable to go into detail. However, Randall did learn that Philip N. Blake Jr. of Exeter, but then of Hampton, is the last person known to have seen the ancient reptile. Blake recalls being with his father in 1926 when the latter came across the turtle, for the second time.

Winnicummett's history runs something like this:

He was first captured by Zaccheus Brown in 1840. Brown scratched his initials on the turtle's shell and released him. In 1857, William Dow came across Winnicummett, and he too, carved his initials and the date on the horny shell. In 1881, Amos Leavitt, then a small boy, found Winnicummett and added his initials and the date to the shell. Over the next two decades, Winnicummett was seen by various people.

Leavitt became an employee of the S. S. Peirce Co. in Boston and often talked of the turtle, claiming great feats for it. When he was faced with a solid wall of doubt, Leavitt made contact with old friends in Hampton, asking that if the turtle was seen again to please send it to him. And so, in 1906, the defunct *Boston Transcript* published the following:

"Twenty-five years ago a bare-footed country lad, playing near the mill dam, in one of the Seacoast towns of New Hampshire, espied a large turtle slowly crawling from the mill dam to a swampy meadow on the other side of the road. The turtle was a fresh water snapping turtle that was well known in the town, for in 1840, in 1857, and again in 1866 he had been caught by prominent citizens, some of whom had cut the dates and their initials in his shell.

"The bare-footed boy cut his initials and the date, 1881, on the shell, and then the turtle was not seen again until 1895. In 1904 and 1905, he made his appearance, still traveling in the Summer from meadow to the mill dam. This year he was caught by a native of the town, who thought that the bare-footed lad, now a Boston merchant, might like to see his old acquaintance. So the turtle was shipped to Boston, and the lad who cut his name on the shell a quarter of a century ago is having a silver plate engraved with the present date which will be attached to the shell and then the turtle will be returned to his habitat. The turtle has excited a good deal of interest among the Fanueil Hall marketmen who sell sea food, and 'Nippy,' as he is called, has received visits from others interested in natural history.

"The consensus is that he is probably about 200 years old. Turtles are capable of subsisting a long time without food and some wonderful stories have been told to Nippy's visitors. This turtle has very strong jaws, very sharp-edged, which cut with ease. He has bitten completely through a notebook an inch and a half thick, and one market man tells of a large turtle that bit an ordinary broom stick in halves. It is said that the body of the turtle will show signs of life for nine days after the head has been cut off, while there is apparently no limit to the remarkable things the head will do under the same circumstances."

When the Blakes saw Winnicummett, the silver plate was gone but the rivet holes still showed. Probably old Winnicummett is long gone. After all, the wild spate of development that has flooded Hampton in the past 60 years has undoubtedly destroyed his habitat, and broken the poor creature's spirit.

Old Billy

While researchers have been able to learn a great deal about the people who lived here years ago, their houses, furniture and other possessions, little is known about their animals. Occasionally, some hint of the places held by various kinds of animals does come through, and from the columns of the *Chronicle* we learn of one of the most unusual horses ever to tread a Portsmouth street.

"We were much astonished, a day or two since (as no doubt many of our readers will be) to hear that the old bay horse 'Billy,' once and long the stylish and serviceable horse of the late James Rundlett, Esq.,—that we supposed had long since gone to the shades of horses—'still lives' and this not in any imaginary or spiritual sense, but as of old only a good deal thinner, and not quite so good looking. Twenty-four years ago he was purchased in Boston, by Mr. Rundlett for a lady's saddle horse—he being then, it was thought, about 20, and sufficiently experienced to be steady and safe.

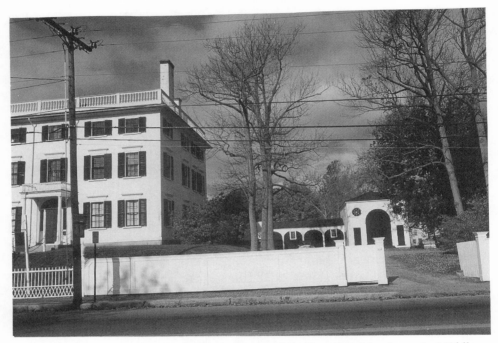

Old Billy's barn. It was in the stable to the rear of the Rundlett-May house in Middle Street that "Old Billy" was sheltered during his long service to the Rundlett family. Author photo.

"For many years he served as the family horse of his owner, and will be remembered by many of our citizens, but of late years, having been supplanted by a younger rival, he has done but little. A grandson of his first owner here, (and grandson also to the prime of the old horse) has driven him a few times during the past winter; but 'his work is now almost done'—and soon all that will be left of old 'Billy' will be the memory of his faithfulness and long service. 'Billy' is thought by his owner to be 40 years old or upwards—horses being like men (or rather women) in this respect at least, but when they reach old age, it is not disgrace or disparagement to allow them their full years.

And "Billy's" time was soon to run out. It came, as it must to all living things, in March of 1857.

"The old dark bay horse 'Billy,' who belonged to the family of the late James Rundlett, Esq., of this city and whom we have once or twice spoken of as a very aged animal, died on Wednesday morning. His age, as near as can be ascertained, was about 43 years—his only ailment, old age. Twenty-five years ago he was purchased in Boston, and ridden to Portsmouth, to be used as a saddle horse in the family of his owner. He was then considered an old horse and was probably about 18 years old.

"From that time, almost to the present, he has done good service in various ways. During the last summer, he was used sometimes under the saddle, and would leap a ditch with his rider, if desired, in a manner which would puzzle most of the younger ones. For a year or two past, however, he has not willingly gone far from his stable—but after going a very short distance, would wish to return. He has not been used or shod during the past winter, but has ate and appeared well, till within a day or two—when he seemed to be paralyzed and quickly died.

"We mention the old fellow thus particularly, as a remarkable instance of equine longevity, and of the endurance of a noble horse when well treated. Many a reader will recollect old 'Billy,' as he might be seen most any time within the last quarter of a century—handsomely doing the pleasure travels of a large family, of which he was the property and almost a member. Peace to his manes!" An old rhyme, highly appropriate, runs like this:

> Old horse John's ever faithful,
> His work is now near done
> He's slow, but ever sure,
> I never can endure
> Parting with my old horse John.

The Kittery Pig Case

By mere happenstance of birth, most of you aren't old enough to remember the famous "Pig Case" in Kittery. The "Pig Case" had its start more than 70 years ago, in July, 1917, to be exact, and more than seven years passed before it was finally settled. Briefly, this is what happened:

Elmer H. Twombly of 60 Hanover St., Portsmouth, a street car motorman by trade, bought a pig from "Keeper Hall of the Kittery Town Farm, which he prepared for family consumption." Before going on, it has to be said that in 1917, the Kittery Town Farm was on Haley Road, about a quarter mile in from the present U.S. Route 1. Further, town farms were, even at that late date, a means the various Seacoast towns used to support their indigents. Portsmouth's Town

Farm, where the New Franklin School now stands, was built in 1834. Kittery acquired 80 acres for a town farm through the beneficence of a member of the Haley family, who bequeathed the land for the purpose.

Former Selectman Leon French says the Kittery Town Farm buildings, however, were actually sited on another, smaller tract, adjacent to the Haley land, and bequeathed by a member of the Lewis family. Now back to the running text: Twombley fed the pig to his family and four members promptly became ill . . . "The attending physician attributed their illness to poison from the Kittery porker . . ." Thereupon, Twombly sued the town for $10,000 and attached the town funds in the New Hampshire National Bank in Portsmouth.

A lengthy paragraph in the *Herald* of Sept. 25, 1924, tells the story:

"The town of Kittery has had four lawyers in the case and the same number has represented Twombly. The death of Attorney (Ralph) Gray caused the first delay, (Twombley's lawyer) and later the death of Attorney Albert R. Hatch, who represented the town of Kittery in New Hampshire sent the case along to another term of court. The death of Horace Mitchell of Kittery Point, who was interested for the town, held it up again. The case was again ready for trial when Judge Aaron B. Cole, representing the town, was called by death. Another army of legal talent then entered the case. Elmer J. Burnham took up the case for Kittery, and Judge (Ernest) Guptill, Arthur A. Sewall and John L. Mitchell carried on the suit for Twombly . . ."

"The last battery of legal counsel decided, in 1924, that it was time 'to get rid of the pig case forever.' They talked it over with Burnham, who, in turn, called in the Kittery selectmen. It was agreed to call a special town meeting at which Twombly was awarded the sum of $32.66. The case was certainly unique. Besides the deaths of four lawyers, several new selectmen and other town officers have been elected in Kittery since the opening of the case and they have all been busy one way and another over the pig suit."

The Town of Kittery still owns the 80-acre Town Farm tract, and it probably will for a long time to come. The Haley who gave the land added a covenant which should protect the land from condominiums for some time to come. His will stipulated the acreage should be used as a town farm forever.

Ironically, the lot on which the town farm buildings were located doesn't carry similar protection against developer devastation.

A Dog Story

Perhaps the story of "Greyfriars Bobby," the passionately devoted little dog in Edinburgh, Scotland, is one of the greatest tales ever told about dogs. However, about 200 years ago, a similar story unfolded on the New Castle waterfront. The *New Hampshire Spy* copied the article from "a Boston newspaper."

"Mr. Joseph Simpson, of New Castle, has, for several years past, sailed in the employ of Messrs. Jacob and James Sheafe, of Portsmouth. About three years ago, Mr. Simpson bought a small dog, and taught him to sit upon his hind legs, smoke a pipe and some other tricks. He made a small hammock for him, and carried him to sea constantly for seven or eight voyages.

"Last spring, Mr. Simpson, on his return from France, was washed overboard with one of the hands, the ninth of May last, a few leagues to the eastward of the Great Bank. After the loss of his master, the dog ran fore and aft, would look over the side and cry in a most surprising manner. A week or two afterwards, the ship arrived, and the dog was carried home to Capt. Simpson's, his master's father, and made very much of.

"They never ate a meal, but he always had a piece of the best; and constantly attended at table. Though there was a vast number of square-rigged vessels up and down the river, he took no notice of any of them. Between two and three months afterwards, the ship was sold to Mr. E. Hasket Derby of Salem and very much altered, having been newly painted and quarter galleries put to her; but the moment she hove in sight, coming down the river, the dog happened to be out, and he knew her. He instantly ran down to the shore, howled and cried, and seemed to be in the greatest distress imaginable to get on board her and continued to till the vessel was out of sight.

"Capt. Simpson afterwards called him to dinner: he would put his head inside the door, but would not come in, or eat one mouthful of anything. In three days after, he lost his senses and would run round in the circumference of two or three yards, for an hour together; and if he struck his head against anything, he would make a soft surprising noise. By forcing vitals down his throat and pouring milk down, they kept him alive three weeks; but he would never eat or drink anything, of his own accord, after the vessel sailed.

Wentworth-by-the-Sea. The majestic old Wentworth was less than a decade old when this drawing was published in the Granite State Monthly. *As the most casual glance will show, many changes in the hotel and its surroundings took place in the next hundred years, and then, ultimately, its partial demolition.*

XVII

The Wentworth-by-the-Sea

WHETHER OR NOT THERE WILL EVEN BE a Wentworth-by-the-Sea—even the pitiful remnant that now exists on the bluff above Little Harbor—is undecided as these words go into print. The Henley Corporation, the owners, and those who want to retain some vestiges of the past are locked in a struggle over its future. Henley wants to raze what's left of the old building, and develop the site for high-priced housing. The opponents of this plan want Henley to turn over the building, as it is, for a nominal price, and they propose to make it a conference center.

With all the controversy in mind, it's intended to offer a brief outline of how the hotel came into being. To anyone who has given a bit of study to the Wentworth, the most amazing aspect of its story is that it didn't get built long before 1873.

That was when Daniel Emery Chase, a Somerville, Mass., rum distiller, acquired the land on which he built Wentworth Hall as he called it. Chase bought the land from Charles E. Campbell, who became associated with the Wentworth as its manager, and ended his years as winter caretaker. What prompted Chase to build the Wentworth isn't known, but undoubtedly he saw in that bluff overlooking Little Harbor, and the whole ocean scene, the possibilities for a successful resort.

Summer tourism, if it could be called that, in the New Hampshire Seacoast was under way by 1820. A hotel, of sorts, was

built at Hampton Beach in that year, and all along the coast residents
began to take in summer boarders.

The major problem, in those days, was transportation, and so the
tide of tourism didn't really start running until the Eastern Railroad
of New Hampshire reached Portsmouth in 1840. Boarding houses
began to flourish on Great Island, as New Castle was known early on,
but getting to "the tight little island community" (as the late Bob
Kennedy used to describe it) wasn't easy.

Three bridges between what is now Pleasant Point in
Portsmouth and Cemetery Hill in New Castle had been built in the
early 1820s. They were toll bridges and usually in a state of "benign
neglect." Over the centuries, several bridges have connected the western end of the island with the mainland. But these came and went,
and often the islanders had to ford across toward the Wentworth-
Coolidge place, or take a boat to get to Portsmouth.

Thomas Laighton, light keeper at the Isle of Shoals, was one of
the first to sense the economic possibilities in establishing a place
where the summer sojourner could eat and sleep in comfort, and enjoy
cool ocean breezes. Laighton had one advantage: all he had to do was
have his guests get to Portsmouth "on the cars," then catch a ferry out
to his islands. There was no coaching, hacking or the like, and, on top
of that, the boat ride itself could be a pleasant experience. Laighton's
Appledore House was a success from the first. In time, partially
because of the poetic fame of his daughter, Celia Thaxter, it became a
retreat for the writers and artists of the day.

Twenty years later, Daniel Chase saw the Laighton success story,
and the end result was that he went into the hotel business. On Sept.
23, 1873, the *Chronicle* reported:

"All things are working nicely in this little village (New Castle),
is the testimony given to visitors, of whom the island had many during the season just closing. In fact, no summer has brought so many
strangers, as this. All the scarce room has been occupied and boarders
could scarcely find accommodations, though willing to accept the most
meager; but during the coming year this should be obviated by the
completion of a large hotel which now is having the foundation laid on
the banks of Little Harbor."

With such encouragement, Chase went ahead with the erection of
his hostelry. On Oct. 21, 1873, the *Chronicle* reported the arrival of
the schooner *Mary Ann McCann*, at New Castle, from Bangor, with
20,000 feet of lumber "for the new hotel." Unloading took ten days.

Today anyone looking at the center tower on the main building has in view timbers brought by the schooner 12 decades ago.

Chase's venture had an added blessing when New Castle, Rye and Rockingham County decided to pool their efforts in building a bridge across Little Harbor. The *Chronicle* wept a few tears because Portsmouth would have to pay for part of the road branching off from Sagamore Road. Work on the hotel was steady and the building was closed in, permitting winter operations. Progress was such that on March 28, 1874, the *Journal* said:

"The new hotel erected by D. E. Chase of Somerville, upon an eminence on the southerly side of New Castle, has taken shape. From the upper stories, besides the excellent seaward prospect, is a fine view of Portsmouth and the surrounding country. The house will be completed in season for summer travel. It is to be elegantly furnished, and contain all modern appliances, including the introduction of gas made on the premises by the Tiffany process. The surrounding grounds will be improved, though in doing this none of the delightful rusticity characteristic of the spot will be lost sight of. This new hotel, as seen from South Street, presents a commanding appearance. Land is changing hands at this seaside resort, and ere long the town will be renown for its summer residences."

The first "ad" for "The Wentworth" appeared in the *Chronicle* on June 15, and set forth all the virtues of the new hotel. Among these were:

". . . Excellent riding, fishing, boating, and bathing facilities; inland, river and ocean being immediately adjacent; pine grove directly behind the house, land-locked harbor of 20 acres for ladies and children's bathing . . ."

The new bridge wasn't finished, so patrons had to come by the way of the toll bridges, and Albert H. White immediately set himself as a stage operator to run between the hotel and the city. A drawing of that original hotel building shows it as a square, block-type structure of three stories with a central tower rising above all. The 1874 season was so successful that Chase made plans to add a wing to the eastern end during the off-season. However, there's reason to believe the new wing was erected on the north side of the hotel.

More work was done in 1876, and the *Portsmouth Times* reported on Aug. 8 that there was a big rush on to get work completed because "the house is jammed now."

In June, "The Wentworth" became the "Hotel Wentworth," and

John Albee, the New Castle historian, claimed the honor of having given the structure its new name. Albee later wrote a history of New Castle, which was subsidized by Frank Jones, the Portsmouth ale brewer, after he acquired the hotel. However, Daniel Chase apparently ran into hard times during the "Greenback Panic," and he leased the hotel to Charles Campbell and Job Jenness, a veteran resort hotel operator. The next operator of the hotel was Gideon Haynes, who took over in May of 1877 and announced that extensive improvements were being made. On June 11, there was a terse item in the *Chronicle* to the effect Daniel E. Chase had failed, and the lumber firm, Thomas E. Call & Sons of Portsmouth, was on the list of creditors at $1,200.

What happened next is well summed up in Albee's town history:

"I have mentioned that the first hotel, about one-third part of the present [1884], was built in 1874 by a gentleman who fell in love with the situation, but did not sit down to count the cost. In the year 1879, it fell into the hands of an owner who did not need to, and who has spared no expense to make it a perfect establishment, within and without."

What better way to introduce Frank Jones? Frank Jones, the Portsmouth brewer, was really only beginning his highly successful business career. Born in Barrington in 1832, he came to Portsmouth to seek his fortune and he found it. Reminders of his days in Portsmouth are on every hand, ranging from the remains of his brewery in the west end of the city to his summer mansion on Woodbury avenue to the National Block downtown. The Frank Jones story has also been told many times, in other contexts, and what's on the present menu is the Hotel Wentworth.

Frank Jones's first hotel was a run-down little inn on Congress street, where the National Block, recently sold, now stands. After he bought it, he improved it and changed the name to the National House. When it was damaged by fire in 1878, he razed it and built the building now on the site. Next he bought the Rockingham House on State street, and that, too, has gone through many changes. The news items concerning the purchase of the Wentworth said the buyers were F. W. Hilton "& Company," and everyone knew who the "& Company" was. The *Journal* on June 28, 1879, published an article that it rewrote from the *Boston Advertiser*:

"The Wentworth at Newcastle which has just been purchased by Messers. F. W. Hilton and Frank Jones, and will be opened July 1st, is destined to take the lead among those beautiful semi-seaside resorts in which the New England coast abounds. Under the enterprising and generous management of Mr. Hilton, whose success at the Rockingham entitles him to all praise, there is every prospect of a brilliant future for this charmingly situated hotel. Its spacious piazzas command views of the Isles of Shoals, the White Mountains, Portsmouth, and the beautiful surrounding country, while in its interior's details no expense has been spared to give every comfort that the most exacting guest could desire. The Hon. Frank Jones, who is associated with Mr. Hilton in this promising undertaking, is a prince of good fellows, and a man of rare tact and business ability; and, with two such favorites at the helm, the Wentworth is bound to sail in smooth waters from the opening day." The basic theme of the Jones era at the Wentworth can be summed up really in two words: constant change. Before the 1879 season even started, the *Chronicle* was hailing the improvements under way:

"One of the features of the new management of the Wentworth house in New Castle will be the increased comfort and convenience of the travellers who visit that historic spot. Messers. F. W. Hilton & Co. have purchased one of the celebrated coaches built by the Abbott Downing Coach Co. of Concord . . . This coach will carry twenty passengers, and is one of the finest ever turned out by the celebrated coach builders. . . ."

One of the new owners' most urgent problems was finding water. They were busy installing bathrooms with water closets, and they needed plenty of water. The Fletcher cottage and land nearby was purchased and a well driven.

It should be said that at this time, the Wentworth didn't have individual bathrooms, there were only two or three to the floor. A later owner, Harry Beckwith, improved on that to a large degree. Cologne was a handy substitute for a shower a century ago.

Before the summer of 1879 was spent, plans were already in progress to expand the westerly end of the hotel by 80 feet. The addition was "to be carried up three stories and topped with a French roof. The house thus enlarged will have a front of 160 feet, with an ell of 140 feet, and room for 300 guests, its present capacity being 170. In the rear of the hotel, a dam has been run across at a cost of $1200, making a large, safe salt water pond for bathing, or the cruising of an inexperienced boat sailer." Pre-fabbed in Waterville, Maine, the frame for the addition was brought by water and was being put in place in October. Additionally, major changes were taking place in the outside surroundings of the hotel. The grade from the bridge was eased; ledge was blasted away; trees judiciously cut away to improve the view.

All of this was hailed by the *Chronicle* which "was glad to know that the great expectations of those who have long desired to see a well-appointed place of resort at this point, which could become second to none in this region." For the next hundred years, the Wentworth lived up to the *Chronicle* prophecy. Today, it is the sole survivor of its kind on the coast north of Boston, albeit the past few years it has been going through a period of genteel rest, like a beautiful old lady in a nursing home. But that won't be so much longer, the old girl is soon either going to be rejuvenated or torn down. In its July issue, 1880, the *Granite State Monthly* published a lengthy article describing the Wentworth and its environs, but its length prohibits republication here. In January, 1880, the *Journal* estimated more than $100,000 had been spent in improving the Wentworth, yet the water problem was still unsolved. That summer Frank Jones contracted with the Portsmouth Aqueduct Company to supply the hotel with water. A two-inch surface pipe was laid from the main at Richards avenue, cross country to the Wentworth-Coolidge place at Little Harbor, thence across to the hotel.

For the edification of the guests, Hilton had seven big searchlights mounted around the hotel, which, as a journalistic wag pointed out did nothing to encourage a little bit of billing and cooing. Entertainment was constantly provided. There were hops, which became so popular that non-guests had to be banned.

More expansion was in order for the 1881 season, and the water line from Richards avenue still wasn't the answer to that problem, so a deeper well was driven, which, at a depth of 250 feet, began producing 2,500 barrels a day. In January, 1882, Frank W. Hilton died. In large part, his early death was due to his war-time service in the Union army. To replace him, Frank Jones brought in George F. Thompson, a scion of a North Country hotel family. Actually, the transition from Hilton to Thompson involved no philosophical changes; after all, the policies and philosophies of the Wentworth were those of the owner, Frank Jones.

Everything that could be done to make the Wentworth an independent operation was done. Jones created an ice pond on the Wentworth road, about opposite BG's Boat House and stored the ice in a building on the site. A couple of hundred yards up the road there is today, an Ice House Restaurant. The Wentworth had its own farm.

Each year a crop of big, fat hogs, not the human kind, but porcine, would be shipped to the Boston market. A truck garden supplied the hotel tables. In the summer of 1882, the Wentworth had its first visit from a president of the United States. Chester A. Arthur of New York, a former colleague of Jones in the U.S. House, had become chief executive after the death of James Garfield from an assassin's bullet. Jones spared nothing to make the president's visit a personal triumph. Jones let Manager Thompson do the honors during a breakfast at the Wentworth, greeting the President at the Rockingham, a little later. Jones offered Arthur, a building lot in the vicinity of the Wentworth, if so desired.

More expansion plans were put forward in the fall of 1882, but never executed in full, although there were plenty of changes and improvements. In 1883, maples were planted along Wentworth road and one or two of them may still be living. Those who know the Wentworth only as a mammoth structure, glistening white in the noon-day sun, will find it hard to believe that in 1883 it had red roofs, and the "body of the house Nile green, while the trimmings will be darker shades." To show there's nothing new in the world, Manager Thompson went to Boston in the spring of 1884 to seek convention business, a practice followed by James B. and Margaret Smith during their heyday as owners of the hotel.

While it never achieved the stature of Newport, R.I., the Wentworth for years staged tennis tournaments that attracted class players. And Proprietor Smith also promoted tennis tournaments during the seasons after World War II.

In January, 1886, George Thompson resigned due to illness, and Jones named William K. Hill to the joint posts of managing the Rockingham and the Wentworth. However, the change again didn't change the manner in which the Wentworth did business. Frank Jones was still on hand.

The seasons came and went. In 1898, Jones finally solved the water problem. The city now owned the old Portsmouth Aqueduct system, and Jones made arrangements to bring an eight-inch main across Little Harbor to the hotel. To this day, the hotel and properties along Wentworth road in New Castle pay their water bills to Portsmouth. Also in 1898, the final additions to the main building were completed. They were tacked on to the eastern end by the means of a bridge. There were two units and the inner one, for a time, featured a restaurant on its top floor.

For a season or two, Harvard College, a football power in the 1890s, had its eleven in summer training and living in the hotel. If nothing else, the football players must have made the place attractive for the summer damsels. Another attraction created in the late 1890s was the golf course. For years it was a nine-hole affair, but in the Smith era it was expanded to the present eighteen holes. Jones added the final portions of the main building in 1898, and his work was nearing completion.

In October, 1902, at the age of 70, Frank Jones died and an era ended. To protect the hotels, Rockingham and Wentworth, he set up a trust fund in which the trustees were enjoined to manage the hotels as "I would if alive." That little clause was put to the test in 1905 when the chief trustee, Calvin Page, wrote to President Theodore Roosevelt offering to host the delegates to the up-coming Russo-Japanese Peace Conference. Roosevelt accepted the offer, and the representatives of the two warring powers were housed at the Wentworth for a month while carrying on peace deliberations at the Portsmouth Navy Yard. Space prohibits getting into the treaty negotiations. Those who wish to read a sensitive analysis can study Peter E. Randall's *There Are No Victors Here*.

The trustees managed the hotels until 1907. On May 2, Frank C. Hall took over management of the Wentworth and the new owners, after all the front men stepped aside, were W. J. McDonald and Loren Towle, but the deeds are hard to follow. Ultimately and briefly, Towle was the owner. For the first time since Jones's day, the Wentworth and Rockingham were owned by different people. More than 40 years later, the Smiths brought them back together.

Towle didn't hold on for even a year. He sold the Wentworth to Albert H. Shaw and Harry H. Priest. The latter became the active front man and promoter. The way news of the Wentworth was played, after the Peace Conference, makes it appear that the hotel was enjoying a jowly middle age. Nothing had more effect on the luxury resort hotel of 80 years ago than the coming of the automobile. From the start, it was the custom for summer urbanites to arrive at their hotel in June, complete with steamer trunks full of clothing; maids, valets, etc.

But the automobile gave the summer visitor a mobility he had never enjoyed before. He could come to the Wentworth, stay for awhile, and then move on to the Mount Washington or the Balsams. The 1910 season was fantastic, but the optimism for 1911 was tempered by bad weather. The seasons moved along and in 1914 the world came apart as the European nations went at each other's throats. The guests were enjoying a Saturday night hop when Europe went to war.

When the conflict was over, the world had changed. But there was still some shooting at the Wentworth. Manager Priest hired Annie Oakley to teach marksmanship and give exhibitions, down near the present ninth tee. In 1919, a group, headed by Harry H. Beckwith, acquired the Wentworth. During his regime, Harry Beckwith built the famous Ship, and he continued operations until the hotel was bought by the Smiths. A high moment in the Beckwith regime at the Hotel Wentworth came in the summer of 1932. Franklin Delano Roosevelt, Democratic nominee to the presidency, anchored his yacht in front of the Wentworth, and in the morning came ashore. Before going into Portsmouth to open his campaign for the White House, Roosevelt chatted with the assembled guests for a bit and said that he had stayed in the Wentworth years before. The hotel was closed during the days of World War II, but had re-opened by the time the Smiths bought it for $125,000 in 1946.

The saga of the Smith ownership could run even longer than the present text. It has to be said that there was but one theme during their ownership: constant change. They constantly poured money back into the operation. Albeit, they made no structural changes, but there were many improvements. Oddly, one of the great highlights of the Smith ownership came in the summer of 1948, two years after they bought it.

That was the National Governors Conference, which will never be forgotten by those who covered it for their newspapers. After all, the next president of the United States was present. Everyone "knew" that Thomas E. Dewey, governor of New York, would wipe the deck with Harry S Truman—everyone but Harry S Truman, that is. The Smiths lengthened the season, the traditional June opening was moved up to May, with emphasis on convention bookings; and the closing ran well into October, again with emphasis on conventions.

In a tragic fire, Fast Day, 1969, the Wentworth's carriage barn and dormitory were destroyed, with death for one employee. The Smiths tried in vain during their ownership to get town approval of expansion plans, but ran into opposition that had the firmness of a stone wall. Finally, as the time must come to all, the Smiths decided to abdicate, and they sold to Pacific Park Corporation, a Swiss firm, in November, 1980, reportedly for $5.8 million. The Swiss firm managed the Wentworth-by-the-Sea for only a season, then shutting it down, and stripping it of furnishings, etc. In a multi-faceted operation, the Wentworth property was acquired by a syndicate—Great Island Trust, which erected a dozen condominiums in the grove east of the hotel. Then it came into the hands of Henley Corporation, one of Michael Dingman's management firms.

The passer-by today sees squadrons of private yachts floating in the marina, and on tap are heady plans for the future of the hotel, getting it ready for the 21st Century. The question is sometimes asked: What would Frank Jones think about all the changes in his proud old hotel?

Frank Jones was a pragmatic man, ever ready to make changes in the product he was marketing—the Wentworth-by-the-Sea. It's the writer's belief that he would have long since taken steps towards modernization.

A Visiting Lord

For months now, the old Hotel Wentworth has been a subject of intense interest, and, if there were sainthood for hostelries, the ancient wooden pile would have long since borne a halo. Although most of its former grandeur now fills the dreams of visionaries, occasionally a humorous story can be told about its more than a century as a stage for the human comedy.

Back in 1917, when the war in Europe was nearing the end of its third bloody year, and the United States was slowly flexing its military muscle to join in, the Wentworth was, of course, crowded with the elegant people from far and near that were its seasonal life. In large part, the bejeweled residents were season-long guests. Many of them came in their chauffeured touring cars; the automobile still lacked the self-starter mechanism that put America on the road some years later.

So the Wentworth's guests clawed their ways to favorite chairs on the spacious veranda, and eagerly awaited some tidbit of gossip that would fill the emptiness of their days. In mid-July, a distinguished gentleman, accompanied by two elegantly gowned ladies, signed the hotel's register. He scribbled "Lord and Lady Harmsworth" and "Lady Hart, London" in the book. The accent he used in his conversation confirmed that the trio were indeed English, and the buzz in the carpeted halls became as near to an uproar as the dignity of the place would stand.

Now these Wentworth guests may have been dilettantes, but they knew their social registers, both here and in England, and they well knew that Lord Northcliffe, the newspaper tycoon, had been Alfred Harmsworth before being elevated to the peerage. And it was easy for the Wentworth guests to assume that the good lord was traveling under a bit of incognito so he wouldn't be annoyed by mere people. Naturally, those guests who had moved in early on the lion were eager in extending luncheon invitations, but about that time a serpent, in the form of a newspaper reporter, crept into the Wentworth's Garden of Eden.

The reporter let it be known that he was acquainted with the kin of Northcliffe's, and so was admitted to a luncheon circle where "Lord Harmsworth" was discoursing on his role at the Battle of the Marne and recent conference with President Wilson. When the reporter began asking questions about the Harmsworth family, the "Lord" suddenly remembered a pressing engagement and left the hotel. Later a query to the British embassy in Washington brought a reply:

"Lord Northcliffe, formerly Alfred Harmsworth, not in your part of the country. Know nothing of any Lord and Lady Harmsworth."

Anyway, the lord and his ladies had one of the best lunches the famed Wentworth could provide, and the people they stiffed could well afford it. When the "I told you so's" subsided, the guests went back to their usual rounds of gossip, counting their money, golf, tennis, cards, and having the famed Annie Oakley teach them how to shoot rifles in case the Germans invaded Rye.

Wentworth Treasure

Few things fire human imagination more quickly than the two words "buried treasure." Everyone has heard of the hole that's been dug on an island off Nova Scotia more than 100 feet deep in a vain search, so far, for a buried pirate hoard. About 30 years ago, the writer was in a small party, under the leadership of the late Lyman D. Rutledge, that went out to the Isles of Shoals simply to check out a rumor of buried treasure.

And when you think of the ancient history of this region, there's plenty of cause to think Spanish doubloons may be turned up somewhere along the coast. However, there are none who can remember a treasure hunt that went on between the Little Harbor Bridge, near the Wentworth Hotel, and the cottage of Charles E. Campbell.

This story began to unfold in October, 1882, when the *Portsmouth Journal* reported that "a party of Boston men have had a diver at work at Newcastle, searching for alleged treasures in the bed of the river lying nearly midway between the bridge leading to the Wentworth, and the island on which is located the Charles E. Campbell cottage." In its first account, the *Journal* said the searchers in mud of the Little Harbor were supposedly being guided "by revelations made in a document in their possession, over one hundred years old, and whose authenticity is undoubted, the full contents of which the holders decline to disclose.

"The work of diving for the expected 'fortune' has been in quiet progress, off and on for several months, and is to be continued indefinitely, but the results thus far of the investigations at the bottom, are kept a profound secret."

The next week the *Journal* reported that another party of Boston men were working in the mud in the channel, seeking the treasure. This group was thought to be a crowd of claim jumpers. More detail was forthcoming the next week:

". . . On Wednesday of the present week, the parties interested made a contract in this city with Mr. Thomas Simonds, the well known dredger, to begin operations immediately at the spot designated, and he was expected to arrive on Thursday at Newcastle, with the dredges and scows from the Chain Bridge near Amesbury, where he has lately been engaged in government work. It has now been divulged that the first revelations concerning this alleged wealth, came from an aged resident of Newcastle, who died some years ago, but who, previous to his death, stated that a document would be found in the lining of one of his vests, giving particulars concerning the burial and location of three chests containing gold, a barrel filled with silver, and a box containing coins.

"This paper was found as stated, and carefully preserved, but the information it contained had for various reasons been kept quiet until now. One of the individuals concerned in bringing to light, if possible, this treasure, states to the Journal representative, that several mineral and other tests have lately been applied by experts to the place designated, every one of which has 'marked' exactly the same spot, and as the company interested have plenty of means at their disposal the work will, he says, be vigorously prosecuted, as each member is confident of finding something rich.

"It is needless to say that the work which now begins under the direction of Mr. Simonds, will be watched with considerable interest by outsiders, and it is already hinted that if anything of real value is brought to light, law suits will result in order to determine on whose land or shore the prize was buried, and hence to whom it belongs."

Apparently the treasure seekers ended their quest for the season with the onslaught of winter, and nothing more about them was reported until May 5, 1883, when it was said that they had resumed operations. They brought down from Belfast, Me., a professional dowser, whose divining rod played fantastic tricks over the same spot that other diviners had found. With that the Boston group was ready to push operations through the summer. If they found anything that summer, it was a better kept secret than operations by the CIA.

Not until September, 1884, was the buried treasure again discussed in the newspapers. At that time, the *Journal* quoted an article that had appeared in the *New York Mail*, and it provided the story behind the story of the treasure: "There has been more or less gossip for a long time in reference to a fabulous amount of money said to be buried in New Castle, Little Harbor. The story of the hidden treasure has, perhaps, for its foundation some facts; at least there are those who accept the visionary tale about buried treasure on our shore, and at different times within the past three years a systematic search for the still unfound gold has been instituted. Those most directly interested in the affair are very reticent when interrogated relative to the story. It is affirmed that many years ago a wealthy clergyman set sail from England, bringing along a large sum of money, which he proposed, as became his benevolent nature, to use in benefitting our forefathers in the name of his Creator.

"Those on board the vessel in which he embarked learned of the wealth on board, and resolved to have control of it. To attain this end the clergyman was forcibly put off the vessel and placed upon one of the Isles of Shoals, and bearing with him for companionship a goat. The crew sailed away, but on account of a severe storm was obliged to put into Little Harbor. How, why or when the gold was buried, or by whom, are points not made clear in the narrative as told to your correspondent. A chart showing the locality of the yet unearthed gold fell into the hands of a school teacher, who, while on a journey, was taken sick, and sought the hospitality of a family in a Maine town. His sickness proved a fatal one, and just before dying he informed his kind friends that he could only repay their kindness by presenting them with a chart which would indicate where much wealth was concealed, and stated that the chart was sewed up in the lining of his vest.

"The party who is now engaged in the search is A.J. Griffin, of Melrose. By marrying into the family, he came into possession of the chart in question, which located the money at one and a half miles below Portsmouth, on the west side of Newcastle Island, 25 rods below the bridge, 20 rods below Black Point at low water, where there is a rock 3 x 4 feet, with the formation of a windowsill on top; on the east side is a barrel of silver and on the west three chests of gold. There are two objects which the chart specifies that cannot be found, namely; the 3 x 4 foot rock and the bridge spoken of. At the supposed spot where the chests and barrel are submerged, an excavation has been made 16 feet deep and 50 feet square. Divining rods have been used, which have only served to add to the uncertainty of the situation; but the holder of the chart is not discouraged, and firmly believes that the money is there.

"Further efforts will soon be made to unearth it. Judging from the amount of expense already incurred, the gold and silver will be eaten up in attempts to obtain it, if the effort is much longer continued."

Thanks to the efforts of the Reference Desk at the Portsmouth Public Library, it has been learned that A. J. Griffin was Dr. Alvah J. Griffin, a physician practicing in Melrose in 1885. Unfortunately, that doesn't give a clue as to where he was able to get the funding for such extended searches of the mucky bottom at Little Harbor. And that leads to a befuddling question:

Given that the crew who stole the minister's money wanted a handy repository for the same, would such people plant it where the tide ebbs and flows twice in 24 hours? It would seem more rational for the treasure to have been buried on the beach between the bridge and Campbell's cottage.

Now, it must be understood that the present bridge doesn't come into play. The old abutments ran more off the late Walter Dunfey's Blunt Island, and there were at least three bridges preceding the present. Anyway, in April, 1886, it was reported that several men were "poking around" on the river side, near the Wentworth Bridge, Little Harbor.

It will be noted that always the reference is upriver of the bridge. Over the past year or two the former Great Island Trust spent oodles of money blasting and dredging out a channel on the ocean side of the bridge. Today the only treasure to be found from that effort, is the fleet of costly yachts that float at the slips in the new marina. Again in 1900, it was reported that "a stranger has been working for two or three days past with a divining rod in the vicinity of the Wentworth House bridge. Hope he will 'locate' it, particularly if it is the long-lost treasure of Capt. Kidd. A few years ago parties were in the same vicinity on a like divining, and this man was of the same company."

Again, if the "treasure" was ever found, it's one of the best-kept secrets of the Seacoast. Perhaps it's time for some other "investors" to have a shot at finding it. All they have to lose is money.

XVIII *More Little Tales Now Told*

OVER THE COURSE OF PORTSMOUTH'S NEARLY FOUR CENTURIES, many wonderful people have walked the streets of the old town. Yet, no matter what the era in which they lived, sainthood shouldn't be bestowed upon them, as so many latter-day revisionists try to do. This chapter will include a few anecdotal yarns about people from all walks of life and generations. Most of the items have never before appeared in public print, for the good reason that there's really nothing historic about them, but they do, in their way, offer glimpses of life here over the years. Some of them are ribald, some pathetic, and others simply remind us that human beings are human beings no matter when they live.

Lord Nelson Tobacco

A few years ago, back when Market Square had a character and atmosphere all its own, Morris "Mike" Levy, a retired shipyarder, dropped in on his friend, Harold Silverman, then proprietor of the Federal Cigar Store, and known to a small circle of acquaintances as the "Sage of Market Square." "The Sage" was mixing up some concoction of pipe tobacco—a bit of this and a bit of that—his own creation, and he asked "Mike" what he should name it.

"What's in it?" queried Levy.

"Mostly light English tobacco," Silverman replied.

"Why don't you call it 'Lord Nelson'," Levy suggested. "He's one of the best-known Englishmen."

Silverman was delighted with the idea. A few days later, Levy again called at Federal Cigar, as was his wont, and Silverman said:

"You know that Lord Nelson tobacco I mixed up the other day?"

"Yeah, why?"

"Well, a guy came in here yesterday and said he wanted to try something new in pipe tobacco, so I suggested he try the Lord Nelson.

"And he said, 'Naw. I tried that two years ago, and it was lousy'."

A Trip to Heaven

The late Andrew Jarvis, whose many years on Market Square had made him dean of the local restaurateurs, used to enjoy needling Sammy Entin, a tailor with quarters in the old Glebe Building, just south of the North Church.

One day Andrew was up to his usual game with Sam when the little tailor turned the tables on him:

"Andrew, I had the most beautiful dream last night. I dreamt that I had died and went to Heaven."

"What was it like up there?" Jarvis asked.

"Oh, it's a beautiful place. I walked around and enjoyed it."

"Did you see any Greeks while you were up there?"

"Andrew, I have to tell you the truth. I didn't look in the kitchen."

A Big Man in Oil

The late U.S. Sen. Tom McIntyre used to delight in telling this little story about his good friend and colleague, the late Norris Cotton, a long entrenched and uninhibited Republican.

In 1968, Senator Cotton faced acrimonious opposition in his bid to return to his Senate seat from Gov. John W. King, the state's foremost Democratic office-holder. Among the charges hurled at Cotton by King was one that labeled Cotton as "the tool of the oil interests." Nevertheless, being a Republican in New Hampshire meant Cotton was re-elected.

Some months after the election, a bill came into the Senate which was favorable to the oil interests. McIntyre was down in the well of the Senate when he heard a stenatorian voice:

"Tom!"

Knowing the voice, McIntyre turned to look at him, and Cotton said, "Tom, you remember when Governor King said I was 'the tool of the oil interests'?"

McIntyre said that he did.

"Well, Tom, I'm about to prove that Governor King was right," and Cotton cast his vote in favor of the oil bill.

Only in Golf

For this little tale of Portsmouth a generation ago, we turn to Francis "Minnie" Regan, a former vice president of the First National Bank. Regan starts his story off by reminding his listeners that both he and his cousin, "Larry" Regan, were in their youth, a couple of good Catholic boys who had been taught that "lying is a sin, and when you get to Heaven they won't let you in."

So it happened that the Regan cousins were caddying at the "Old Portsmouth Country Club," which, after three decades of U.S. Air Force modifications and management, is the Pease Country Club, and is again under civilian control. Be that as it may, on the day in question, Larry Regan was carrying for the late estimable A. B. Duncan, and it's Minnie's recollection that his principal was the late Harry Winebaum, the great merchandiser of news journals. Whatever—the duo was playing the tenth hole, still a par three through the woods on either side.

Finally, the moment of truth arrived. The players holed out. A. B. Duncan's opponent asked, "What did you have there, A. B.?" Now, let it be understood that A. B. Duncan was noted for years in Portsmouth for his integrity as a dealer in jewelry (in the shop where Alie's is today); he had also generated some notoriety for his forgetfulness on the golf course—a fault not uncommon in golfers. After a moment of deep thought, Duncan admitted to having used five strokes on the par three. His opponent voiced some skepticism. Finally, in desperation, Duncan turned to his caddy, Larry Regan, and asked, "Son, how many shots did I take?"

The honest Catholic boy, visions of hell-fire racing through his mind, said, with tears streaming down his cheeks, "Mr. Duncan, you had seven." Then young Regan broke and ran for the caddy shack as though Lucifer himself was in hot pursuit.

How to Lose a Customer

Portsmouth has never lacked for those on the alert to make a buck, and may it always be so. One of the faster operators in the mid-20th Century was the late Ira A. Brown, a man of many parts, and one who played them all to the full. More than half a century ago, he was the city's dealer in Packard automobiles. In its time, the Packard was the equivalent of a present-day Lincoln Continental. Brown's place of business was on old Vaughan street, to the west of where the Portsmouth Stone is now located. Later it became Seybolt's.

Judge Thomas H. Simes, a legal light of no dimness, bought a Packard from Brown. The car developed the usual new-car symptoms, and the judge took it back to dealer Brown, ever willing to listen to a customer.

"Judge," said Brown, "you'll have to leave the car for us to work on it, and we will fix it. I promise."

"But when can I get it back? I want to go to the mountains this weekend."

"Well, judge, it's Friday, and we can't get to it until next week."

Unhappy, but reconciled to his fate, Judge Simes made other arrangements and went off on his trip to the White Mountains. Riding down through Crawford Notch on Sunday afternoon, the judge was startled to see a familiar-looking Packard at the famed Willey's Slide. Sure enough, it was the judge's Packard, with a beaming Ira Brown at the wheel, steering a group of leaf-peepers through the mountains.

It ended a once happy business association.

Under Her Bed

One of Portsmouth's most eminent historians and personalities used to tell this little story about herself.

Former Portsmouth Librarian Dorothy M. Vaughan, L.L.D., has devoted her long life to research in local history and into the lives of those who lived here long ago.

An oft-used source of such information for her is Charles W.

Brewster's *Rambles About Portsmouth*, a two-volume collection of essays about the "Old Town By the Sea." On the occasion of one of her talks before a local group, Miss Vaughan was asked how she was able to amass so much information.

Without thinking of any other implication, Miss Vaughan replied, "I keep Brewster under my bed." Her answer prompted laughter in which she joined.

A couple of years later, Miss Vaughan was introduced to a woman who said, "Oh, I know her. She's the lady who keeps Brewster under her bed."

Business Is Business

Some years ago, the bar of the old Rockingham Hotel was a hangout for Portsmouth sports.

Also patronizing the premises at times were various ladies of the night. On one occasion a sport became involved with one of the delightful creatures. Finally, he proposed that they adjourn to a pad he maintained in an area motel. Because that was part of her business, the lady acquiesced.

Once in this haven of sybaritic luxury, the professional person suddenly sensed her escort wasn't fully aware of the commercial aspects of the liaison. Before matters went any further forward, she said, "You know this is going to cost you $100?"

With quick wit, the sport asked:

"Is that for the night, or for the season?"

The professional person herself told the story, but didn't say how it came out.

Only in the Army

From the military world comes the following:

During World War II, soldiers of the 22nd Coast Artillery manned the Harbor Defenses of Portsmouth. Some units of the 22nd were stationed at Ft. Foster, across the harbor on Gerrish Island in Kittery Point, Maine. One dreary, freezing, wet, sleeting night, a soldier on sentry duty at Ft. Foster, while walking his post in a military manner, as prescribed by the drill book, slipped and fell. As he did so, his M-1 rifle discharged. This brought the Officer of the Day out of the warmth and security of the BOQ to look into the matter. Finding the sentry okay, other than the scrapes and bruises attendant on such a fall, the O.D. returned to his quarters. The telephone rang. On the other end was a familiar irascible voice demanding to know:

"What in hell is going on over there?"

It was the major commanding the Harbor Entrance Control Point at Ft. Stark in New Castle. The wind, unfortunately, was out east, and the major heard the rifle shot.

The Ft. Foster O.D. explained that it was an accidental discharge of a rifle brought about by a fall on ice; and then listened to acerbic comments on his mental competency from the major sitting in the warm, dry safety of the HECP, and went back to bed.

The next day, the orders issuing from the 22nd C.A. headquarters at Camp Langdon dictated:

"There will be no more accidental discharges of firearms in the Portsmouth Harbor Defenses."

Horse Deal

A man living in Portsmouth's North End, back in the days when it was a community, before the blitz of Urban Renewal, owned a horse and a wagon with which he traveled around the city selling garden produce.

Time went along, and the faithful equine went blind, but was still capable of work. However, the North Ender decided to sell the animal, and soon found a willing purchaser. Within a day or two the buyer discovered he had bought a blind horse. In outrage, he went after the seller, and their meeting resulted in fisticuffs, and the seller was taken to court.

Judge Ernest Guptill, appointed to the Municipal Court in 1915, was presiding. For various reasons, Guptill wanted to make the case as easy as possible on the accused.

So he asked sympathetically, "Well now, you didn't know the horse was blind, did you?" His hope was that the defendant would answer, "No, your honor!"

But the judge had little choice but to find the man guilty when he answered, "I sold the horse to work, not to read."

The Doctor

A generation or so ago, a convivial group of Portsmouth residents had the practice of gathering at J. L. O. Coleman's antique shop on outer Market street for a quiet tipple or two. The shop stood about where the scales for Granite State Minerals are now located. It was a long, narrow building that has since disappeared.

It was the custom of the group, each having his own special nickname, to have their "ailments" prescribed by "The Doctor," who was, in real life, Clarence E. Montgomery, a piano tuner. His habit of carrying a little black bag containing the tools of his trade had earned him the sobriquet. Having written out prescriptions for each of his patients, "The Doctor" would often repair to Dr. Green's, as the local liquor stores were often called in those days, and get them filled by the "druggist" on duty.

When the patients had completed the first dosage of the prescriptions, a candle was lit and stuck in an empty bottle. With the completion of the second round, a second candle was lit. A third round of treatment resulted in a third candle, and when consumed, the members adjourned to Ham's restaurant on High street for dinner.

Soft Sell

In the dear dead days beyond recall, as the trite saying goes, Portsmouth merchants were of a different breed than the modern go-getters. Not for that older generation was the hustle of the market place, but rather a more leisurely approach. Nothing illustrates the point better than an anecdote about the James F. Borthwick Co., once an ornament to Market street.

A shipment of feminine under-fripperies came into the store, and, despite being modestly displayed, attracted much attention —Portsmouth women have always liked to be in touch with the swinging world south of Rye. So many sales were generated that one of the sales people felt it necessary to approach Mr. Borthwick to tell him of the success.

The merchant thought a moment and then said, "I think we'd better slow things down. If we don't, I'll have to reorder very soon."

No Man's a Hero to His Wife

One of the literati who became infatuated with the Piscataqua Basin was William Dean Howells. Howells became a noted journalist, novelist and pundit, who has belatedly, been enjoying a mild renaissance. He was native of Ashtabula, Ohio, a town New York Central Railroad express trains used to run through—non stop.

But Howells persevered. In the latter part of the 19th Century, he became the senior literary figure in Kittery Point, a neighborhood of no great physical dimensions, but plenty of room for a bit of debate with his wife. They argued whether "lunch" or "luncheon" was correct usage.

Howells decided "lunch" was preferred and went to a reference book to sustain his point. Triumphantly, he returned to announce he was correct.

Mrs. Howells asked who wrote the reference cited, and Howells proudly replied, "William Dean Howells."

"But he's no authority, " opinioned Mrs. Howells sweetly.

Rip Van Winkle

Quite truthfully the following anecdote is borrowed in full from the *Portsmouth Herald* of February 28, 1905.

In the years before the Civil War, a Portsmouth native resided in Providence, R.I. In that community he operated a small, neighborhood shop—"Mom and Pop" as it would be called today.

Time and other vicissitudes of fortune crept up on William Plaisted, and he retreated to the place of his birth. Finally, in 1905, at the age of 90, he came to realize that various people in Rhode Island still owed him money. So, one day in February, he climbed on a train at Portsmouth Depot, and went to Providence to collect his due bills. The *Boston Evening Record* reported what happened:

"When he landed in the town, he was struck with the changes which confronted him. . . . After all, he hadn't been in the town in 40 years. The poor old man wandered on and on, finally went into a drug store, sat down and fell asleep. The police were called and he quite lucidly explained to them why he was there, and named his debtors. Sadly, most of them had been dead for years, many having been prominent citizens."

While at the police station, Plaisted regaled his hearers with tales of Indians who had their camps on Sagamore Creek and over in Kittery only 40 years before. The Providence police put him on a train back to Portsmouth. William Plaisted died Nov. 30, 1906, at the age of 92.

Not a Reference

Our majestic and heavily over-membered State Legislature takes itself and its doings quite seriously.

And considering the burdens it often inflicts on the long-suffering property taxpayers, it really should.

One day in 1877, a federal judge offered a view that probably wouldn't be appreciated by today's legislators any more than the members of the General Court did when the following was published on May 26 by the *Portsmouth Journal*.

During a trial in the old court house, the former federal building on Pleasant Street, a lawyer was trying to establish that because his client had been a member of the State Legislature, he was a man of some probity.

The judge opinioned that such a line of reasoning was gratuitous and not germane to the matter in hand. The lawyer persisted:

"But I think, Your Honor, it is evidence of respectability to have been a member of the Legislature of this state."

To which, His Honor replied:

"Hm! Well, I have my doubts about that!"

Astutely, the lawyer yielded:

"I will not press the point, Your Honor," while the assemblage enjoyed this exchange.

XIX Some Portsmouth Navy Yard Yarns

Ship Yard Strike

A THREE-WEEK STRIKE at the Portsmouth Naval Shipyard would be hard to imagine today, yet there was one nearly 150 years ago. The story is one of those weird convolutions that only federal officials, left to their own devices, can get themselves into.

In November, 1854, the Portsmouth Navy Yard was running in full thrust to meet the demand for new vessels, created by the return of aging warships from overseas. Articles in the Nov. 24 issue of the *Chronicle* dwelt on the progress of construction of the *USS Santee* and the *USS Franklin*. Yet there was a worm even in that garden of military preparedness. Word of it came on Dec. 2, in the *Chronicle*. It said:

"A STRIKE—We learn that on Friday morning the ship carpenters and blacksmiths employed on the Navy Yard near this city were informed that their wages from that time would be cut down twenty-five cents per day, leaving the ship-carpenters $2 per day and the blacksmiths about the same. When the roll was called after dinner, not one carpenter answered; and it was said that all the blacksmiths were to quit last night. The carpenters are to hold a meeting to consider the matter this forenoon, at 10 o'clock, at Mr. Hayes' on the Foreside."

Apparently that little insurrection was quelled. The *Chronicle* said on Dec. 4 that the strikers had gone back to work, at their old rates, "satisfactory evidence being presented to the Commodore, that their wages were no higher than was paid in private yards. The pay-roll of the yard remains about 750 names." The ship carpenters had met on Dec. 2 in Hayes' Hall, Kittery, and had adopted the following resolutions:

"Resolved 1st that we consider the reduction in our pay unjust and uncalled for, and we will not submit to it.

"Resolved 2d that we view with contempt the conduct of those who continued to work.

"Resolved 3d we render thanks to the brother mechanics not employed at the Navy Yard, for their sympathy and efficient aid in our behalf.

"Voted to choose a committee to inquire into the expedience of establishing a rate of wages for the future and report to a subsequent meeting; and Charles Simpson, Joseph Williams and Elisha Clough were chosen.

"Voted to choose a committee to wait on the Naval Constructor and inform him that we would resume work at 1 o'clock p.m. at our former rate of pay as proposed by him. R.C. Newsom, T. Shapley and J. Remick were chosen.

"Voted that the secretary cause the proceedings of this meeting to be published in the Portsmouth N.H. papers."

For a daily paper the *Chronicle* seemed a step or two behind the times. The shipyarders had to buy an ad on Dec. 8 to straighten out one reportorial error:

"The strike at the Navy Yard—The mechanics at the Navy Yard who remonstrated against having their wages reduced, a few days since, wish to correct a misstatement made in your editorial columns that next morning after they left work and repeated by 'Trim, Jr.' in a letter published in the *Saco Democrat*. The statement in both instances was that when the afternoon-roll was called, not a man of those branches whose wages were reduced, appeared; but there were a few who did go to work, against the wish of the great majority—and whose conduct in so doing was strongly censured by the meeting after-wards. Their names were Charles Williams, Wm. W. Brooks, Alpheus Brooks and Ira Delano."

Then the Navy's bureaucracy compounded the on-going stupidity:

"We understand that orders have been received at the Portsmouth Navy Yard, to discharge all those persons who were publicly mentioned by name in the proceedings, as officiating at the late meeting held by the carpenters after their late strike. We are informed that, after the reading of the above order at the muster on Tuesday afternoon, most of the carpenters declined to answer to their names at the calling of the role; and that a meeting was held to consider the matter. At this meeting a committee was appointed to wait upon the Commandant and inform him of the reason for their declining to answer, viz, the issuing of the above order."

Pressure built up on the command function at the Navy Yard, and the carpenters were restored to their jobs and wage structure. But the naval officers, sailing with a "damn the torpedoes" attitude, fired the men whose names had been listed as participating in the meeting. The *Chronicle* said on December 14:

"This was followed by another strike on Tuesday, which we noticed on Wednesday morning. We now learn from the *Messenger*, that the discharge of these men for such a cause aroused the indignation of their fellow workmen, who have generally ceased from their labor on the yard, and refused to return until the proscribed men are restored. They held a meeting Wednesday morning, which was participated in by the blacksmiths and joiners, and a committee of one of each trade—Chas. W. Stimson, Theodore F. Rowe and Acanthus Young, was appointed to repair to Washington to ask justice at the hands of the Secretary of the Navy."

On Dec. 19 the *Chronicle* reported that the committee sent to Washington "to settle their difficulties, have returned, and reported to their constituents on Tuesday afternoon (Dec. 19). The men will probably return to their work soon, and all difficulties will be removed." On Dec. 23, the *Chronicle* heralded the end of the strike. Apparently the local committee interviewed the naval secretary, and was assured that if the case had been presented to him, he would have resolved it.

"At a meeting of mechanics held at Hayes' Hall to hear the report of Messrs. Young, Stimson and Rowe, Committee to represent their grievances at Washington. M.P. Post called the meeting to order and James Trefethen was chosen Secretary, pro tem. The committee then made their report which was accepted.

"Voted, that the former committee on resolutions be requested to draft a new set of resolutions which were subsequently reported as follows, and unanimously adopted:

"Whereas being fully convinced from the report of the committee from Washington, that had the mechanics continued at work, and represented their case to the Secretary of the Navy, that justice would have been done them in the premises therefore.

"Resolved that we, having full confidence in the Secretary of the Navy, should have submitted our case to his hands.

"Resolved that the thanks of this meeting be tendered to Messers. Kittredge and Hibbard, members of Congress from New Hampshire, for their kind interest on our behalf.

"Resolved that the thanks of this meeting be tendered to the committee to Washington for their faithful services.

"Resolved that the proceedings of this meeting be published in the Portsmouth papers."

In essence what the meeting decided was that complete capitulation to the Secretary of the Navy was the best course that could be followed. By surrendering, they were rewarded with an order restoring them to employment. The *Journal* commented:

". . . We presume at the old rates of wages, but this is not expressed in that order. They will commence work again on Monday next, having been absent nearly three weeks. The number who suspended work is about four hundred, and the value of labor lost is about $15,000. This is the present position of the result of the strike; and in view of the whole proceedings we doubt not that many who united in it will take a more judicious course under like circumstances in the future. It is very evident that the men were receiving no more wages than they were justly entitled to, and that a reduction of their wages was neither politic nor just. The first course which should have been pursued was an appeal to the regulating power and a true representation of the case made.

"If this had not succeeded, the workmen had the privilege of seeking employment elsewhere. And if any workmen, who are not bound by any definite articles of association, could do better at the reduced rates than they could elsewhere, for remaining at their posts they were not deserving the public censure of those who retired. All past experience shows that those who are the leaders in matters of this kind are directly or indirectly sufferers. Cases can be cited where workmen have combined against their employers, and re-opened in distant places where confidence between the employer and the employed could be sustained."

Franklin Shiphouse

In a way the Franklin Shiphouse at the Portsmouth Navy Yard had much in common with Oliver Wendell Holmes' famed One-Hoss Shay. It too lasted about a hundred years and a day, and then disappeared. However, the Shiphouse went up in a mighty orgy of flame and smoke. That was March 10, 1936. A local man, then a boy of 10, recalled the fiery scene as the most awesome event of its kind that he has ever seen. He watched the destructive flames from the safety of Pierce Island in a chilly dawn.

What was the Franklin Shiphouse?

In its heyday it was the most imposing structure on the old Portsmouth Navy Yard, one of what were once three such buildings, almost alike. Under its skylighted roof, many of the Navy Yard's most historic events took place. As is the way of the Navy, the Franklin Shiphouse was long in coming into being.

Shipbuilders on the Piscataqua had known for generations that the construction of vessels in the winter months was hard labor, and often unproductive when wind-driven snow, sleet and extreme cold prevailed. The private yards suffered too, but they didn't have federal money with which to shelter their projects. There was long talk about building such a structure as the shiphouse, but it wasn't until 1820 that the concept began to take shape. But it was many years before it was completed. An item in The *Portsmouth Journal* of August 19, 1837, reports:

"The old frigate *Congress*, now condemned, was built at the Portsmouth Navy Yard about 38 years ago. Her place is to be supplied by another frigate of the same name, the keel of which was laid in the new house at the Navy Yard in this harbor, on Wednesday last, under the supervision of Capt. Thomas W. Wyman. The length of the keel is about 160 feet. The new Ship-house in which she is to be built, was completed a month or two since, and is one of the best to be found in the Union. It is 250 feet long, 130 feet base, and its roof is covered with about 150 tons of slate . . ."

Detailed specifications of some of the materials that were to go into the finishing construction of the shiphouse filled a column in a July, 1836, issue of the *Journal*. When they were all in place, the Franklin Shiphouse, at first unnamed, began a century of service. In 1854, the shiphouse was lengthened so that the keel of the frigate

Franklin Shiphouse. Two views of the venerable Franklin Shiphouse at the Portsmouth Navy Yard are offered. Above, from the Patch Collection at Strawbery Banke, is shown the launching of the USS Franklin, *for whom the structure was named, Sept. 17, 1864, and, facing page, a rear view of the old building from the collection of Fred Lightfoot, Long Island, NY.*

Franklin could be laid in it. The *Franklin* was the biggest wooden warship built at the yard, but it was on the ways for ten years. And that long gestation period gave the shiphouse its name.

A full recital of all that went on under the roof of the old Franklin Shiphouse is impossible in this space.

However, it was here in 1915 that the most significant keel-laying in the yard's history took place. On February 24th, naval officials drove the first rivet in the keel of the submarine *L-8*, the first submarine built in a government shipyard. The *L-8* was the first of more than 130 submarines built at the Portsmouth Navy Yard, and dozens of others have been repaired or rebuilt there.

For one local man, she was the first submarine on which he

worked. That was in 1921 when the *L-8* came in for repairs. The late Wilfred L. Gillespie finished his yard career by working on the *USS Albacore*. Before the *L-8* many vessels of all shapes and sizes were fabricated under the Franklin Shiphouse roof. Among these was the *Boxer*, the last sailing vessel built at the Navy Yard.

An off-beat event took place in the shiphouse while the *L-8* was still on the ways: the Navy Yard built a balloon for the Imperial German Navy. Still another unique occurrence came in the 1840s when the largest temperance rally ever held in the Piscataqua Valley took place in the building. The temperance movement was then in full spate, and on hand to assail "Demon Rum" with great vigor was Elder Joseph Davis.

The Franklin Shiphouse had a narrow escape from destruction in the 1890s during an economy wave in government. The other two shiphouses, Alabama and Santee, were razed but the Franklin was saved.

One of the features of the old building were galleries high on its walls where spectators could watch launchings and the like. It was in the north gallery, then used for storage, that the fire started at 5:30 a.m. Within an hour, a century of service to the Navy had gone up in smoke.

Water Mishap

It is a story that has to be told, if only because it is, in present-day terms, unbelievable. Once upon a time the Portsmouth Navy Yard depended on ponds around its grounds for its water supply, plus what could be collected of rainwater falling on roofs. Back in the early days, no major source of water was available to the Navy Yard. If fact, very early on, even the ponds weren't available, only what water that could be captured in cisterns. For those who want to see the real thing for themselves, such cisterns are still in service in Key West, Fla., where water is a precious commodity.

Occasionally, in seasons of extended drought, the Navy Yard's ponds and cisterns would go dry, and the Navy had to find other sources. One occasion was Sept. 20, 1870. In such times of crisis, it was customary to send an anchor hoy, a utility boat of no war-like pretenses, up the Piscataqua to where potable water could be found—obviously above the high-tide level.

The present story gets under way with a quotation from the *Daily Chronicle* of Sept. 22, 1870:

"SHORT OF WATER—The tanks at the Navy Yard and the natural reservoir on Seavey's Island, having then exhausted of water, the authorities at the Yard put a steam fire engine on board the 'anchor hoy' and sent her up the river to Durham, Tuesday [Sept. 20], in tow of the U.S. tug *Port Fire*, to bring down a load of fresh water in bulk, for the use of the machine shops, etc., at the Station.

"The huge anchor boat will hold water enough for several weeks consumption, and it is fortunate that the at present precious liquid can be procured with no great trouble or otherwise work would have to be suspended at the Yard. There is probably some rain left yet, somewhere, and some of it would be welcome in this vicinity just about now."

Commodore A. M. Pennock was yard commandant and Capt. D. McN. Fairfax was captain of the yard. The tug *Port Fire* was under the command of her pilot, Horatio Trefethen, and his fireman was Charles A. Bowden. The steam fire engine was the *Union*, and she had Edwin C. Neally as her engineer. However, the expedition didn't go to Durham, it went to South Berwick, where it was arranged, after some delay, to get water piped down from the factories on the Salmon Falls River.

The events that took place after the *Union* had pumped about 100,000 gallons of water into the tanks on the hoy, had everyone in the Piscataqua Valley laughing, except the Navy. Years later, the accounts of what happened were collected, edited, and became part of the Piscataqua story. First, with the huge amount of water in her tanks, the hoy was so deep in the water that she had less than a foot of freeboard. When the *Port Fire* and her tow started downstream, they caught the first of the ebb, and, about a quarter of a mile from Dover Point, the *Port Fire* grounded, and hung up for the next 12 hours.

The tug *Clara Bateman* was sent up to get the hoy. She started downstream but was held up by the incoming tide. At high slack, both tugs began hauling the floating water tank down the river. Again they met the incoming tide, which buried the hoy's bow and washed overboard a six-inch hawser. That fouled the *Port Fire*'s propellor, and the entourage rode the tide back to an anchorage.

Parenthetically it should be noted that the *Clara Bateman* was new on the river. She had been bought by a local firm and her captain was Albert Rand, former carpenter's mate on the clipper ship *Sierra Nevada*. Before long the *Clara Bateman* became the nucleus of the Portsmouth Navigation Company. (Although no longer locally owned, Portsmouth Navigation provides tugs and pilots for traffic on the Piscataqua. Woodard D. Openo, a local historian, has published a definitive work on Piscataqua tug boat operations.)

In the darkness of midnight the anchors on the hoy and the *Port Fire* began to drag, and they went down river to about where the Sarah Mildred Long Bridge spans the river today. At the time, a wooden bridge was in place, which had a small draw to permit the passage of vessels. As the hoy and the *Port Fire* went down the Piscataqua, the *Clara Bateman* managed to keep them clear of

Boiling Rock, but the bridge, always difficult to navigate, was a different story. The hoy struck the bridge, went on her beam ends and sank in 60 feet of water. In so doing, she landed in some way on top of the steam engine.

Then the *Port Fire* struck the bridge, and was hung up there until the *Clara Bateman* untangled her, and towed her to the Navy Yard.

Both the hoy and the steam engine were eventually salvaged. They were dragged into shallow water and raised. However, the *Union* suffered great damage from having the hoy ride ashore on her.

They were repaired, but the *Union* was soon dismantled and junked. She had given long and faithful service, but enough was enough.

By now the reader is probably asking the same question that was on everyone's lips in Portsmouth: Why didn't the Navy simply come across the river and get water in Portsmouth?

The *Chronicle*'s account of the incident made that point:

"This account is the result of about fifteen different stories sifted to the best of our ability. We hear that Mr. Horatio Trefethen, the pilot of the *Port Fire,* protested against making the trip.

"The result of this trip made the cost of the water obtained exceed by two bits (a quarter) what it could have been purchased for in Portsmouth—and isn't obtained now.

Nothing changes in the federal government.

Homeward Boat Races

For generations beyond count Portsmouthians have marveled over the passage, to and fro, of Portsmouth Naval Shipyard workers as they go about their daily duties. In the mornings, when all should be bright-eyed and bushy-tailed, well rested and eager to tackle the day's problems, they move toward the yard at a sedentary pace, knowing that the day's programs will have their tasks right where they left them the day before.

It is in the evening when the day's stint is done, that a frenzied animation stimulates the homebound traffic. Today, of course, three bridges are available to expedite the cross-Piscataqua vehicles as the thousands of shipyarders beat their weary ways. More than a century ago, the scene was much more colorful than today. For decades there were two ways of getting to the Portsmouth Navy Yard: the long way round by crossing the Piscataqua Bridge, or by boat. That bridge was located in the general vicinity of the present Sarah Long span, which meant that anyone using it had to walk over to Noble's Island, cross the bridge, tramp through Kittery, and then onto the yard.

So, being water-minded people, most yard workers for years used the direct approach: boats. This practice apparently reached a climax of sorts during the Civil War, when as many as 500 boats—wherries, yawls, seine boats . . . even 12- and 14-oared cutters made the eventide passage. In a day when people weren't transfixed to their idiot boxes by such delectable entertainment as "General Hospital," the evening run would bring hundreds of spectators to the Portsmouth banks of the river. As a news article said:

"The leisurely stream of the boats in the morning offered nothing extraordinary in the way of interest; but the afternoons saw daily a liberal portion of the Portsmouth and New Castle populace collect along the waterfront to witness the most exhilarating boating scene to be found in America. Even the Isle of Shoals steamer would lie to in order that the passengers should not miss the coming race."

Let it not be thought that the homeward dash was a happenstance thing. Every angle was exploited among the contenders.

"When the workingmen arrived in the yard in the mornings, they moored their boats in dense numbers around the landing stages, or hauled them ashore above the high-water mark." To show that nothing really ever changes, privileged parkers in the high-perk spots on the Navy Yard, now moor their four-wheeled craft in front of their name plates, waiting only the 4 o'clock whistle to charge to them.

In boating days "oars, row locks, gratings and rudders were carefully secured; lest they take wing unto themselves; and bow and stern fasts, and fenders were gotten out and hitched as only old-timers could do such things." With their home-ward passages well protected, then the workmen could begin work on vessels such as the famed *Kearsarge*. Labor they did. But real animation began when a bell tolled the end of the working day:

"There was a stampede for the waterfront. That for which the crowds of spectators along the Portsmouth-Newcastle shores had assembled was on. The wave of running workmen broke at the shore line, dividing into groups striving to launch the hauled-up boats, and swarms leaping from one moored craft to another to reach their own. Oars and gear were swiftly unlocked and shipped; shouts went up for belated members of the crews; painters and stern fasts were cast off; boats shot ahead and out. Warm language was the order of the day. It was no place for a sensitive soul.

"There were two classes of men who went in the boats, 'rowers,' and 'sitters;' the rowers of course pay, but they also rowed; the sitters sat and that is all they did do. During the year the sitters paid a dollar a month for their transportation across the river. The rowers in the seine boats and the big government boats which carried a dozen or 20 sitters each, paid nothing; their labor being considered an equivalent. In the smaller boats, which carried but few sitters, the sitters paid a quarter of a dollar each month; and in some of the whale boats and such racers as the *Skedaddle* and the *Joe Hooker*, the rowers paid the full dollar a month besides working their passage."

As water seeks its own level so did the various boats, all 500 of them. Each knew and had its natural opponent(s). Remember there was no Memorial Bridge, so the scene below Badger's Island was one of frenzied pandemonium as half a thousand human-driven waterbugs each fought to get to the Portsmouth shore first. Collisions were frequent, and yet skillful boatsmanship was evident everywhere, as the various coxswains fought to take advantage of every eddy of current.

The competition built to the point where there were two boats that dominated the afternoon fun. Because of the rivalry, the two crews began to lavish more and more money on their craft. One was the *Skedaddle*, the other the *Joe Hooker*. It will be remembered that Joseph Hooker was the Civil War general whose name became synonymous for ladies of easy virtue.

"Much more money changed hands. Rivalry became intense. The most powerful oarsmen among the yard's workmen sold their own boats and took thwarts in the favorites. Both of the racers became yacht-like in splendor of paint and brightwork.

"After much see-sawing of results, the *Skedaddle* began to experience bad breaks of luck, and the crew went into conference. It was decided to trim the boat down a bit by the head; so an extra hand was place in the bow. Sure enough, the *Skedaddle* seemed to do better. She held her own in the first stretch; and, as Four Tree Island was neared, began to drop the *Joe Hooker* astern.

"This was too much for the human ballast in the bow. Leaping to his feet and swinging his hat above his head, he began three lusty cheers. Two of the three were given in handsome style, but the third is unvoiced to this day, for the *Skedaddle* struck a submerged rock with great force and came to an abrupt stop, while the animated figure-head continued on the way."

That grounding wrecked the *Skedaddle*. However, it wasn't long before another rival to the *Joe Hooker* took her place. This one was named the *Ku Klux*. She didn't keep that name long; the yard commander requested that it be changed.

The great river rivalries are all but forgotten in this day of madly dashing automobiles. But the old spirit is there as the yard workmen fight traffic to get away from the yard as fast as possible. Even that is more sedate today than it was back in World War II when 22,000 workers were jammed into the limited confines of the Portsmouth Navy Yard.

Shipyard Pay

For nearly two centuries of its existence, the Portsmouth Naval Shipyard, or Portsmouth Navy Yard as it was known earlier, has been the core industry for the greater Portsmouth community.

Today, with wages and fringes at their highest levels in history, it's amusing to look back at the wage scales prevailing a century ago. Of course, the job titles were related to the days of wooden ships and iron men, but the comparison of 1886 and the present is striking.

The wages listed are per diem: $5, shipwrights; $3.20, millmen; $2.70, sawyers (pit); $3, painters; $2.70, boatbuilders; $2.88, coopers; $3.08, machinists; $2.94, writers; $3.31, riggers; $2.90, watchmen; $3.08, blacksmiths; $2, laborers; $1.78, laborers (second class).

In 1862, when there were 1,100 men on the yard, the payroll for July was $36,000. By trades they were paid:

Foremen, $4; shipwrights, $2; millmen, $2.25; millmen (second class), $1.75; sawyers (pit), $1.75; painters, $1.75; boatbuilders, $1.75; coopers, $1.75; machinists, $2; machinists (second class), $1.75; writers, $2; writers (second class), $1.50; riggers, $1.50; masons, $2.25; watchmen, $1.25; blacksmiths, $2; laborers, $1.12; laborers (second class), 90 cents.

XX More Deadly Fires

1845

FIRE HAS EVER BEEN A DEADLY SCOURGE for Portsmouth. Three times in the first two decades of the 19th Century fire struck the center of town, bringing sweeping destruction of property. The stories of the fires of 1802, 1806 and 1813 have oft been told, but the story of the one that swept through part of Market and Hanover streets in 1845 is not so well known.

From the outset, it was agreed that the fire was not as damaging as its three predecessors, but quite probably that was due to the fact the town had acquired better fire-fighting equipment, and the presence of a railroad line made it possible to mobilize outside aid very quickly. The fire started early on Sunday morning, May 4, and spread rapidly. It was believed that sparks from a chimney fire in the vicinity the evening before threw off sparks that caused the fire.

At 12:40 a.m., a small wooden dye house, near the junction of Hanover and Market streets was discovered burning. Before any kind of fire equipment could get to the scene the fire spread to a cabinet shop owned jointly by Edmund Brown and Alfred T. Joy. It fanned out in the opposite direction to the house of Mary Lunt, widow of a former sea captain, Thomas Lunt. Both structures were destroyed. The *Journal*'s account continued:

"The conflagration spread rapidly to Hanover street, where four dwellings were burned on the south side, and all the buildings in the rear to, but not including those in Ladd street. All the buildings on the west side of Market street being of brick and four stories, from the store of Mr. Charles W. Clark to the M'Intire block (excepting the store of Mr. S.J. Dodge), were consumed.

"On the east side of Market street, the fire communicated with the store occupied by S. Rowe & Co., adjoining that of Wm. Jones & Son, and consumed the stores to the corner of Bow and Penhallow streets, all four stories; and a three-story brick block on the west side of Penhallow street. The following is a more particular description of the property destroyed: Three-story Dwelling House on Market-street, occupied by Mrs. Lunt; brick block, Market street, owned by Benjamin Cheever and David Kimball, and occupied by Benjamin Cheever, Clothing Ware-house, David Kimball, Druggist, and Brown & Joy, Furniture Ware House;

"A part of a brick block, Market St. belonging to John Haven, and occupied by John P. Lyman, Iron Store, and J.M. Mathes, Grocery Store; Brick block, Market street, owned by Nehemiah Moses, and occupied by Nehemiah Moses and Charles W. Clark as Clothing Ware Houses. Waldron's brick block, Market Street, occupied by Kittredge Sheldon, Provision store; C.E. Myers, Clothing Warehouse; N.K. Walker, Hat-store; Francis Dupray, Confectioner; S.G. Folsom, Grocery store; Seamen's Home; and in Penhallow street, store occupied by Conseder Derby, and dwelling-house occupied by J.G. Rand. Brick store in Market street, owned by William Rice, & occupied by Samuel Rowe & Co., Grocery store; McIntire brick buildings, Market-st., occupied by Samuel P. Wiggin, Provision-store; Lewis Bruce, Paint shop, J. Holmes, J.W. Fernald, John Pinder and Mr. Johnson, Dwelling-houses:

"In Hanover-st., a Two-story wooden Dwelling House, occupied by Capt. Edward Kennard and Mrs. Place; a Two-story Dwelling House occupied by Hall Varrell; a Two-story wooden Dwelling House owned by Robert Gray, and occupied by John Sanborn and William Shapleigh; a Two-story wooden Dwelling House owned by Marsh Estate, and occupied by Samuel P. Wiggin."

The *Journal* pooh-poohed other news accounts which put the total losses as high as $90,000, and added the belief that the total wouldn't exceed $65,000. The newspaper also ascertained that the insurances, distributed among seven different companies, totaled about $65,000. So concerned with its analysis of the losses, the newspaper let go until the end of its account two of the really dramatic moments of the great fire. While the modern concept of saturation efforts to battle fires through mutual aid had yet to be born, towns that were threatened by a major fire often sent messengers for help. And that was where the Eastern Railroad made a major difference in fighting the 1845 fire. Ichabod Goodwin, who would later be the state's first Civil War governor, was a director of the ERR, and he sent a locomotive to Newburyport to get help. In less than two hours the locomotive was back, bringing with it three fire engines and nearly 400 men:

"It was a grateful sight—the time might not have been one for full expression of the grateful feelings of our citizens, yet the remembrance of the act will never be erased. May we never be needed to reciprocate the kindness. The facilities afforded by the Railroad Co., which were gratutitous, should be borne in grateful remembrance."

The *Journal* also omitted mentioning the contribution of the garrison at Ft. Constitution. Equipped "with an excellent fire engine," the soldiers battled the flames along Penhallow street. The sight of uniformed men fighting a Portsmouth fire must have been reminiscent for older citizens of the aid given by sailors and Marines in fighting the Great Fire of 1813. Sent across the river by Commodore Isaac Hull, of "Old Ironsides" fame, the sailors and Marines not only fought the fire, but their presence kept the inevitable looting to a minimum.

In fairness to the *Journal*, it must be said that paper didn't mention until near the end of its article that its plant in Ladd street had been threatened by the march of the fire. Helpful friends packed up the paper's type, removed it from the office and then returned it, "without breaking down a line, or making an ounce of pi." The fire also prompted the *Journal* to sound a stenatorian call for patrols of the town's streets:

". . . The Town ought never to be without a Night Watch or Patrol, in Summer as well as Winter.

"We do not undertake to assert that the late fire would have been early discovered and put out by the means of such a watch; though this not improbable. But we do maintain, what may be easily demonstrated, that a perpetual night watch, as a preventive measure, against both fire and thieves, is always worth more than its cost in a town of this size. The existence or lack of such a watch ought to affect premiums of insurance, as it certainly does affect the comparative danger or safety of property. It is hoped that this watch may by some means be revived—and that no pennywise economist may ever be able to abolish it."

Immediate plans were under way to rebuild, but no amount of rebuilding could replace the loss of the North Parish's 800-volume library. A year after the fire, in its issue of May 9th, the *Journal* commented:

"The ashes of the fire of 1845, desolating through they seemed to be, have been like the sprinkling of guano on the torpid roots of a flower garden—our town has been invigorated, and its luxuriant branches are shooting out in very direction, which will grow with increased vigor as soon as the first sprouts of the Concord Railroad appear on the surface."

When built, the Portsmouth & Concord Railroad never did achieve the success visualized by the builders; it came too late—but that's another story that might be told some day.

1865

This story begins on the morning of Nov. 30, 1865, when one of the worst fires in the community's history destroyed the Congress Block on Congress street. It took only a few hours for the flames to destroy the three-story brick building, but it took weeks for all the name calling, charging and counter-charging as to blame to die down.

In its Friday issue, Dec. 1, 1865, the *Chronicle* well told the fire story:

"One of the most disastrous fires with which we have been visited for years, broke out on Thursday morning soon after 4 o'clock, in Congress Block; and in a few hours the whole three-story brick building—one of the handsomest and best blocks in the city—was in ruins." Thereafter followed the real pyrotechnics, perhaps stimulated by the *Chronicle*'s next paragraph:

"After diligent inquiry, we see little reason to doubt that the fire originated from some unknown cause in Mr. J. H. S. Frink's law office, in the chamber in the second story, over the stores of Messers (J. F.) Shores and (W. R.) Preston. When first discovered below, the fire was very small, in Mr. Preston's drug store, and confined to an upper shelf on the side adjoining Mr. Shore's book store. Gentlemen who were present state that on water being thrown on the small body of fire, a shoot of flame rapidly spread along the store. As bottles in that part of the store contained mostly alcohol or preparations thereof, it is probable that the sudden spread of the flames was caused by breakage in some of those bottles.

Congress block. The building, until recently occupied by J. J. Newberry, is the successor to the structure burned in 1865. And this successor itself was badly damaged by fire in 1956, and its two top stories removed. Next left of it is where the Old Bell Tavern stood until destroyed by fire in 1867. Author photo.

"On the other hand, we are informed that a gentleman who entered Mr. Preston's store very early, says the fire was on a shelf near the front, a hole was burnt through the floor above, and fire was dropping down. An early newspaper boy saw a bright light above, before the fire was cried. From these circumstances, added to the fact that Mr. P's windows had no shutters, it seems the fire must originate above. There was great delay caused in giving the alarm after the fire was discovered, from the fact that the night watch had gone to their homes, (as usual at 4 o'clock, so it is said) and the key to the church (North) kept at the station house could not be obtained!

"Axes were procured, but even then the heavy doors of the North Church presented strong resistance. Below we give a statement of losses and insurance, which we think will be found correct in the main:

FIRST FLOOR

"J.F. Shores, Jr., had a large stock in his bookstore, but as much was removed, his insurance of $3000, in the Home Ins. Co., of New York, will probably cover his loss. Wm. R. Preston, apothecary, has insurance $2800, in the Home, of New York, on a loss of $6,000 or $8,000. F.D. Morse, clothing and fancy goods, is insured for $2000 in the Phenix, Hartford. Many goods saved in chaotic condition. Wm. H. Laws, express office, everything saved, almost.

SECOND FLOOR

"J.S.H. Frink, law library and office furniture. Loss $1500, insured $500, in City of Hartford Co., by John Sise, Agent. F.L. Salen, photographic artist, loss say $900; insured for $400 in the Home of New York. Mrs. Moran, hair worker, loss, $800, and no insurance.

THIRD FLOOR

"Ineffable Grand Lodge of Perfection, No. One; Council of Princes of Jerusalem; DeWitt Clinton Commandery of Knight's Templar; Washington Chapter, No. 3; St. John's and St. Andrew's Lodges. The loss in regalia and paraphernalia cannot be less than $20,000, the regalia of the Commandery alone being worth $4,000."

The Congress Block was about 20 years old, having been built in 1845, at a cost of $20,000, by Samuel E. Coues, a prosperous merchant and dabbler in science. Coues was also a partner with Ichabod Goodwin in ship ownership and other mercantile pursuits. Coues was carrying $14,000 in insurance on the building. But contractors estimated it would cost three times that amount to rebuild.

Then came a battle of letters in the *Chronicle*, as William R. Preston, an apothecary on the ground floor, tried to pin the blame on a young law student, J.B. Butler, in the office of J.S.H. Frink. Preston was adamant in his conviction that the fire must have started in Frink's office, and Butler was equally contentious that it had emanated in Preston's store.

Butler admitted that he had been in the Frink office until nearly midnight, and had, he said, early on, smoked his pipe. But he said he carefully "raked over the spittoon" before he left for the night Although he later explained that he didn't empty his pipe into that utensil. Like most such disputes, this one was never resolved. Preston apparently came off the winner because his insurance agent accepted his theory of the fire's cause, and paid off the policy.

One remarkable vignette came out of the fire. It was laid in the actions of William H. Laws, proprietor of an express service. Laws was called to the fire, and managed to save all the goods entrusted to his care, having done that, Laws then took the train to Boston on his daily run. For more than 12 years, he had never missed the trip, and a mere fire in his place of business didn't break the habit. The lot and ruins of the Congress Block were bought in January, 1866, for $10,000, "and the new building which will be erected, it is reported, will comprise, among other things, a Masonic Hall, which will no doubt be fireproof."

Benjamin F. Webster, the city's leading contractor, headed the syndicate that bought the property. Associated with him were Albert R. Hatch, Joseph Parry, Frank Jones, Washington Freeman, John R. Holbrook and Charles G. Pickering. The syndicate was given a bit of advice by the *Chronicle*, which urged that "the new block be extended so as to reach to Fleet Street; and we hear that the new owners of the old Bell Tavern building, are ready to enter into an arrangement which will leave them, in exchange for their present property, each of a new store (of a single floor) in a new structure. . . ."

Ironically, the *Chronicle's* advice was ignored as regards the Bell Tavern property, and it, too, was soon destroyed by fire.

Later it was disclosed that Frank Jones held 40 percent of the interest in the new Congress Block and others were in for a tenth each. In March, 1867, the Masonic bodies again occupied quarters in the Congress block. Elaborate ceremonies were held marking the occasion. The historian emeritus of St. John's Lodge, Gerald D. Foss, says that St. John's Lodge remained in Congress Hall until 1920 when the Hackett property, at the corner of Miller avenue and Middle street was acquired, and a new temple built. The other Masonic bodies continued downtown until the 1930s when they became tenants in the buildings owned by St. John's.

Eventually, the late Andrew Jarvis acquired the Congress Block, and its major tenant for many years was the J.J. Newberry Co. now closed. In January, 1956, the building was severely damaged by fire and in the reconstruction most of the two upper floors were removed.

BELL TAVERN

The Bell Tavern, built in 1743, was one of the city's oldest buildings when it was destroyed by fire on Feb. 25, 1867, a little more than two years after destruction of its neighbor, the Congress Block.

At the time the original Congress Block was leveled the, *Chronicle* urged strongly that the developers buy the Bell Tavern and extend the Congress Block all the way to Fleet street. Three stores occupied the old tavern, and they were out of business. Ferguson & Frye had a grocery in the eastern third of the building; Henry M. Clark had a provision store in the middle; and Charles E. Shedd & Co., a clothing firm, was in the west end.

"The building was owned by Henry M. Clark, Aaron Akerman, and S.S. Frye; and was insured for about $6000 at Messrs. Harvey's agency. Mr. Clark's stock was insured at Messrs. Harvey's for $1000; mostly saved. Ferguson & Frye's stock, at Mr. Sise's agency, for $1500; total loss.—Shedd & Co., for $3000 at Sise's and $2000 at Harvey's; mostly saved, but much damaged. The stock in the store where the fire began, was of course all destroyed or ruined. The other stores were cleared, mostly, but rather in a hurry. Besides the above, the International Telegraphy Company probably made a small loss in fixtures, etc. in their office at Mr. Shedd's store.

"Mr. Philip Meisner occupied the dwelling above, and his household effects (which we regret to hear were not insured) were considerably damaged in removal, and his library, which he much prized, was burned with many other articles. He is master pattern maker at the Navy Yard, and is a member of the Portsmouth Cornet Band, and the cornet he played hung behind his entry door, and was no doubt destroyed. It was the property of the Band and the City."

The Bell Tavern had, of course, long since ceased to function. For a century, it had been one of the chief inns, in the ancient town. It was, therefore, a center of community life. But times altered and the old structure was changed into the three stores destroyed in the fire. The owners quickly decided to rebuild and on April 4, it was reported that Isaiah Wilson, a carpenter, had prepared plans for a two-story brick building with quarters for three stores.

Over two of the stores would be living quarters, but Henry Clark elected to use his upstairs space for storage. The report added:

"The stories are of good height, the finish tasteful, and the new structure will be a great ornament to that part of Congress street. The roof will be flat, so as to shed snow and water from the street (sic). A French roof would look finer and comport better with Congress Block."

1876

In 1876, one of the city's more interesting buildings was destroyed on Christmas Eve. The building thus ruined, called The Temple, once stood on Chestnut Street at the corner with Porter Street where The Music Hall stands today.

While not yet known as The Temple, the structure came into being in 1803, and the guiding hand behind its construction was probably that of Elder Elias Smith, a hard-working preacher of evangelistic bent. He came to Portsmouth in December of 1802, and became associated with a religious group known as "The Christians." Smith's flock met first in a school house, then in the Court House, which stood in Congress Street outside the doors of the North Church, a more staid congregation. It might have been complaints about the enthusiastic singing, or whatever, but Smith's group looked around, and in Smith's own words, they "purchased a lot on which stood a house 25 feet wide and about 45 feet long. This was turned into a convenient place for meetings by making a plain pulpit, pews and a gallery." Unfortunately, nothing survives to tell us what that early church looked like, and very little is known of the appearance of the building on the site that became The Temple.

Besides developing the church and society, Smith also founded the world's first religious newspaper. That was in 1808. Elder Smith in his introduction said: "A religious Newspaper is almost a new thing under the sun. I know not but this is the first ever published in the world."

Elder Smith and his supporters organized in 1803 as the First Baptist Society, with formal incorporation in 1806. The group worshipped there until 1840, when it moved to a new church structure at the corner of Pleasant and Livermore Streets, which is now an apartment house. In 1828, the society installed an 844-pound bell and erected a belfry at a cost of $480.67. The bell, made by the Boston Copper Co. and purchased for $295.40, was brought to Portsmouth on board a coasting vessel, the *Planter*.

By 1844 the all-out religious character of the old building had changed, and it was extensively remodeled and enlarged to a point where it could seat up to a thousand people. The Temple was devoted to some religious activities, but any worthy groups would have access to it for meetings. The owners were Benjamin Cheever and Joseph M. Edmonds.

Tiny couple. General Tom Thumb and his wife, the world-renown midgets, appeared at the Temple on Sept. 15, 1876. Courtesy of James Dolph.

Apparently The Temple began to suffer from benign neglect by March of 1853 when the *Journal* reported:

"The old Temple, which had begun to look like 'time worn and rusty,' has recently been undergoing some improvements in its appearance, such as frescoing, painting, &c.

Edmonds and Cheever had sold the building in 1847 to the Washington Total Abstinence Society, "composed of men pledged to the total abstinence from partaking of intoxicating liquors . . . . Many a man was rescued from a drunkard's grave by their efforts . . ."

Why the temperance people sold the hall back to Cheever and Edmonds isn't known, but they did in 1848. The two partners owned it over the next decade, and then Cheever sold out to Edmonds. In 1864 Clement March and George W. Haven bought out Edmonds for $6,000. Still later, John W. Stavers became part owner and manager of the building.

During Staver's regime, The Temple was the constant scene of professional stage entertainment, and Stavers worked assiduously to improve it. On Sept. 18, 1875, it was reported: "Our citizens will appreciate the efforts of Mr. Stavers to furnish such a hall for their benefit as shall make it a pleasure to attend the winter evening's entertainments, of which the lyceum lectures this season will be a prominent feature. These lectures, by the way, are to open Nov. 6th with a lecture by Carl Schurz." [Schurz, a naturalized German, was at the time a U.S. senator from Missouri.]

Stavers booked in some of the leading entertainers of the day, not the least of which was Henry Clay Barnabee, a native of Portsmouth and one of the great comedians. Still another star to play The Temple was Edwin Forrest, considered one of the leading tragedians on the American stage.

In July 1870, Stavers daringly booked in an all-female troupe of minstrels. The *Chronicle* commented:

"There is enough of the 'naked drama' about it to make it interesting, and it is said the music is good, both vocal and instrumental. It is a big company, numbering 19 performers. . . ."

How 'naked' the performance was was never divulged, at least not in public print, but Stavers was ever a promoter. For instance, that same year he installed a bowling alley in the basement that could be used by both men and women. Stavers and The Temple continued to prosper until Christmas Eve, 1876. The *Chronicle* reported on Monday, Christmas Day, and its account depicts a scene of wild confusion: "About half-past five o'clock, Sunday evening, fire was discovered in the Temple, and an alarm was given.—in a rather undecided and intermittent manner, the 'hollering' and bell-ringing being far from first-class, and the brewery whistle not joining in until after several of the steamers had got streams on the burning building.

"In fact it was the meanest alarm we ever experienced—and we would suggest that the first bell to ring out a fire alarm should be kept ringing for say 10 minutes or so, as two minutes is hardly long enough to rouse the people. . . ."

"The engine horses had all they could do (and much more than they should have to do) to haul the machines into position for service, and we suppose snow-shoes for the wheels will now be procured; they should be anyway.

"As soon as it was evident the building would go, an attempt was made to save the piano, but the dense smoke compelled the men who were carrying it to drop it, and it was burned with the rest of the contents of the house. The Reform Club were to hold their usual Sunday night meeting in The Temple that evening; their organ was saved.

"The Rockingham House pump kept the wood work of that establishment wet down on the side next to the fire, so that the paint was hardly blistered. The Market Square reservoir gave out before the fire did, and the engine stationed there was transferred to the School street reservoir.

"The fire was well managed by the Department, and was confined to The Temple, Mr. Peirce's stable (which adjoined it on the rear) and the Kearsarge House being little harmed."

Little time was lost in replacing the highly useful Temple. In May, 1877, the site was bought by William A. Peirce and others, and work began immediately on a new theater building which was opened to the public in January, 1878, but that's a story for another day.

1896

On March 28, 1896, one of the city's more disastrous fires ripped through the Universalist Church on Pleasant street, a site that is today a parking lot for the First New Hampshire Bank, formerly BankEast.

Before the flames could be subdued more than 40 houses had suffered damage from the flying sparks. A passing city workman noticed flames at around 11 a.m. and promptly informed the police. An alarm was sounded but the gong refused to work, so response to the call was slow. The exact cause of the fire wasn't determined, but it was believed that it came either from an overheated chimney or a spark flying onto the roof.

Nearly 90 years old, the timbers in the church building were easy prey for the flames, and the unavoidable, slow response of the firefighters let the blaze get a good hold. The firemen, under Chief Engineer John D. Randall, battled stubbornly to quell the fire, and volunteers did yeoman work. The *Chronicle* reported:

"Willing hands rushed into the church as soon as the doors could be opened and the stripping of the edifice of everything movable was commenced. Lines were formed and the pews stripped. Into the gallery rushed the little band of property savers and the huge organ was tackled. Bit by bit the instrument was taken apart and the pieces carried to a place of safety. Meanwhile the flames, fanned by the raging northwest gale, which seemed to increase in its intensity every moment, crept into the belfry and soon that portion of the church was ablaze. The flames leaped to the very top of the dome and licked the weather vane which moved jerkily in different currents of air. The interior of the church became a veritable burning caldron.

First Church. The Universalist Society erected this building in 1808, moving over from a structure in what is now the Vaughan street parking lot.

"As the support of the belfry grew weaker, the crowd, who still stuck to the work of saving property from the front of the church, were warned that their lives were in danger. They fled and none too soon. They had hardly reached the opposite sidewalk when the bell, which only a few moments before had been pealing forth its mournful notes, fell with a crash. Ten minutes later, the belfry toppled over and crashed into the street. . . . Almost immediately fire was discovered on the roofs of other adjacent structures. Everybody took a hand in the saving of property and impromptu bucket brigades were formed."

A decisive factor in limiting the damage from the fire was something commonplace to today's property owners, but untried in a serious situation until then. That was the recently completed hydrant service. Fire companies were assigned hydrants and buildings within reasonable distance for safeguarding. The hydrants were credited by the *Chronicle* for saving much of the city's South End. Social attitudes

Second Universalist Church. This photo of the second Universalist Church was proba-
bly made shortly after the Church was built in 1896 to replace the first church on the
site. Strawbery Banke photo.

have changed a bit since 1896, and so the next paragraph in the
Chronicle's account may irk some readers:

"... The women were as brave as the men in fighting the flames,
and while the latter mounted the roofs, the former carried bucket
after bucket of water up ladders and handed it over to be turned on
the smouldering shingles. ..."

And when one sees pictures of the heavy, entangling clothing
worn by women in that long-ago day, the thought strikes that they
deserved far more credit for their work than given them by the
Chronicle. Like one of television's favorite sports devices, an instant
replay of the 1896 fire took place on Jan. 11, 1947, a story that is told
next.

1947

Falling snow may well have saved neighboring buildings from fiery destruction in a 1947 blaze that destroyed the Universalist Church. The Jan. 11 fire was a grim reminder of an 1896 conflagration that struck a church on the same site and also damaged dozens of nearby homes.

Like its predecessor 51 years before, the 1947 fire apparently started near the furnace room and had a strong hold before it was discovered by Miss Kathleen Farnum, a Rye school teacher who had rooms in the Universalist—Unitarian parsonage next door. Miss Farnum alerted the Rev. William W. Lewis and his wife and they turned in the alarm.

The Rev. Mr. Lewis and Fire Chief George T. Cogan attempted to save materials from the burning church, but were forced out of the building by a wall of flame. Some files and two typewriters were saved.

The fire caused the church bell—cast by Paul Revere and recast after the 1896 fire—to drop from the belfry through the floors and into the basement, where it lay in the rubble.

The *Portsmouth Herald* reported:

"Remembering an earlier church fire of half a century ago on the same site which caused a hundred fires in the South End, neighbors were alerted to watch for sparks which might start roof fires. Chief Cogan said only the fact that there was a snow storm in progress and there was no high wind prevented a similar conflagration. . . ."

The many spectators who witnessed the fire will never forget the sight of the late Richman S. Margeson on the widow's walk of his home, the historic Thomas Thompson house across the street, guarding against any chance sparks. Margeson, senior partner in the Margeson Brothers, a furniture store, later became mayor of the city, while his wife, Miriam, served on the school board.

The *Herald's* report continued: "Chief Cogan said it was evident on arrival that the church building was doomed and until the heat of the fire died down he concentrated on safe-guarding the surrounding wooden buildings . . .

". . . Chief Cogan trained his hose lines on the eastern end of the parsonage less than 50 yards from the flaming structure. At times the end of the rectory was so hot that water steamed off it, but the boards didn't reach the kindling point . . ."

A bit of irony in connection with the fire—parishioners were planning to celebrate in April the 50th anniversary of the dedication of the church.

XXI Post Riders, Stages, Early Railroad, Steam Boats

Post Rider

ONE OF THE PORTSMOUTH ATHENAEUM'S most valued treasures is a small metal box that was used by Deacon John Noble to carry mail between Portsmouth and Boston.

The deacon rode that route before the Revolution and until a more formal postal system began. Weather permitting, Noble left Portsmouth on Mondays, arriving in Ipswich that night; by Tuesday evening he would be in Boston. Wednesday and Thursday, he spent executing any errands that might have been entrusted to him. Friday he left Boston for home, arriving in Portsmouth Saturday evening. Aside from the importance of mail, it must be remembered that Deacon Noble was also the most reliable link Portsmouth's worthy burghers had with the outside world. The stages to Boston finally drove the deacon out of business.

Mail has, of course, been a vital concern for centuries. Benjamin Franklin once served as postmaster general, but that was before the Revolution and before Franklin visited Portsmouth. Tradition has it that he "pulled" a page on the press of the *New Hampshire Gazette*, and also that he installed a lightning rod on the Warner House. Neither of these little tasks would seem to have much to do with the

Letter box. Deacon John Noble carried mail between Boston and Portsmouth once a week in this box, which is made of tin, four inches high, four inches wide, ten inches long. The stage coaches finally put him out of business in 1783. The box is now a prized possession of the Portsmouth Athenaeum, having been given to that institution by the Noble family.

development of a postal system, but then, people weren't as frantic about time as they are today.

Exactly for whom the man worked isn't quite clear, but Hugh Finlay, in 1773, did a survey of the postal system, starting at Casco Bay. Finlay kept a journal, which came to light in 1868, and reported in the *Portsmouth Journal,* affords a wonderful word picture of the operation of Portsmouth's post office when Finlay arrived on Oct. 5.

The post office was managed by Eleazar Russell, an eccentric soul who lived on outer Market street. Finlay noted:

"His office is small and looks mean, his books are in good form and up to this day; he is a careful regular officer, he understands his business and seems to have the interest of the office at heart. The Post from the Westward, that is the mails from Virginia, Maryland, Pennsylvania, Jersey, New York and Boston arrive at his office at 11 o'clock in good weather—in winter after a fall of snow, or heavy rain, he seldom arrives before ten o'clock at night, when the wind blows hard from certain points, he is detained at the ferry at Newbury Port, for there's no passing there in a high wind.

"One Stavers some years ago began to drive a stage coach between Portsmouth and Boston; his drivers hurt the office very much by carrying letters, and they were so artful that the post master cou'd not detect them; it was therefore judged proper to take this man into the pay of the office, and to give two mails weekly between Boston and Portsmouth. This was of no disadvantage to the Post office because the mails brought by the stage coach did rather more than pay 10 pounds, Stavers's yearly salary.

"At this day there's many stages between this place and Boston, and they hurt the office much. Mr. Russel says that the drivers cannot be detected, they have small sham bundles with each letter or they are given to the Passengers in the coach, who will without hesitation say that they are letters of recommendation which they carry.

"Mr. Russel advises to keep Stavers in pay because the people have been so long accustomed to having two mails weekly, the publick wou'd raise a clamor were one taken away, and as Stavers's salary is paid from the amount of the letters he brings to the office, it is best to let things remain as they are for present.

"The coach mail (Stavers) should arrive on Saturdays at midday, but it is very irregular, depending entirely on the state of the roads, so that Mr. Russel is oblig'd to attend at his office for this mail from midday until midnight to receive and deliver the letters, for it is a rule with him to do no business on Sunday—yet hitherto he has carried home all Publick letters that were not sent for in time and he has delivered them even on Sunday at his own house. By the books it appears that the stage mails amount from 6 to 30 dwt. Thus Mr. Russel's time as Post Master is taken up.

"On Monday evening the mails for the Westward are made up, the stage leaves Stavers's at sunrise the next morning. On Wednesday the Post arrives from the Westward—in winter much attendance is requir'd on these days. On Thursday at Noon the Falmouth Post arrives; there's frequently no letters in summer. The benefit arising from this Post is but small, for correspondence is entirely carried on by the coasting vessels in the summer. When they are laid up in winter for two or three months there's tollerable mails between Boston and Falmouth. On Friday the Mails for the Westward and Eastward are made up. For Newbury, Salem, Boston at 11 o'clock and for Falmouth at 10 o'clock. On Saturday as has been mention'd the stage mail arrives and long attendance is requite in Winter.

"Mr. Russel prays that he may have a quarterly allowance in lieu of the liberty he formerly enjoyed viz. to frank his own letters, sent or received, and that allowance may be made to him from the time that Mr. Parker's circular letter depriv'd him of that prerequisite. He declares on his word that it was a saving to him of 6 pounds to 8 pounds of lawful money yearly. He also for his own sake prays, that it may be had in remembrance, that he is oblig'd to deliver the Governor's letters without receiving the postage—in the common run of the Provincial publick business he cannot receive the amount of his account under 12 months, because it must pass in Assembly. He fears that his slowness in remitting the balance of his account may appear in his disfavor."

Finlay left Portsmouth on Oct. 9, and went to Newburyport. Eleazar Russell continued as postmaster and customs officer until 1798. It was said of him that he was so fearful of contracting tropical diseases that he made mariners hand papers in to him with tongs. Ironically, he died of yellow fever during the 1798 epidemic.

Stage Coaches

The counters in the various Seacoast area post offices are now adorned with electronic gadgets that are undoubtedly intended to speed up the process of mailing. One wonders, with so much electronics, why, not long ago, it took six days for a letter to come down from Burlington, Vt., but that's another story, and a far cry from the handling of mail nearly two centuries ago.

In those antediluvian days, the mails between the various communities were either moved by stage coach or post rider. Previously, it was related how Deacon John Noble took two days to take mail to Boston and two days to bring mail back from that center. Long before the deacon's day, the Isles of Shoals were a clearing house for mails, which were often dropped off out there for trans-shipment to the mainland.

But that's not the subject of today's history lesson. As everyone knows, if a man devises a means of making a little money, he will soon have imitators. Deacon Noble's competition rose in the form of a stage line to Boston founded by Bartholomew Stavers, brother to the proprietor of the Earl of Halifax tavern. And it wasn't long before Deacon Noble and his little tin mail pouch were out of business.

By 1803, the stage business had prospered to the extent that an "Every Day Stage" was advertised in the *Portsmouth Oracle* on April 16, that was intended to travel on the "upper road to Boston. The Proprietors of the Mail Stage from Portsmouth to Boston thro' Exeter, Haverhill, Andover, Wilmington and Woburn, to Boston, inform their friends and the public, that they have commenced running their Stage to Boston everyday in the week (Sundays excepted) and they wish the patronage of a generous public.

"This stage will start from Davenport's Tavern, Buck street, every morning, and arrive there at evening. . . ." Davenport's Tavern was located on the northeast corner of State and Fleet streets, a site now occupied by the First National Bank. The building itself is at 70 Court street, and used as business offices. (A little anecdote about John Davenport, the proprietor, will be tacked onto the end of this article).

To resume the text of the ad:

"Passengers shall be taken from and delivered to their houses at any part of the town. Those gentlemen who should have no particular business thro the sea-ports, will find it to their advantage to travel this way more especially at this season of the year, when the beauty and agreeableness of the country far exceeds anything that can be experienced through popular towns or cities.

"Gentlemen who may have business at Exeter, can be accommodated very conveniently by going in the morning and returning at night every day: And should it so happen, as it is the case at times, that the Stage should be full, they shall be furnished with private conveyances at the same price as stage fare, and be attended upon in the same manner.

"They have provided themselves with extra Carriages, purchased a number of good horses, procured new Drivers, steady men, who are experienced in the business, therefore they put confidence in their friends for encouragement in this new arrangement.

"Stage books will be kept at the following places, for those who wish to take passage in the above Stage, viz.—Davenport's at

Portsmouth, Hutchins' at Exeter, Mr. Nath'l Bradley's at Haverhill, Mr. Evans' Ann-street and Mr. Kendell's State street, Boston.

John Davenport

Ezra Hutchins

There was, however, one little fly in the proverbial ointment:

"N.B. Though they have been denied the privilege of having a Stage-Book at Maj. Walker's, by some of the proprietors of the other stage yet those who travel in this line and wish to quarter there (the Bell Tavern) shall be landed there or taken from thence with as much pleasure as elsewhere.

"Roads on this line are now good, public houses excellent, expences low, and added to all the fare 75 cents less than the other road. Time of departure and arrival will be the same as on the other line, though the distance is shorter." In other words, the existing stage line, as is the way of things between the airlines today, was trying to keep the competition away from the stage coach center which was at the Bell Tavern on Congress, west of where the former J. J. Newberry's now stands.

But John Davenport was a practical man and an accommodation was arrived at. In fact, Davenport once proved he could cope with any situation—even bereavement.

On the occasion, the court was in session and his tavern was loaded with patrons: lawyers, judges, litigants, jurors and witnesses, were all crowding for sleeping rooms.

In the midst of all the hubbub, Davenport's wife was inconsiderate enough to die. Time couldn't be spared for proper obsequies, as funeral services were once called, so the genial tavern keeper put the body down in the cellar until the court session was over.

A practical man—John Davenport.

First Train

On Nov. 9, 1840, Portsmouth's way of life changed forever.

On that day a stubby little locomotive pulling a string of small cars along an iron track, chugged into a temporary depot a few hundred yards from the Powder Magazine on Islington street, and discharged passengers. In a very brief article noting this important occasion, the *Portsmouth Journal* said on Nov. 14:

"The Eastern Rail Road, as will be seen by the advertisement, is now in full operation to Portsmouth. The cars commenced running on Monday last. Notwithstanding the week has been the most unpleasant in the year, we do not think there has been a much greater amount of travelling through Portsmouth on any week for months past. Our citizens can now leave Portsmouth after breakfast, spend about four hours in Boston, and be home at six to tea. The cars ran from Boston to Portsmouth yesterday morning in two hours and three quarters. We understand a line of stages runs regularly from the Portsmouth depot to Dover."

Because railroad travel was so new to the majority of its readers, the *Journal* copied a set of "hints" for railway travel from the *Boston Merchants Journal*, which was printed below the item about the first train into the town:

1. If you love comfort and safety, never travel by night.

2. Always arrive at the depot at least twenty minutes before the time. You can then choose your seat, and make at leisure any other arrangements as may be necessary.

3. Occupy the seat near the centre of the centre division of the train. The motion is less in that situation; and you cannot thrust your head or arms out of the window.

4. Never quit your seat, or car when making a temporary stop, unless it is absolutely necessary—for the engineer waits for no man—and a person seldom looks so awkward, or feels so foolish, as when chasing a railroad train.

5. Never get in or out of the cars while the train is in motion, however slow.

6. Never smoke or chew tobacco, or sleep in the cars.

7. At the first notice you have of the train's running off the track, or coming into collision with another train of cars, throw yourself suddenly into a heap, resembling as much as possible a sphere, curtail your legs and arms, instead of extending them as is too often the case—and await with patience and philosophy the result."

Imagine being able to go to Boston and back in a day and be able to spend four hours in that teeming city before returning for your evening meal at home! Oh, it wasn't as if there had never before been ways and means of travel between the coastal towns. For more than two centuries, the colonists had used the ocean as a means of getting around, but that mode of transport was rather limited in its appeal, and, while being dependent on tide and wind, was a rather erratic business.

Going by land was a hazardous process at best. In his diary, Judge Samuel Sewall tells of riding his horse to Portsmouth while en route to Kittery and York for court sessions. That item was entered on May 12, 1714:

"Went to Brewster, the Anchor in the Plain; got thither about 11. . . . Took Joseph Brewster for our guide, and went to Town. . . ."

It's hard for moderns to believe a traveler would need a guide to get into downtown Portsmouth from The Plains, but Islington street didn't open up all the way out in the line it now follows until 1797. Judge Sewall rode the court circuit throughout Massachusetts and into the District of Maine for years.

Tradition has it that a Portsmouth baker, Robert Macklin or Robert Metlin, who had a shop on Congress street in the vicinity of the former J.J. Newberry's store, was accustomed to walking to Boston in a single day, crossing on the Charles River ferry about sunset. He would buy flour for his bakery, put it on a coasting vessel, and then walk home the next day. Anyway that saved him paying for a ride on the coaster, and perhaps, depending on wind and tide, walking was quicker. Tradition also has it that Macklin lived to be 115, so perhaps walking is sort of a "fountain of youth."

In 1761, John Stavers, proprietor of the Earl of Halifax Tavern, Court Street, established a stage line between Portsmouth and Boston. The stage was to leave Portsmouth on Tuesdays, overnight at Ipswich and be in Boston Wednesday evening. It made the return run on Fridays. By 1763, Stavers was calling it the "Portsmouth Flying Stage Coach." The fare was 13 shillings, six pence.

Additionally, there were "post riders," a man with his horse carrying mail and the like between Portsmouth and Boston; later post riders penetrated into the interior.

Steam Boats

Another real change came with the advent of steamboats. Coasting vessels, under sail, had operated for generations, but on Sept. 2, 1817, a steamboat, the *Massachusetts*, poked her bow into the harbor and steamed up the river to the old Portsmouth Pier, which was located at the upper end of Prescott Park, and was really an extension into the water of present-day State street.

The *Massachusetts* confined her activities to taking out curiosity seekers at 50 cents a head. How many venturesome souls paid the fare isn't known, but it must have been obvious to all that a new way of travel was at hand. One of the first steam vessels to ply the river on a regular basis was the *Tom Thumb*. On Sept. 3, 1836, 19 years after the first appearance of the *Massachusetts,* the *Journal* reported:

"The *Tom Thumb* now plays regularly every day between Portsmouth and Dover, and is, we understand, doing a pretty fair business—The excursion from Portsmouth to Dover is but a short one, and anyone who wishes to enjoy the beauties of the river scenery at the present season, has an opportunity for a pleasant excursion at a very cheap rate. . . ."

In our time, the *Thomas B. Laighton* offers upriver trips to admire the fall foliage. Robert Whitehouse, in his definitive *Port of Dover*, said the *Tom Thumb* worked three seasons in upriver passages, and then quit because of the difficulty in getting through the draw of Portsmouth Bridge. However, it is more likely her Dover excursions ended in November, 1836, when she was lost at Boon Island. However, before that unhappy event, the *Tom Thumb* had been the first steamer to tow a sailing vessel out of the Piscataqua into open water.

But all the while those concerned with steamboats and sailing vessels were plying their trade, there were those strenuously promoting railroads. For example, in 1834, the *Journal* applauded proposals to build a railroad from Portland into northern Maine and New Hampshire. On Sept. 12, 1835, the *Journal* reported:

"The survey for the Railroad from Boston through Lynn, Salem, Ipswich and Newburyport to the N.H. line, has so far progressed, that the engineer states a remarkably level and straight road may be made, not exceeding by more than a mile, the route made by the Newburyport turnpike. The survey of the route from the line to Portsmouth will be, we believe, at least as favorable, and indeed, more so."

And on Jan. 9, 1836, the *Journal* published a report on the survey by Joshua Barney, the engineer, in which it offered alternate routes for the railroad. One of them is interesting because it brought about publication of the famed "Error Map" in the 1839-1840 *City Directory*.

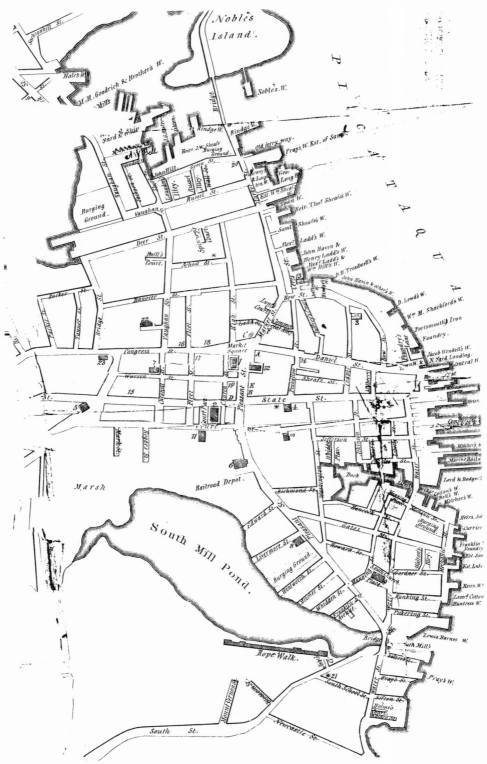

This map from 1839-1840 Town Directory is known as the "error map." At that time, people were convinced the Eastern Railroad would enter the town at an angle that would take it across the South Mill Pond, with the depot located about where the offices of First New Hampshire and BankEast are today.

Why an "Error Map?"

Because the depot for the new railroad was shown on the map as being located near the present-day First New Hampshire Bank building on Pleasant street.

That came about because Barney's "Eastern Route" started near the Universalist Church on the bank of the South Mill Pond, ran across the pond in a southwesterly direction and then on toward Hampton. His "Western Route," which, ultimately, came closer to what was actually laid out, went from Noble's Island at the foot of the Portsmouth Bridge in a general westerly direction, and somewhat parallel to Islington street.

Index